$3.50

Problems of race and segregation have brought tension and conflict to the Union of South Africa—as they have in the United States. This is a study of the potent weapon that some of the politically disinherited South African non-whites have turned to: passive resistance. Leo Kuper, professor of sociology at the University of Natal, explains their Gandhi-like movement and the larger issue behind it by examining the events of one year in which Africans and Indians took their measures against laws regulating relations between races. In the disturbed situation that arose from government counteractions, he detects the development of new and unexpected attitudes; and he contends that it is out of these frequently paradoxical reversals of role and opinion that the races must fashion the country of the future.

PASSIVE RESISTANCE
IN SOUTH AFRICA

PASSIVE
RESISTANCE
in South Africa

by
LEO KUPER

NEW HAVEN
YALE UNIVERSITY PRESS
1957

PRINTED IN GREAT BRITAIN

CONTENTS

ILLUSTRATIONS

Nos. 3, 4, 5 and 6 are reproduced by permission of Mr. G. R. Naidoo, press photographer, Durban.

ACKNOWLEDGEMENTS

INEVITABLY, in a work such as this, one relies heavily on the help of a great many people. I cannot acknowledge them all by name, but would express my special indebtedness to my wife Hilda, Mr Julius Lewin, Miss Muriel Horrell and Professor A. Keppel-Jones for their criticism of the whole manuscript, and to Dr Leonard Doob and Mr Alan Paton for their comments, and assistance in publication. I am grateful to Advocate Rex Welsh, Miss Violaine Junod, Professor Charles Nixon and Mr Manilal Gandhi, who read critically some of the chapters and assisted me in discussion. Mr Ismail Meer was most helpful in his analysis of the campaign from the point of view of the resistance leaders and introduced me to the resistance literature. The South African Institute of Race Relations kindly made available its library of documentary sources, and legal acquaintances assisted with the loan of court records. I should like to thank the University of Natal for a grant of thirty pounds for typing, and Miss Beth Meikle and Mrs Anne Ross for their patient work on the manuscript. Two of the theoretical chapters were published in *Social Forces* and the *British Journal of Sociology*, under the titles of 'The Control of Social Change: a South African Experiment' (*Social Forces*, Volume 33, October, 1954), and 'The Background to Passive Resistance' (*British Journal of Sociology*, Volume IV, September, 1953) and I wish to acknowledge permission to use these articles. It is particularly important in dealing with so controversial a topic that I should emphasize that the interpretations given are my own, and do not necessarily reflect the approach or conclusions of those who have helped me.

LEO KUPER.

DURBAN.
November, 1955.

INTRODUCTION

IN South Africa, race relations are often characterized by violence and bitterness, yet it was in South Africa that Mahatma Gandhi first developed his philosophy of passive resistance. A method of non-violence, based on an ethic of universal love, it contrasted sharply with the techniques used in the many Kaffir wars and the Boer war, and with the outlook behind these destructive conflicts.

Passive resistance ceased as a method of struggle in South Africa from the beginning of the first world war, when Mahatma Gandhi returned to India, until the end of the second world war. There were no South African resistance campaigns during this period in which Gandhi perfected his method in the struggle for Indian independence. It was not until 1946 that the South African Indians revived passive resistance in an attempt to gain relief from what they described as the 'Ghetto Act'.

Passive resistance is usually regarded as compatible with Indian philosophy, an expression of Indian asceticism and quietism. Among South African whites, at any rate, it is thought to be in the nature of the Indian that he should resist passively. The 1946 campaign, almost entirely Indian, did not disturb settled convictions. When, however, the African National Congress and the South African Indian Congress united in sponsoring the 1952 campaign, and Africans, Indians and Coloureds responded, there was confusion. A non-white united front challenged the stereotyped patterns of South African thought, based on assumptions of mutual antagonisms and fundamental differences among Africans, Indians and Coloureds.

The reactions of the whites were most varied: some described the campaign as an inevitable consequence of mounting discrimination under apartheid, and others saw in it the influence of communist agitation or the designs of Indian imperialism. A constant theme was the widening of the gulf between whites and non-whites, and the urgent need to build bridges before it was too late. Present in many minds was the early possibility of open and violent conflict, while proposals to avoid the crisis ranged from minor concessions or round-table conferences to forcible suppression.

Amid this confusion of viewpoints, it was difficult to get reliable, factual information. The English press, fearing Government censorship, was guarded in its coverage of resistance news, and the Afrikaans newspapers, though more outspoken, gave the official point of view. Some additional information could be gained from the non-white weekly periodicals, but the different sources, white and non-white, presented a very incomplete picture. Moreover, public discussion was limited as a result of the extension of police activity and the control of public life. A variety of new procedures (the 'naming' of persons as communists, bans against attendance at public meetings, the belief that telephones were being tapped, instances of the interrogation of servants about the activities of householders) spread fear among many opponents of Government policy, and effectively restrained the presentation of the resisters' case to the public.

Yet, notwithstanding the many restraints, it was largely through public meetings that the leaders spread the message of the passive resistance campaign among the non-white masses. These meetings were often the starting-point for acts in defiance of the law. Since the situation evoked such conflicting images and interpretations, an account of a resistance meeting, and of the sequence of acts which constitute passive resistance, will help to define more concretely the subject matter of our discussion. I have selected for the following description a meeting I attended in Durban.

This meeting had been called by the Natal branch of the African National Congress and the Natal Indian Congress for November 9th, 1952, at Nicol (Red) Square, Durban, but the City Council had forbidden the use of the land. Not knowing this, people arrived to find the square empty, except for a few armed policemen on motor-cycles. On a nearby corner, as though in warning, was a hoarding with the words 5 KILLED 39 INJURED IN EAST LONDON RIOTS.[1]

People moved on to Lakhani Chambers, the headquarters of the Natal Indian Congress, realizing that a decision as to the venue of the meeting would be taken there. The leaders of the resistance movement were already in consultation. The decision rested with the President of the Natal Indian Congress, Dr G. M. Naicker, and other leaders. Dr Naicker is firmly dedicated to non-violence, in the tradition of Mahatma Gandhi, and has served terms of imprisonment in two passive resistance campaigns.

With Dr Naicker was the secretary of the Natal Indian Congress, Mr J. N. Singh, a handsome man with military carriage, trained at the University of the Witwatersrand, and practising as a lawyer in Durban. Mr Singh had been selected to lead a corps of volunteers in the defiance of law that very afternoon. Someone asked him cheerfully whether he had taken his vitamins and he replied that he had. Dr Naicker explained to me that resisters went into training so as to ensure that they were physically fit to withstand the rigours of a term of imprisonment. Resisters were punished by the loss of a meal, if they displeased the warders, 'and they are easily displeased with us'. A young student who had recently served his resistance term added that resisters were set to breaking stones or digging rubble, and were penalized by the loss of a meal if the task were not completed at the end of the day. He spoke with revulsion of the prison diet (which he described as mealie-meal in the morning with one teaspoon of sugar, one quarter-loaf of bread with a teaspoonful of fat for lunch, mealie-rice with

---

[1] This was the second disturbance in the Cape Eastern Province.

boiled beans for supper) and his difficulty in following the advice of the long-term prisoners to 'press it down'.

Meanwhile, a number of resisters both African and Indian, who were to participate in the meeting as stewards, speakers or volunteers, were active on a variety of missions. As they passed each other on the stairs or in the corridors, they exchanged the resistance movement's greeting. This takes the form of the call 'Afrika', the 'a' pronounced as in English 'bath', with a resolute emphasis on the first and third syllables. At the same time, the right fist is clenched, with thumb held erect, and moved up towards the shoulder. Word and gesture symbolize the unity of the peoples, and the return of the country to them. Some of the men wore armbands, which signified that they had served, or were about to serve, terms of imprisonment for defiance of the laws.

The decision in regard to the venue of the meeting was difficult to take and long delayed. Too ready a compliance with official edicts would make it impossible for the leaders to function publicly, and would indeed undermine the spirit of resistance. On the other hand, the pattern of recent disturbances in East London and other parts of the country, resulting in considerable loss of life and destruction of property, might be repeated in Durban, if the resisters attempted to meet on the forbidden Red Square. Inevitably some measure of responsibility would attach to the resisters, even though they themselves behaved with disciplined non-violence.

Finally, Dr Naicker announced that the meeting would be held on a privately-owned piece of ground, not subject to the City Council's control. The route to the new meeting-place lay through the Indian section of this multi-racial city, past an Indian mosque, the Bantu Social Centre and a block of flats, Indian-owned but unoccupied because the authorities had not yet decided for which racial group they would reserve the area. Only a few people were walking toward the meeting-place, and it seemed that the long delay and uncertainty had dissipated enthusiasm. Yet by the time the leaders arrived, there was a crowd of some four thousand persons, indicating the effectiveness of the resistance organization.

The crowd was composed of Africans and Indians of all ages, men and women, the Indian women in colourful *saris*, the African women in various European-styled clothing. On the outskirts stood a 'ricksha boy' in gorgeous beadwork, his head adorned with plumes and painted ox-horns. The narrow street was lined by a few cars, in one of which sat a number of white men from the political section of the South African police. A huge flag, with the symbolic colours of the African National Congress, black for the people, green for the land, and gold for the wealth, marked the platform, a wagon.

From the beginning, the first act as it were, the organizers asserted the peaceful nature of the meeting. One of the vice-presidents of the Natal Indian Congress, who had already served a term of imprisonment, mounted the platform and exhorted the crowd to sit. The meeting could not begin, he called, till everyone was seated. To stand would create an impression of disorderliness which had to be avoided. This was a peaceful meeting; the campaign was non-violent. Gradually, leisurely, most of the people sat down on the ground. This seemed to create a feeling of good-humoured relaxation and of solidarity.

Almost immediately, a deep bass voice from somewhere in the crowd began a Zulu chant '*Mayibuy' IAfrika*'. The whole crowd, Indians as well as Africans, joined in this song of the resistance movement, and instead of Amen, shouted '*Afrika!*' Throughout the meeting '*Afrika*' was used in this way – a fervent affirmation whenever a speaker emphasized the principles of the defiance campaign, or attacked discrimination or indeed made a good joke.

MAYIBUY' IAFRIKA!	LET AFRICA RETURN!
Thina sizwe esinsundu,	We black people,
Sikhalel 'iAfrika,	We cry for Africa,
Eyathathwa amaNgisi;	Which was taken by the English,
Sisese6umnyameni.	While we were still in darkness.

Chorus: Mayi6uye, mayi6uye, Mayi6uy'iAfrika!	Let it return, let it return, Let Africa return!
Eyathathwa amaNgisi; Sisese6umnyameni.	Which was taken by the English, While we were still in darnkness.
Chorus: Mayi6uye mayi6uye, Mayi6uy'iAfrika!	Let it return, let it return, Let Africa return!
Eyagqilazwa amaBunu; Sisese6umnyameni.	Which was enslaved by the Boers While we were still in darkness!
Chorus: Mayi6uye, mayi6uye, Mayi6uy'iAfrika!	Let it return, let it return, Let Africa return!
Eyadayiswa amaMbuka, Sisese6umnyameni.	Which was sold by traitors, While we were still in darkness.
Chorus: Mayi6uye, mayi6uye, Mayi6uy'iAfrika!	Let it return, let it return, Let Africa return!
Makaphel'amapasi; Sithol'inkululeko.	Let the passes end; So that we find freedom.
Chorus: Mayi6uye, mayi6uye, Mayi6uy'iAfrika!	Let it return, let it return, Let Africa return!

Then they took up '*S'yayifun'inkululedo*' (We want freedom) and '*Vula Malani*' (Open, Malan).

S'YAYIFUN'INKULULEKO	WE WANT FREEDOM
S'yayifun'inkululeko; (twice) S'yayifuna, s'yayifuna! S'yayifun'inkululeko.	We want freedom; (twice) We want it, we want it! We want freedom.
We! Malani.	Listen! Malan.
S'yayifun'inkululeko; (twice) S'yayifuna, s'yayifuna! S'yayifun'inkululeko	We want freedom; (twice) We want it, we want it! We want freedom.
We! Verwoerdi.	Listen! Verwoerd.

(Etc., all Cabinet Ministers sung to in turn).

VULA, MALANI!	OPEN, MALAN!
Vula Malan, siyangqongqoza: (four times)	Open Malan, we are knocking: (four times)

Vuka Luthuli, Luthuli we-Afrika (twice)	Wake up Luthuli,[2] Luthuli of Africa (twice)
Awusoze wale nxa uthunyiwe (twice)	You will never refuse when you are sent (twice)
Maka6ongwe uJehova! (four times)	Let God be praised! (four times)
Wenzeni na umnt'onsundu?	What has the black person done?
Mayi6uy'iAfrika (four times)	Let Africa return! (four times)

The ready good humour and the rich spontaneous song gave an impression of strength and solidarity. The sentiments seemed to be rooted in the emotions and music of these people, and not something foreign, peddled by agitators. Throughout the meeting, one or other of the thousands of men and women would suddenly be moved to song, and unite the whole crowd in melodious harmony. The speeches were interwoven with song, as sermon with hymn. And the slightest of jokes, a mere turn of phrase, would draw tumultuous laughter.

Dr Naicker came to the wagon and took up the theme of non-violence, while Mr M. B. Yengwa, secretary of the Natal branch of the African National Congress, interpreted into Zulu. Dr Naicker began by saying that as he looked at the faces round him, he saw on them no violence, yet the meeting had been prohibited on the Red Square. The excuse given was that there might be violence, though for weeks and months meetings had been held on Red Square without any violence. But the police were 'trigger-happy', and so he had given up the public meeting-place to prevent a possible attack, 'not by us, by them'. '*Afrika!*' shouted the audience.

He spoke of the need for racial co-operation, and of the deliberate unreliability of the White press. 'In to-day's paper,' he said, 'there is another white lie. I'm not sure whether this means the same as when a European talks of white lies. I'm not sure what sort of lies those are, saying that India is giving two million pounds to our campaign. This is an attempt to make

[2] Chief Albert Luthuli is the President-General of the African National Congress.

this movement appear to be directed from outside, led by Nehru, backed by non-South Africans. This is done to divide us non-Europeans and destroy the unity and friendship which we are steadily building. England, America and India are sending us money, but only token sums, not to support us financially, but to show their sympathy with us. And we will go on, winning the co-operation of all Christian men. We are civilized people, preaching no hatred, men with love and brotherhood in our hearts, as well as on our lips. It is said that at first the Europeans had all the Bible and the non-Europeans had all the land, but now the non-Europeans have all the Bible, and the Europeans have all the land. Yet we will not take it by force; we do not use nor advocate force.[3]

At one stage, a police officer came up to the platform, and Dr Naicker, after a few minutes, announced that there were complaints about noise, and asked that the loud-speakers should be toned down. Someone in the crowd swore. His neighbours turned quickly on him.

Indian and African speakers alternated, and the speaker after Dr Naicker was from the African National Congress. He developed a favourite theme with non-white political audiences, the deceit of the white man. He emphasized that Europeans interpreted national unity as unity between the different European parties, which was absurd since it left out eleven and a half million non-Europeans. '*Afrika!*' He described the poverty of the reserves, and the effect that culling the cattle would have on an already land-hungry, cattle-hungry people. With ironical humour, he commented on the white man's myth that the discriminatory laws are for the benefit of the people discriminated against. 'The laws they say are good for us. The pass-laws – they are good for us. When they take away our cattle – it is good for us. When they take our houses – good for us. They say, no rights till you're civilized. It's like saying you can't go into the water until you can swim perfectly.' He

---

[3] Notes were taken in longhand throughout the meeting and, though the quotations are not verbatim, they are very close to what was said.

drew a round of loud applause when he said 'the policy of apartheid is a policy of banishment, but we will not be banished from our homes. South Africa is not gaol, it is our home. *Afrika!*'

Mr J. N. Singh was then announced as 'leader of to-day's batch', and he stepped forward to the microphone. 'We are civilized men,' he declared, 'not barbarians, and we must not rest until the Europeans respect us and our women.' Standing quite still a little behind him were his wife and her sister and Mrs Naicker, a matron draped in deep red. 'We will not let ourselves be terrorized, nor will we accept moral degradation. In Port Elizabeth and Kimberley, East London and Johannesburg, the police have shot and killed our people like animals. I ask you to stand and think for a short time of those who have died and to sing softly in prayer.'

The crowd sang and, when the song ended, Mr Singh discussed the rights of non-whites to live like human beings. This, and not lawlessness, he said, was the aim of the campaign of defiance against unjust laws.

Dr Naicker stood up and spoke with clear emphasis: 'I want you all to listen very carefully. Mr Singh and his batch are now going to walk to the Berea Road station to be arrested. None of you must follow him. Demonstrations are no longer allowed under the Riotous Assemblies Act. Stay here peacefully till the meeting is over.' As Mr Singh and his company moved away, accompanied by an observer from the meeting, the crowd watched without stirring from the ground. A police car drove slowly off.

A youth-leader of the African National Congress stepped jauntily up to the microphone. His words, aggressively self-assured and demagogic, were very different in tone from those of previous speakers. 'We must not look to the past,' he cried, 'but forward. *Afrika!* Those who look behind will fall and be walked over. But those who look ahead can win a glorious future, which is ours if we fight for it. Rather let us be killed fighting than live as slaves of fascists.' The interpreter found it difficult to keep pace with the speaker, and the crowd was not particularly interested, but listened politely enough. It was like a blind pulled over a luminous room, hiding the main actors. It began to drizzle.

A loud noise, like a shot, suddenly rang out, once and again. The crowd tensed, heads turned. A police car moved slowly round. Eyes showed the unspoken fears. I understood then how easily a crowd can stampede to action and self-destruction.

But the speaker was unperturbed. After commenting on events in Kenya and other parts of Africa, he ended on a note of triumph: 'To you who are young and whose blood is hot, we say catch the bull by its horns. *Afrika!*'

At this stage, Dr Naicker announced the arrest of the resisters. 'I rejoice to tell you that our people have been safely arrested. *Afrika!*' The crowd relaxed. Then Dr Naicker commented on the position of the governing Nationalist Party and of the opposition United Party, the similarity of outlook on the non-European question, and the United Party's pandering to race-prejudice to catch votes; and he predicted that the United Party had already lost the next election, because it had no policy. 'If the Nationalist Party told the United Party to go to the toilet, it would go. [Laughter.] *Afrika!*' But he pointed out that there were a number of liberals, homeless Europeans. 'Let them join the defiance movement, let them become a power that could drive out of Parliament the real enemies of the country, and build it on true worth. Not this year or next, but in five years time, the movement could succeed, for with it would be the majority of the people, the non-Europeans.' He then called on Mr Yengwa to read out a resolution of protest against discrimination. It was acclaimed by a show of hands and the call '*Afrika*'. Concluding his speech, Dr Naicker urged the crowd to give the campaign active support. 'Well, there are still two more things to be done. To make this campaign a success, one member of every family, a brother or sister, a father or a granny or a grandfather must join the African or Indian National Congress. That is what will give us our support. And we have the affairs of the campaign to help; we have built this movement, not with money from overseas, but with the pennies and the shillings you have given. Will you, while we sing our song, and the African National Anthem come and give us what you can?'

The crowd sang 'Let Africa Return', and all the time men and women moved forward and made their contributions. Then they sang the African anthem, *Nkosi Sikelel'iAfrika*.

NKOSI SIKELEL'IAFRIKA	LORD BLESS AFRICA
Nkosi Sikelel'iAfrika!	Lord bless Africa!
Maluphakanyis'udumo lwayo!	Exalted be its fame!
Yizwa imithandawo yethu!	Hear our prayers!
Nkosi Sikelela!	Lord grant thy blessing!
Woza, moya,	Come, spirit,
woza, woza,	come, come.
Woza, moya,	Come, spirit,
woza, woza,	come, come,
Woza moya oyingcwele,	Come, Holy Spirit,
Usi sikelele, thina lusapho lwayo!	And bless us, her children

Long after the singing had stopped, a tiny child of not more than three or four, held in the arms of a proud father, kept on repeating the call. The meeting dispersed in small groups. There were no incidents.

The arrest of Mr Singh was the second act in the development of the drama of passive resistance, and, since it took place off-stage, I am giving an account of a subsequent arrest at the Berea Road railway station, a favoured area in Durban for the defiance of apartheid laws.

In Durban, the resisters had a 'gentleman's agreement' to notify the railway police in advance of the intention to commit a breach of railway apartheid regulations, so that the arrest would be effected with a minimum of disorganization. On the following Sunday, Mr Ismail Meer, one of the vice-presidents of the Natal Indian Congress, led a batch of resisters from the meeting-place to the Berea Road station, only to find the entrance barred by the police. In a truck near by were more police fully armed and there were also police in the cars which had followed the resisters from the meeting-place. Since it was impossible to enter the European waiting-room peacefully, Mr Meer returned with his fellow resisters to the meeting, and reported what had happened. He described the incident as a breach of faith, and as a victory over apartheid. The non-Europeans were now so politically conscious that the South African Government was obliged to use the police in order to prevent non-Europeans entering the European section. Under a free South Africa, he declared, the police would not be wasting their time at the Berea Road station. South Africa would require a very, very big police force to enforce all its apartheid laws. 'Let us celebrate our victory with our salute—*Afrika! Afrika! Afrika!*'

Far from being complacent in their 'victory', and relieved that it had been gained without suffering, the resisters felt frustrated by the miscarriage of their plans, and resolved to repeat their act of defiance, without first notifying the police. On the next day or the day after, they drove up to the Berea Road station in two cars. No policemen barred the entrance, and Mr Meer led fourteen resisters without hindrance into the waiting-room marked 'Europeans Only, *Alleen vir Blankes.*' There were seven Indian men, apart from Mr Meer, and seven Africans—four men and three women. Mr Meer arranged the batch on the three benches in the waiting-room, placing Indians at the ends of each bench, and settled down to wait for the police.

At first, the resisters were restrained, sitting very still and occasionally speaking quietly. Then, as the minutes passed and nothing happened, there were obvious signs of tension. Some wiped perspiration from their brows; they began to smoke; they responded quickly to unexpected noises outside the waiting-room, clearly bracing themselves for arrest. Then after a time they seemed to relax a little, and moved around talking to each other, or they read, trying to appear unconcerned. At one stage an African, with a beautifully dressed baby in his arms, seeing non-Europeans in the waiting-room, almost came and sat down, but someone called out to him and he quickly removed himself.

At last, after the resisters had waited almost an hour, three white policemen, armed with revolvers, suddenly marched into the waiting-room. They asked for the leader and Mr Meer stood up and spoke quietly to them. The police then placed all the resisters under arrest for trespassing in the European waiting-room. As the police vans arrived and the resisters were taken away, a crowd of white people collected in the doorway; some non-Europeans gave the resistance salute; others laughed as if in amusement over the whole episode.

From then on, the resisters were under the control of the police, and the next acts followed the ordinary process of law. The resisters did not ask to be released on bail, but spent the night in the cells. The following morning they were brought up for trial before a magistrate. The court was packed with a mixed group of supporters. There were also two Europeans, but the usual apartheid in seating arrangements was not observed. The Clerk of the Court read the charge, and the resisters all admitted guilt. Mr Meer was asked whether he had anything to say, and, following precedent, he explained the reasons for the defiance of apartheid regulations. Then the magistrate sentenced Mr Meer to seven days' imprisonment and the other accused to fourteen days' imprisonment, with the option of a fine, which they all declined.[4] The resisters were removed from court, and the crowd slowly dispersed, having been prohibited from demonstrating support.

The separate acts, which together constituted passive resistance, were familiar to South African society. The

[4] This was an unusual sentence. The more usual sentence in Durban for this offence was either twenty-one days' or one month's imprisonment, and it was not the practice to show more leniency to the leaders. Mr Meer later spoke of his sentence with obvious embarrassment. Ready to sacrifice himself, subjected to the strains of uncertain police and Government retaliation, the leniency of his sentence came as an anti-climax, almost as a humiliation.

non-European political meeting, with its analysis of white domination, its aspirations for 'liberation', was not new. So too, prosecutions for minor statutory offences are a familiar aspect of the structure of South African race relations: every week, the South African courts dispose of thousands of non-European statutory offenders. Even the arrangements for the imprisonment of short-term offenders sufficed also for the passive resisters.

The motives of the resisters were, however, profoundly different from those of the ordinary statutory offender. They felt themselves to be dedicated. They deliberately defied the laws, and the breach of statutory regulations became charged with new meaning. They voluntarily sought imprisonment, and imprisonment became a mark of achievement. It was to this spirit of resistance that the whites responded with active emotions of hate or sympathy. and not with their normal indifference to non-European statutory offenders. For the whites, too, the breach of statutory regulations became charged with new meaning.

The significance of passive resistance is, therefore, not to be found in the acts themselves, but in the meanings given to them. Passive resistance was symbolic of an ideological conflict heightened by apartheid, and it was modelled on an ethical and political technique evolved by Mahatma Gandhi. An understanding of the background of South African political theories and policies, and of the philosophy of passive resistance, is necessary for the interpretation of the 1952 campaign. These considerations have shaped the arrangement of this book, with the broad analysis of South African society and of passive resistance preceding the account of the events.

The scope of the study is the sociological analysis of the 1952 campaign in the context of South African race relations, and also the analysis of South African race relations as illuminated by the varied reactions to the campaign. Part I contains the more general chapters, in which I have tried to introduce necessary background information in such a way as not to offend the reader who knows something of South African affairs. Chapter I gives an account of the ideological background to passive resistance and of the pressures on the white group to renounce democratic values. The renunciation is expressed in the dominant ideology of apartheid, to which the campaign was, partly, a reaction. Accordingly, Chapter II, 'Communism by Statute', discusses apartheid legislation and the extent to which the renunciation of democratic values may be carried. The reactions of the non-whites to apartheid are also analysed, and the issue raised whether, in consequence of apartheid, communism may prove a rival ideology to African nationalism. Chapter III, 'The Sociological Nature of Passive Resistance', deals with the nature of a passive resistance as a political technique and poses the specific question of a violent or non-violent solution to the South African conflict. Throughout these chapters, I have suggested the possibility of a resolution of the conflict along liberal, evolutionary lines.

Part II (Chapters IV–VIII) is an historical account of the 1952 campaign. Chapter IV deals with the preparations, and Chapter V with the events, of the campaign; Chapters VI and VII analyse the reactions of different sections of the South African population, and Chapter VIII describes the counter-action of the Government, and the contemporary manifestations of the struggle. The concluding chapter is an assessment of the significance of the passive resistance movement, and of broad trends in South African race relations. I have included, in Appendix A, a letter addressed by the former Prime Minister, Dr D. F. Malan, to an American pastor, setting out the Government's political philosophy, and a reply to this letter by the South African Institute of Race Relations. These should help the reader to gain his own perspective, and enable him to see South African events in other than the local shades of black or white.

Inevitably, my approach has been selective, and some important aspects are not included in this study. Observations should have been made in the main centres of resistance, the

Cape Eastern Province and Johannesburg; and an analysis of the leadership would have been valuable. The reactions of the rank-and-file resisters are of considerable interest. How did they perceive passive resistance, and what was the effect on them of their voluntary sufferings? The role of ex-communists in the resistance movement became a significant factor in Government counteractions, and some information on this issue is readily available, though it is difficult to assess the extent of communist influence. I have not dealt with any of these problems, but limited the scope of the work to what I could reasonably accomplish. On the question of communist participation, I did not feel that I could discuss identifiable individuals in these terms, since the advocacy of communism is an offence under South African law. While this record is therefore by no means complete, I think it gives a sufficient picture for the analysis of the passive resistance movement and its significance in the context of South African race relations.

PART ONE

THE SETTING OF
PASSIVE RESISTANCE

I

THE IDEOLOGICAL BACKGROUND TO
PASSIVE RESISTANCE

THE ideological problem in South Africa is what to do with democracy. It is deeply valued by the whites for the purpose of regulating their own relations, but is not applied in the governing of the non-whites. If the whites ceased to monopolize democratic rights, and extended them throughout South Africa, the non-whites would be freed from domination. Hence the anomaly arises that there is considerable pressure on the whites to abandon the democratic creed which they value, and which they themselves introduced to the non-whites, while it is among the non-whites, the borrowers of this culture pattern, that we find the staunchest and most uncompromising support of democratic values. In others words, democratic values serve quite opposite functions in South African society. They undermine the aspirations of the white exporters, the group for whom these values are, as it were, home products, and they sustain the ambitions of the non-white importers. The subordinates have selected from the culture of the dominant group precisely those items which are subversive of its domination; they have forced the dominant group to choose between the sharp modification of its own cultural heritage and the abandonment of race domination.

It is unfortunate for the whites that they should have inherited from their European forebears a political philosophy so unsuited to the local situation. At the same time, the blessings of democracy are also somewhat mixed for the non-whites. Democracy holds out the goal of equality to them, but denies the means for its realization. Two of the basic tenets of a democratic creed, respect for law and respect for constitutional procedures, stand in the way of equality, since domination rests on the constitution, on the laws of the country, and on the sanctity of law.[1] Hence, too, there is pressure on the non-whites to reject a creed which would seem to offer them the realization of their aspirations. For both white and non-white, democracy is both 'meat and poison', though in very different proportions.

We may regard the democratic creed, then, as a potentially disruptive strand in South African society, and look at the political ideologies of white and non-white as different ways of handling this creed. For the whites, the problem is to retain democratic values, but to make them safe (i.e. consistent with domination) by introducing new components. The task of the non-white is to detach these democratic values from their cultural moorings, so that they become applicable to all sections of the population.

'White' Ideologies

A number of ideologies attempt to make democracy safe for the dominant white group. The technique is to combine democratic values with interpretations of the difference between the groups and of the tempo of social change. This is done in such a way as to render the equalitarian political philosophy of democracy compatible with a theory of race domination. The ideologies emphasize the manifest differences between the groups, defining them as either racial or cultural, and stress a time-perspective, extending into a remote past or into a future beyond the span of human perception. These

[1] Realization of the role of law in South Africa is shown in this extract from an editorial in the anti-Government newspaper, the *Natal Daily News* (March 11th, 1953), which dealt with a criticism of the Appellate Division by a Cabinet Minister. 'Respect for the law and those who administer it in any form is the foundation of society, *above all in South Africa*. It is not only a question of our young people at political meetings having to listen to these remarks about the Judges. *It is also a question of the effects such remarks have on the non-Europeans.*' (Author's italics.)

interpretations are linked with different concepts of space (integration into a common area or separation into geographically distinct areas), and different theories of human motivation (the essential goodness of man and his responsiveness to higher ethical imperatives or, on the other hand, the fundamental sinfulness of man). The varying combinations of ideas give rise to the political theories of trusteeship, partnership and apartheid. Only trusteeship and apartheid are relevant in South Africa.

Trusteeship is an ideology which combines with democratic values the elements of cultural difference and an extended time-perspective. Its moral basis lies in the fact that the wards are in process of adaptation from a rural tribal culture to the industrial civilization of the trustees. There is no conflict with democracy, since the wards are promised progressive liberation from tutelage, as they acquire the white man's culture, until finally they achieve equal rights in an integrated society.

At the same time, trusteeship reconciles white domination and democratic values by continually postponing the extension of rights, and by projecting the equalitarian idea into the infinite future. As long as the non-whites have faith in the good intentions of the whites, trusteeship promotes domination. Because of the interdependence of the groups and the great numerical differences between them, the ruling ideology must not only have a moral value for the white minority, but also secure a measure of acceptance from the non-white majority. The testing time for trusteeship comes when the non-whites have acquired skills in the white man's world, and demand that the ultimate be translated into the here-and-now. The rulers cannot indefinitely defer consideration of these demands without undermining the confidence on which trusteeship depends. They are obliged to choose between democracy and domination. At this stage, trusteeship no longer serves the function of maintaining white supremacy.

Dr James S. Moroka, the first leader of the passive resistance movement, describes conversion to Christianity as serving a somewhat similar function to the ideology of trusteeship.

'Why', he asks, 'have the Europeans succeeded in the past three hundred years to keep you down? (*a*) One answer to this question is to be sought in the introduction of Christianity to you. To you was preached a religion of love and mutual trust. You believed implicitly in all that the Bible teaches about the character of a good man. You trusted your neighbours as good Christian men and women ought to do. When, afterwards, anybody suggested to you that you would do well to think of the things of this world, for those who brought you that religion thought first of the things of this world, you would not believe.'[2]

In the same way as with trusteeship, the difference between Christian theory and practice has stimulated a critical appraisal of the role of Christianity.

Trusteeship, a dominant ideology in South Africa for some years, is now rarely mentioned. It has been replaced by apartheid, which is a product of the impact of liberal equalitarian ideals on an earlier fundamentalist ideology.

This fundamentalist ideology rests on the assumption of timeless racial differences. Biblical sanction is claimed for the doctrine of the permanent racial inferiority of the non-whites. Race stratification is therefore not simply a secular matter, but a divine dispensation and a sacred duty – an absolute doctrine, regulating race relations from the infinite past to the ultimate future. This ideology provides a rationale for the timeless petrifaction of the *status quo*. Moreover, the ideology is logically consistent. The whites can enjoy both democracy and domination, since democratic values can have no relevance for the non-white substratum of humanity.

Absolute doctrines do not necessarily make for static social orders. The advocates of these doctrines have been obliged to adjust them to the changing relationships of the races, as a result of industrialization and the achievements of the

---

[2] Speech quoted at page 322 in the transcript of the evidence given at the preparatory examination of Dr J. S. Moroka on a charge under the Suppression of Communism Act.

non-whites. They have been forced to respond to a liberal creed, expressed not only within the country but crystallized in the Charter of the United Nations Organization and in its deliberations. In consequence, while the belief in permanent racial inferiority is still widely held, churchmen, politicians, professors and intellectuals were driven to evolve the contemporary solution of apartheid.

Apartheid, in theory, rests on difference, not on inferiority. It thus recognizes the liberal rejection of the dogma of racial inferiority, and the inability of scientists, no matter how adequately motivated, to establish racial inferiority.[3] The adoption of difference as the basis of discrimination introduces, however, the dilemma of finding a satisfactory criterion of difference. Race differences are relatively permanent, or at any rate long enduring, but discrimination based on race invites world criticism. Cultural differences, again, even if acceptable to outside critics, may be very transient, and therefore provide only a shifting foundation for the maintenance of the *status quo*. The dilemma is that of using the differences between the racial groups in a form acceptable to world opinion on the one hand, and in such a way as to permit the perpetuation of the *status quo* on the other – a challenging dilemma.

The most recent reconciliation of these conflicting compulsions relies on an analogy with the nationalism of the nation-states of Europe. Apartheid, so the argument runs, must be acceptable to a world which has embraced the nation-state, and which has recognized the justice of nationalism in a number of partitions and in the right of nations to self-determination. At the same time, the national differences between the groups may be interpreted as an expression of the divine will which created them.[4] There is accordingly a duty to maintain these

[3] See, for example, the work of Dr Ben J. Marais, *Die Kleur-krisis en die Weste* (Johannesburg, 1952, Die Goeie Hoop Uitgewers). Marais apparently accepts contemporary findings in regard to race, but his conclusion nevertheless merely reaffirms his initial implicit premise, the necessity of apartheid, which he justifies by emphasizing the conservative over against the radical principles in Bible teaching.

[4] Naturally, as manifested in the post-"Tower of Babel" era.

differences in perpetuity and, since man is inherently sinful, the maintenance of difference must be ensured by penal laws. That nationality and race tend to coincide in South Africa is fortuitous; the emphasis is not on the discreditable criterion of race, but on the legitimate aspirations of nations.

This most recent solution of the ideological problem was used by the Prime Minister, Dr D. F. Malan, at the beginning of the 1953 election campaign:

'Apartheid, both in principle and application, is not a specifically South African product, and much less a creation of the Nationalist Party for political ends. Europe itself, the matrix of Christian civilization, is the outstanding example of apartheid. The map resembles a Joseph's coat of some twenty-five sections, each represented by its own nationality, and for the most part also its own race with its own tongue and its own culture. . . . Apartheid is accepted in Europe, and in the rest of the world, as natural, self-explanatory and right. And now we rightly ask, why then should it be regarded as a deadly sin in South Africa? . . .'

The Prime Minister, while acknowledging that all men are equal before God, finds it difficult to see what relevance this has to an equal franchise. In any event, that cannot be the end of the matter. 'Apartheid is also founded in another act of Divine creativity . . . in the natural differences between race and race, colour and colour, incorporating for the most part differences also in nationality, language and culture.' He concludes with the argument that apartheid is morally justified, since it promotes friendship and co-operation, and avoids exploitation.[5]

The rejection of racial inequality is linked with the adoption of a further liberal assumption, the right of individuals or of groups to develop their inherent capacities to the full. Since apartheid is entirely negative in the implication of geographical

[5] Translated from *Die Burger*, March 6th, 1953.

separation for its own sake, the term has been given the more positive connotation of distinctive evolution for the various groups – '*eiesoortige ontwikkeling*', that is development along their own lines, and in their own areas.

In theory, then, apartheid incorporates some elements of a liberal creed – the recognition of differences, not as a basis for subordination, but as the foundation of varying potentialities for development and self-expression. A new group coming to power has been forced to adjust its views to a prevailing world-philosophy, and to the influence of this philosophy on its predecessors in power. The painful character of this adjustment is indicated by the continuous attacks on liberalism and the anathema directed against liberals. 'Liberalisties' is a term of abuse. But the adjustment is primarily at the ideological level and even then in essence the main assumption is still that of permanent racial inferiority.

Thus apartheid rests on an absolute, timeless, sacred difference between 'nations'. Since the advocates of the apartheid ideology are an extremely ethnocentric group, difference *is* inequality. This is the meaning of the Prime Minister's reply to the request by the leaders of the passive resistance movement for the abolition of discriminatory laws. He writes:

'. . . it is self-contradictory to claim as an inherent right of the Bantu, who differ in many ways from the Europeans, that they should be regarded as not different, especially when it is borne in mind that these differences are permanent and not man-made. If this is a matter of indifference to you, and if you do not value your racial characteristics, you cannot, in any case, dispute the Europeans' right which, in this case, is definitely an inherent right, to take the opposite view and to adopt the necessary measures to preserve their identity as a separate community. It should be understood clearly that the Government will under no circumstances entertain the idea of giving administrative or executive or legislative powers over

Europeans, or within a European community, to Bantu men and women, or to other smaller non-European groups.'[6]

Since the Bantu are different, the demands for the abolition of certain discriminatory laws and for direct representation in Parliament are self-contradictory; that is to say, difference necessitates discrimination. Super-ordination of a non-white over a white is totally excluded; non-whites are to be permanently debarred from administrative, executive or legislative powers in white South Africa. It is clear that in an area occupied by whites and non-whites there is no distinction between difference and inequality.

Even the promise of separate development for the non-whites in their own areas, and along their own lines, cannot readily be realized. It gives rise to the same inherent conflict as trusteeship, since it involves the allocation of resources to non-whites, and seems thus to limit the rewards which the whites might reasonably anticipate in an expanding capitalist economy. Also, complete territorial separation into a reproduction of the checker-board of Europe runs counter to industrial trends. The demographic facts are that the urbanization of the Bantu is a product of industrial development, and also, if we exclude the possibility of large-scale European immigration, its necessary basis. Indeed, complete territorial separation has been rejected by the political leaders as impracticable, at any rate for many years to come.

Moreover, what is involved in apartheid is not the self-determination of nations, but the self-determination of the white group. Because of the interdependence of the groups, the corollary to the self-determination of the whites is the other-determination of the non-whites. Thus, the Prime Minister asserts in the letter quoted above, if the non-whites do not value their racial characteristics, they cannot in any event deny the Europeans the right to preserve their identity. The description of European self-determination as 'a right, which in this case

[6] See Appendix B, p. 236.

is definitely an inherent right', throws doubt on the legitimacy of a refusal to maintain a separate racial identity. Since the differences are permanent, not man-made – that is to say, since they are part of a divine order – the preservation of racial characteristics is a sacred duty, and not subject to free choice. In any event, from the point of view of the perpetuation of white domination, the reduction of the non-whites into a number of mutually exclusive units is a functional necessity, and apartheid provides the moral justification for counteraction against an emergent non-white unity.

What remains then is the old dogma of racial inferiority (with some questioning of its validity), and stratification in an integrated society (with some recognition of an obligation to provide controlled opportunities for the development of non-whites in reserved areas). While the ideology is still subject to pressure and is still protean in form, its current meaning is given in the following statement by the former Director of the State Information Office:[7]

'We Nationalists believe that we must maintain White supremacy for all time. A policy of partnership must lead to Black domination. . . . We want the Bantu people back in the reserves where they come into their own and where they will be given self-government – under white trustee-ship. We cannot have independent Bantu States to threaten White South Africa. We must keep some Natives in the White areas for a very long time to do the work. I am being quite candid with you, but we are sincere when we say that we want the Natives to develop in their own areas.'

'Non-White' Ideologies

Since the Utopia which apartheid offers the non-white is the ultimate reconstruction of his traditional society, it appeals to those non-whites who have a sentimental attachment for, or a vested interest in, the past. It is no accident, then, that the Bantu National Congress was launched at a meeting of African

[7] Quoted in *Press Digest*, No. 8, February 26th, 1953, pp. 77-8.

herbalists, a group whose position will be undermined by the spread of Western medical practices.[8] Organized to assist the government in carrying out apartheid, the Bantu National Congress supports laws already passed for the segregation of the races, accepts a horizontal colour bar as right and inevitable in an integrated society, and looks to a future territorial separation as the only possible basis for fuller self-expression.

From the white supporters of the apartheid doctrine, the Bantu National Congress has borrowed the organizational form – it is a nationalist movement, by and for Africans – and a racialist technique. Characteristically, aggression is directed against the white man's licensed scapegoat, the Indian, and the emphasis is on the danger of miscegenation[9] – an illustration of the non-rational character of culture-borrowing, since the fear of miscegenation arose from the fact that small Afrikaner groups settled amongst populous African (Bantu) tribes.[10] It is entirely inconsistent with the numerical preponderance of Africans (roughly eight and a half million) over a negligible Indian minority (little more than one-third of a million).

The effective influence of the Bantu National Congress is certainly small. The non-white leaders took no active steps to combat the movement and attached little significance to it, even though they were somewhat embarrassed by the Government's use of the Congress for propaganda. With the conviction of the President-General of the Bantu National Congress on charges of theft, fraud and forgery, the movement has been discredited. Yet apartheid has some appeal not only for such non-whites as herbalists, but also for a number of chiefs whose

[8] The Bantu National Congress is federated to the Supreme Council for the Federation of Bantu Organizations. In the present discussion, I shall not draw a distinction between these two groups.

[9] 'And what is the sole Indian aim about the Native? It is simply the admixture of the two races. . . . The Indians insist on miscegenation and immorality with Native women-folk. . . . The Indian landlord polluting your daughter.' Quotations from 'Clarion Call to the Bantu People of Natal', the invitation by the Natal Native Medical Council to the meeting at which the Congress was founded, *The Torch*, February 26th, 1952.

[10] African, Bantu and Native are used as synonyms in South Africa. Native is the official designation; African is the term preferred by the people themselves.

orientation is to the traditional tribal structure, for some men of ability or education, frustrated by the colour bar and hoping for more extended opportunities under separate development, and generally for those whom the Government is able to attract by the rewards at its disposal. An interesting instalment of these rewards is the opportunity for advancement given to non-white policemen, a group whose identification is with their white superiors, and not with their own people.

This non-white apartheid movement, then, shows little concern for democratic values. Policy is based on racial separa- tion and antagonism, and on the acceptance of permanent inferiority in the white man's world. Superficially a nationalist movement, even its nationalism is spurious. There is no revival of ancient customs, as a rejection of the white man's ways, or as a magical restoration of the golden age before the white man's coming. Nor is 'black' nationalism set in opposition to 'white' nationalism. Instead, the movement seeks a preordained place for Africans in an order established by the whites and under their protection. Indeed, this dependence on the whites for the realization of African apartheid is inevitable. Almost two centuries of culture-contact have left their impact on the African in the modification and breakdown of tribal structure. He is now oriented to Western values and to the urban in- dustrial life which he has helped to create. Since apartheid means the reversal of this long process of acculturation, the only possible mechanism for its imposition on the non-whites is the superior force of the white man.

While the Bantu National Congress has adopted apartheid in terms of its apparent meaning – its promise of a realizable Utopia – a second mode of assimilating the doctrine is in terms of its real meaning, as an ideology of race domination. In this second form, Afrikaner nationalism finds its counterpart in African nationalism, and in the slogan 'Africa for the African'. It is, indeed, only these two groups, the Africans and Afrikaners who are in sufficient numerical strength to find nationalism attractive. Yet African nationalism is largely in abeyance at the present time, partly because of the influence of the Indian minority whose security rests in intergroup tolerance; partly because of the feeling among many non-whites that their advancement depends on unity (as the South African emblem phrases it, 'Union is Strength'),[11] and partly, no doubt, because of the abhorrence of many non-white leaders for the manifestations of extreme chauvinism. But it remains a possible, and indeed from the point of view of the white man an inevitable, development, since he projects his own concept of social phenomena in terms of race conflict and domination.

The very antithesis of the Bantu National Congress is the Non-European Unity Movement, which rejects apartheid and all forms of differentiation, on the assumption that differentiation is synonymous with discrimination. Its policy is based on a programme of non-white unity, of non-collaboration with the Government and refusal to work the 'machinery of oppression',[12] and on an affirmation of democratic values, which are detached from the ideologies of apartheid and trusteeship and are to be realized, not progressively in the liberals' evolutionary timespan, but simultaneously by a revolutionary assumption of power.

The leaders of the Unity Movement follow certain Marxist theories in their analysis of political philosophies. They interpret these philosophies, that is to say, as more or less automatic expressions of class interests, in contrast to the prevailing South African modes of analysis in terms of moral purpose and deliberate deception.

Deceit, is, in fact, deeply rooted in South African politics. Thus charges and countercharges by the two main white political parties of fraud, falsity, misrepresentation, double-dealing, and indeed outright lies, have been a dominant theme

---

[11] This is an item of culture which the whites naturally wish to reserve for themselves.

[12] 'This . . . means that we must *now* reject inferior institutions, that we must *now* refuse to work the machinery which oppresses us, that we must *now* in the struggle for our aims, refuse to collaborate with our oppressors, the rulers, the Herrenvolk, from Nationalist to liberal, that we must *now* isolate the agents of the Herrenvolk – the Quislings – in other words, that our method is the policy of non-collaboration.' Article on 10-Point Programme of N.E.U.M., *The Torch*, April 22nd, 1952.

in recent elections. This falsity stems primarily from the race relations of contemporary South African culture. A number of factors contribute to undermine public morality: the close identity of the racial programmes of the two main white parties, so that politicians are obliged to demonstrate that the opposition policy is not what it seems; the emotional character of political rivalries founded on racial prejudice; and an ignorant electorate. Also, white politicians act on the assumption that the African is a simple untutored savage, to whom any explanation may be offered, a *tabula rasa* on which any writing may be engraved. With the development of political understanding among Africans, the rationalizations offered to them are clothed in slightly more sophisticated terms. But the process is cumulative; the increasingly subtle deceptions progressively evoke increasingly subtle analysis, and the politically oriented non-white of to-day shows keen critical ability. Political statements have not kept pace with the development in non-white leadership; there is still not enough flesh to camouflage the real intent.[13]

Deliberate deception implies also the possibility of a change of heart, and it is precisely this assumption which the Non-European Unity Movement rejects. To the liberal theory of human motivation, based on a belief in the freedom of the human will and the ultimate power of truth over human behaviour, the Unity Movement opposes the largely determinist theory of Marxism. Distortion is regarded as an inevitable product of material conditions, and it cannot be exorcized by goodwill; political philosophies express material interests. While the liberals believe in the possibility of transcending these material determinants, and of maintaining co-operative relations between the races, the philosophy of the Unity Movement implies a radical rejection of the white man, his laws, and his ideologies, whether apartheid, trusteeship, liberalism, 'neo-liberalism', or other variants of

[13] A colleague suggested the analogy of a pantomime ass, with its large clumsy bones moving under the loose skin.

'Herrenvolkism'.[14] Though membership of the Unity Movement is open to whites, and the ultimate goal is an integrated society, the immediate practical effect of its programme is to range non-white against white in an irreconcilable conflict of interests.

The ideology of the Unity Movement has a number of elements in common with apartheid. It is based on a determinist theory of human motivation as in apartheid, but rooted in the class (i.e. race) situation, and not in the fundamental nature of man. It shares with apartheid a dogmatic approach to social phenomena. Again, as in apartheid, the basis is the antagonism of white and non-white, flowing, however, from different material interests, not from cultural or biological factors. In the same way that apartheid aims at the consolidation of the whites under Afrikaner leadership, the goal of the Unity Movement is non-white unity. The curious anomaly is that the Unity Movement acts in fact as a divisive force, since it will only tolerate unity under its own auspices. In contradistinction to apartheid, the Unity Movement is oriented to the present, to the auspicious revolutionary moment when full democratic rights, and the abolition of all discrimination on the basis of race, colour or creed are to be achieved simultaneously.

While the Government is sympathetic to the Bantu National Congress, it also shows a measure of tolerance for the revolutionary Non-European Unity Movement, presumably on the principle of 'divide and rule', since both organizations are

[14] Some indication of the spirit of the Unity Movement appears from this quotation, extracted from an editorial in *The Torch* (August 19th, 1952), the official journal of the Movement. 'Imperialism – Herrenvolkism has no "conscience" or "soul" or "sense of decency". It is not moved to pity or reform by the misery and suffering of the oppressed and exploited people. It causes and lives off this oppression and exploitation, of which poverty, tyranny and suffering are inevitable and inseparable parts. It has no respect for those who seek to end its régime of oppression and exploitation. In fact, it passes laws against, builds jails for, and generally hounds and persecutes those who seek to liberate the impoverished, rightless and voiceless mass which is the foundation of Imperialism – Herrenvolkism. It never repents, because repentance would mean suicide. It never parts with anything voluntarily. It gives up only what is forced from it. It never departs from the scene of its own accord. It fights with every means at its disposal. It disguises itself when and where it can. It uses any agency or person it can, and in the end, it has to be beaten to its grave by the active, unified, organized, principled and militant struggles of the oppressed and exploited people.'

antagonistic to passive resistance, though for diametrically opposite reasons. The Bantu National Congress rejects the passive resistance movement on the grounds that it is working for non-white unity and against the Government's beneficent apartheid dispensations, through which fuller democratic rights are to be achieved. The Unity Movement attacks passive resistance on the grounds that it is *not* working for unity; that the present co-operation it has achieved between African and Indian is unprincipled, based on a temporary expedient serving different ends; and that the objectives are trivial concessions and rewards of office under an oppressive régime, not a full programme of democratic rights in an integrated society. Indeed, the attacks directed against passive resistance by the Unity Movement equal those of the Government in their uncompromising hostility.

The structural roots of the ideologies appear clearly in the establishment by African herbalists of the Bantu National Congress; in the espousal by non-white teachers of the perfectionist, dogmatic, arm-chair educational Unity Movement; and in the imposition of apartheid laws by Afrikaner nationalists, still culturally rooted in their patriarchal, semi-feudal, rural communities and conceptualizing a complex, racially-integrated industrial society in the semi-sacred categories of the backveld. But the application of a structural analysis to the passive resistance movement is more complex.

The passive resistance movement is supported primarily by the two main non-white political organizations, the African National Congress and the South African Indian Congress. These aim at the extension of full democratic rights to all races in an integrated South African society. The members of the African National Congress vary in political outlook from Marxists, at one extreme, through liberals and moderates, to African nationalists, at the other. The South African Indian Congress is almost equally varied in the political composition of its members, though there is no Indian nationalist movement.

The mixed pattern of reactions to passive resistance gives some indication of its ideology. The most vigorous opponents are the Bantu National Congress and the Unity Movement among the non-whites, and the followers of apartheid among the whites. The main non-white supporters are the African and Indian Congresses. Among the whites, only small groups, mainly liberals and non-Afrikaner churchmen, openly expressed their sympathy. This suggests that the ideology of passive resistance represents a middle road between the conservative Bantu National Congress and the revolutionary Unity Movement, a course which is acceptable to the politically varied membership of the African and Indian Congresses, and involves a non-revolutionary rejection of apartheid, compatible with Liberal and Christian thought.

We can determine the main ideological characteristics of passive resistance more precisely from its programme (as set out in the initial plan and the correspondence with the Prime Minister),[15] and from the steps taken to carry out that programme.

The passive resistance leaders demanded the abolition of the Pass Laws, limiting freedom of movement; Stock-limitation (a rural rehabilitation scheme, which the resistance movement claims has added to the misery of the African peasant); the Suppression of Communism Act (Communism being redefined, as the law stands at present, to include movements directed at bringing about *any* political, industrial, social, or economic change, by unlawful acts or omissions); the Group Areas Act (variously described in terms of segregation, separation, ghettoes, or expropriation, depending on the political perspective); the Bantu Authorities Act (oriented to a revival of tribal structure); and the Separate Representation of (Coloured) Voters Act (designed to remove the Cape Coloured voters from a common to a separate roll). The last four Acts mentioned were passed by the present Government and are interpreted by the resistance movement as retrogressive, negating the promise of progressive advancement implied in trusteeship. The objective of the resistance campaign is to eliminate these laws, to set in motion progress towards equal

[15] See Appendices B and C, pp. 233-56.

status, and to secure an earnest of goodwill in the abolition of passes. No immediate claim is made for direct political representation or for full democratic rights, which are held out as a goal for the future. The time-element is thus conceived in the spirit of liberalism. It is evolutionary, but with a perspective within the span of perception – 'during our lifetime', as the leaders of the resistance movement phrase it, and not extending, as in trusteeship, to an infinitely distant future.

The resistance acts take the form of deliberate breach of selected pass-laws and apartheid regulations, and express the apparent anomaly of the acceptance of a democratic creed and the rejection of one of its basic tenets, respect for law. The rejection, however, applies to specific laws and not to the legal process as such. Indeed, the resisters court arrest and the attendant penalties, justifying their defiance, at the ideological level, in terms of a higher ethical imperative, the allegiance owed to God over against the duty to Caesar, and on the grounds that the rejected laws do not rest on the will of the majority of the people and offend against the dignity of man.

This belief in the power of ideas of justice and of the human personality to motivate the non-white resisters also provides a basis for co-operation between white and non-white, in contrast to the determinist theory of the Unity Movement. The defiance acts themselves were so planned, and for the most part so executed, as to give the minimum offence to the sentiments of the whites. The rationale underlying the dignified acceptance of punishment is that the noble sacrifice of self-interest for an ideal would stir the 'higher orders' of the mind, the moral conscience of the rulers.[16] The hope for co-operation is

---

[16] Thus the President of the South African Indian Congress, concludes a letter to the Prime Minister announcing his organization's support of the African National Congress, with the expectation 'that unbiased justice will prevail and that laws which offend the dignity of Man and retard the progress of South Africa will be repealed' (p. 36 of the Court record cited above).

The contrast with the approach of the United Movement appears in this quotation from *The Torch*, June 10, 1952: 'And now, because Malan wouldn't resign on Leap Year's Day, as Moroka told him to do, he will jolly well have to resign because a few extra Non-Whites are inviting themselves to gaol. At least, that is what the Joint Planners are asking the oppressed people to believe. In

expressed in the appeal to Government for the repeal of its own discriminatory laws, in the ready assumption that large sections of the white population are opposed to apartheid, and in the repeated invitations to whites for support in order to prevent the antagonistic separation of the races.

In opposition to all forms of racialism, a central theme in the campaign is that the defiance is directed against unjust laws, not against any racial group. This non-identification of the white man with his laws flows from Gandhi's philosophy that

> 'man and his deed are two distinct things. Whereas a good deed should call forth approbation and a wicked deed disapprobation, the doer of the deed, whether good or wicked, always deserves respect or pity as the case may be. "Hate the sin and not the sinner" is a precept which though easy enough to understand is rarely practised, and that is why the poison of hatred spreads in the world.'[17]

The opposition to racialism arises partly from the need which many non-whites feel for unity in their own ranks, and the consequent need to combat the antagonism of Africans, Coloureds and Indians to each other. It also expresses, however, a democratic ideology, the goal of an integrated inter-racial society. Race-difference is accepted, race-pride acknowledged, but the apartheid corollary of race separation and discrimination is rejected.[18]

South Africa, is there anyone but a fool or a crook who really believes that Malan and Co. will lose any sleep because a Dadoo or a Kotane or (and this is indeed a wicked thought) a Moroka is in gaol? . . . Or the tens of thousands of non-white innocents who go to gaol every year? Every politically-minded person knows that the conscience of the South African ruling class lies locked up in the Reserve Bank and the Constitution, and is guarded by the sjambok, the police force, the gaols, the *skietcommandos*, Parliament, the Law Courts high and low, and by every member of the Herrenvolk—whether organized in the O.B., the Broederbond, the Torch Commando or the United Democratic Front.'

[17] *The Story of my Experiments with Truth*, Ahmedabad, Navajivan Karyalaya, 1933, Vol. II, p. 53.

[18] In reply to the Prime Minister's confounding of biological differentiation and social discrimination during the initial correspondence between the parties, the President of the African National Congress carefully distinguishes race and culture. 'The question at issue is not one of biological differences, but one of citizenship rights which are granted in full measure to one section of the population and

Clearly, the immediate aims, and the assumptions under-lying the resistance movement, are consistent with the spirit of liberalism. The ultimate objectives of the participants, however, the ends to which the resistance movement is but a means, will vary with their political outlook – liberal, Marxist or nationalist.

Rejection of Democratic Values

At the present time, neither trusteeship nor apartheid solves the problem of so combining democratic values with other components as to maintain white domination. Trusteeship fails because its time-perspective has been narrowed by the non-whites and will be increasingly retracted to the present. Apart-heid is a transient doctrine, since it is invalid in the sense that it is not consistent with the social structure and does not allow for the accommodation of action to the new and changed situa-tion of industrial integration. Its promise of self-development in separate areas is illusory for the great mass of non-whites and ignores the effects of two centuries of culture-contact.

The non-white ideologies have not succeeded in detaching democracy from its insulation. The Bantu National Congress accepts a subordinate position in South African society, and is not concerned with the achievement of full political status. The complete rejection of the white man by the Non-European Unity Movement provides no mechanism for the realization of shared values in collaboration with whites; it is revolutionary, and would presumably produce the counter-response of the further explicit abandonment of democratic ideas. As for the passive resistance movement, the attempt to free democratic sentiment by the deliberate breach of selected laws has had the opposite effect, at any rate as far as legal rights are con-cerned. And the movement is now arrested by the heavy

completely denied to the other by means of man-made laws artificially imposed, not to preserve the identity of Europeans as a separate community, but to per-petuate the systematic exploitation of the African people. The African people yield to no one as far as pride of race is concerned, and it is precisely for this reason that they are striving for the attainment of fundamental human rights in the land of their birth.' (Letter signed by Dr J. S. Moroka, February 11th, 1952, p. 28 of the Court Record cited.)

penalties imposed under the Criminal Law Amendment Act.

The crucial issue is the course which the two sponsors of the passive resistance movement, the African National Congress and the South African Indian Congress, will pursue. They may move towards Unity Movement doctrine, or the Africans may move towards extreme nationalism spurred on by the success of the Afrikaner. In either case, the possibility of a peaceful solution seems remote. On the other hand, they may stand firm on a liberal ideology, and seek to realize their objectives by lawful means. Whether they will take this latter course depends on the answers they give to the following questions: Are there effective legal means for realizing their aims? Since an integrated industrial society depends largely on co-operative participation, will the Government be obliged to make concessions in order to secure the consent of the governed, or can it maintain its position without consent? Is the assumption of the Unity Movement correct that all whites are inescapably *Herrenvolk*, or are there a substantial number of whites who will be motivated by equalitarian ideals? And, finally, can the moderate leaders maintain their influence and following?

As a result of the interdependence of the groups, the literal acceptance by non-whites of democratic values, with their subversive implications for white domination, has influenced the whites towards the rejection of democracy. Ultimately we may expect the whites to return to a clear democratic ideology, since the numerical proportions of the races in Africa are such that the future of the whites depends on the acceptance by the non-whites of the principle of racial equality. In the meantime, the ardent adoption of this very principle by the non-whites has set in motion an attack on democratic values. It is expressed in a wide range of apartheid laws, and in the progressive redefinition of communism as synonymous with non-discrimination on the basis of race or colour, a process not yet completed. The immediate problem is the extent to which this rejection of democracy will be carried, and the nature of the response by the non-whites.

II

COMMUNISM BY STATUTE

GOVERNMENTS generally seek to control social change in such a way as to render their own power more secure. The techniques for control vary with the conditions in the society and the political philosophies of the rulers. Governments, in an attempt to further their own interests, may guide and initiate change, or they may emphasize the sanctity of tradition and resist all forms of social change. Either technique may fail in its objectives and set in motion unanticipated changes in the structure of power.

The policy of the South African Government is to control social change in such a way as to maintain the traditional structure of race domination, characteristically expressed in the patriarchal rural household – with its white overlord, and with its non-white servants living in primitive shelters far removed from the homestead, bartering labour for the use of land and small rewards, entitled to nothing as of right within the patriarchal domain but receiving limited and revocable concessions by grace of the master.

At the same time, the economic basis of South African society is changing rapidly. The percentage of the national income attributable to secondary manufacturing industries now exceeds that of either agriculture or mining, and the Government is, in fact, encouraging the industrial development of the country.

The Afrikaner rulers, in their interpretation of the relationship

47

between economic institutions and social structure, place an almost Marxist emphasis on the determining power of the economic institutions; race equality and indeed biological amalgamation are predicted as the consequence of non-white advancement in a developing and integrated economy. But the rulers assert that these consequences can be avoided by deliberate policy, by the application of a system of ideas – in this case, the ideology of apartheid. The objective of their experiment is, therefore, to use the ideology of apartheid in such a way as to hold race relations constant, while promoting economic change and expansion. Ironically, a partial accept-ance of Marxist theory, which provides an ideology for under-privileged groups, has stimulated the South African Government to the preventive action of quarantining the non-whites in their present subordination.

Passive resistance is a reaction to the techniques used for stabilizing race domination. We need therefore to analayse these techniques, and to assess their consequences, in order to see passive resistance in its broad South African perspective. Is the Government's contention correct that a semi-feudal system of race relations can be maintained in a capitalist industrial society? If not, will the whites subordinate industrial develop-ment in the interests of apartheid, or modify apartheid in the interests of economic expansion and thus set in motion un-predictable changes in race relations? Or will the whites persist in the policy of apartheid and economic expansion and in this way perhaps provoke a revolutionary challenge to the whole structure of race domination?

Stabilizing Race Domination

The instruments designed to achieve stability of race domina-tion are: (1) the systematic perfecting of unequal status contact between the races; (2) the removal of non-white affairs from politics to administration; and (3) the monopoly by the whites of all constitutional means for initiating social change.

48

(1) *Unequal Status Contact*

In the outside world equal-status contact is accepted as a technique for reducing prejudice and discrimination; in South Africa unequal-status contact is used to heighten prejudice and perfect discrimination. The South African counterpart of the United States experiments in promoting intergroup understanding by equal-status contact is legislation designed to ensure that only the minimum contact takes place and that such contact is unequal.

'For points of contact inevitably produce friction and friction generates heat which may lead to a conflagration. It is our duty therefore to reduce these points of contact to the absolute minimum which public opinion is prepared to accept. The paramountcy of the white man and of Western civilization in South Africa must be ensured in the interests of the material, cultural and spiritual development *of all races*'[1] (author's italics).

Systematically, starting with the maximum degree of intimacy, the Nationalist Government is eliminating the possibility of equal-status contact. Its first statute for this purpose was the Prohibition of Mixed Marriages Act, No. 55 of 1949. This provides that a marriage between a European (white) and a non-European (non-white) may not be solemnized. The object cannot be to check blood mixture and to promote racial purity, as stated by the Minister of the Interior,[2] since there are, by general acceptance and policy in the Union of South Africa, four races (in hierarchical order, European, Coloured, Asiatic, and Native), and the Act allows intermarriage between three of them. Its real purpose is rather to close the membership of the ruling group, to limit the recruitment of new members to children of the rulers and to approved immigrants, and to erect a barrier against the race mobility of the Coloureds.

---

[1] The Minister of the Interior, May 1950 (*Hansard, House of Assembly Debates,* Vol. 70-73, p. 7,453.)
[2] *Ibid.,* Vol. 66-69, p. 6,164.

But intermarriage is a small producer of potential recruits as compared with the mass production of miscegenation, and the second stage in this Utopia by legislative enactment is the Immorality Amendment Act, No. 21 of 1950. The principal Act, the Immorality Act of 1927, stripped European males of their traditional prerogative of 'illicit carnal intercourse' with women of all races and prohibited acts of miscegenation between European and Native, imposing penalties on both partners. Europeans still retained the right to miscegenate with Coloureds, while Coloureds had complete freedom of miscegenation. The amending Act, passed by the present Government, substitutes the word 'non-European' for 'Native' in the principal Act. Its effect is, therefore, to whittle away further the European prerogative, with the result that Europeans now have the right to practise 'illicit carnal intercourse' only among themselves. As far as the Coloureds are concerned, they are denied the privilege of miscegenation with whites, their sexual status is rendered as incriminating as that of the Native, and the avenue of race mobility by miscegenation is partly closed.

Clearly, both these Acts are directed largely at setting a barrier between the whites and the Coloureds, and this raises the perplexing legal and biological problem of defining the characteristics which distinguish a coloured person from a white person. It is significant for an understanding of the psychology of apartheid legislation that the test of ancestry which is applied in the United States to define a Negro is not used in either of these Acts. Indeed, a distinction based on ancestry would mean the substantial reduction of the white group, in consequence of the long history of miscegenation and of 'passing' in South Africa. Instead, the legislature, following legal precedent, has relied on appearance or social acceptance. Thus for purposes of the Immorality Amendment Act, ' "European" means a person who in appearance obviously is, or who by general acceptance and repute is, a European'. In other words, the test is that of 'successful passing', regardless of ancestry.

The third phase in the plan for eliminating equal-status contact is the Group Areas Act, No. 41 of 1950, which provides the machinery, 'by compulsion, if necessary',[3] for the physical segregation of defined groups, for residential purposes or trade. A further aspect of apartheid policy emerges in the definition of the groups. Under the sexual-contact statutes the distinction is between European and non-European. But the consolidation of the non-European groups would threaten white domination because of the numerical disproportion between white and non-white, and the Group Areas Act provides the machinery to break down the non-Europeans into more manageable units. A classification in terms of white, native, and coloured replaces that of European and non-European, while express power is vested in the Governor-General to further differentiate the native and coloured groups, *but not the white*, into 'ethnical, linguistic, cultural' or other subdivisions. Indian, Malay and Chinese groups have already been separated out from the coloureds, and the indications are that the natives (Africans) will be sub-divided on a linguistic basis.

The statutory definition of the groups emphasizes again the test of 'successful passing' for whites. The phrase 'any person who in fact is' a member of a particular group – that is, by the biological test – forms part of the definition of a native, but it is not used to differentiate whites, whose membership in the ruling class is validated by obvious physical appearance or general social acceptance. Indeed, of these two criteria, acceptance as a white man overrides the physical criterion, since a person who is obviously in appearance white but who is accepted as coloured falls outside the white group, while, conversely, a person who is not white in appearance may

[3] The Minister of the Interior. *Ibid.*, Vol. 70-73, p. 7,433. Racial segregation is no invention of the Afrikaner group but a present reality. The contribution of the Government lies in the systematic planning and extension of segregation and in the removal of deviations. Indeed, the main impetus for the Group Areas Act came from the English-speaking people of Natal and more particularly from the city of Durban. It is the 'race-zoning experts' of the Corporation of the city of Durban who have produced the most thoroughgoing proposals.

establish membership in the white group by proof of general acceptance.

These statutes lay the foundations for the avoidance of the more intimate equal-status contacts, but there still remain many other areas of contact on a basis of relative equality.

The churches deviate somewhat from apartheid, and Government spokesmen have attacked the liberalism of the English churches.[4] The Government is beginning to take over the education of Natives from the English missions, and exercises some control over mission churches in native urban locations. It seems unlikely, however, that the Government will impose religious apartheid, especially since there is some questioning of the apartheid practices of the Government among its own supporters in the Dutch Reformed Church. Though the Dutch Reformed Church acts in many ways as the spiritual wing of the Government, it shows increasing signs in race relations of an independent development of ideas stimulated by religious doctrine rather than by the desire for domination.

Educational apartheid is relatively complete. There are, however, two deviations: the Universities of Cape Town and of the Witwatersrand, which accept non-white students, and had, in 1954, an enrolment of under 500. Both universities assert their academic freedom and resist the bleaching process. The Government is thus faced with the difficult problem of devising the necessary formulae and procedures for the reconciliation of compulsory apartheid and academic freedom.

Finally, fraternization, in the sense of personal human contacts, of mutual visiting and companionship, is not illegal and does take place. It is assisted by higher levels of education

[4] However, the Prime Minister, Dr D. F. Malan, appeared to be fairly satisfied with the position. 'To a large extent there is apartheid even in the churches, and I want to say here that even the host of political bishops who are bubbling over with holy indignation and who are holding up their hands in horror because Christian principles are being violated by discrimination do not practise in their own churches and schools what they preach. Even in their own churches separate seats have been allocated to Europeans and non-Europeans, and in their European schools the Coloureds have been systematically refused admission.' *Hansard, Joint Sitting of Both Houses of Parliament*, July 15th, 1953, p. 37.

among the non-whites, and there have also been interracial experiments in the way of holiday camps open to all groups. The extent of fraternization is, however, relatively small.

The significance of these contacts lies not so much in their quantity, but in the fact that they tend to erode colour prejudice, and that they constitute a deliberate breach of the general principle of unequal-status contact. Visiting and companionship are avoidable contacts, and their voluntary character directly challenges apartheid.

While the legislative enactment of unequal-status contact is thus incomplete, the administrative basis for its implementation was laid in the Population Registration Act, No. 30 of 1950. This provides for the compilation of a register of the people of South Africa, classified into white, coloured, and native, with such subdivisions of coloured and native into ethnic or other groups as the Governor-General may prescribe. It will solve the difficulty in distinguishing between white and coloured which now impairs efficient administration of apartheid doctrine. Officers presiding at marriages, police arresting persons who have engaged in illicit carnal intercourse, principals admitting children to school, officials in control of seaside resorts and sports fields, proprietors of bottle stores, and local authorities concerned with group areas will be assisted in their duties by a system of identity cards based on the register and will be saved the invidious task of identification by physical appearance or social acceptance. This task will be carried out once and for all by the Director of Census. The ultimate test of a white person is again that of 'successful passing', as shown in the definition of a white person and the assurance given to the whites by the Minister of the Interior that

'. . . if an objector says that he knows that another person's great-great-grandfather had Coloured blood, the objection will not be valid, because the Act stipulates that a person's appearance or social associations will be the deciding factor in the classification. Therefore objections

53

founded on ancestry will not even be referred to the judicial Board. Such objections will immediately go to the wastepaper basket where they belong.'[5]

When all objections to classifications have been settled, the list will be final.

'All those important facts regarding the life of every individual will be combined in this book and recorded under the name of a specific person, who can never change his identity. It is only when the last page in that book of life is written by an entry recording the death of such a person that the book is closed and taken out of the gallery of the living and placed in the gallery of the dead.'[6]

The population register is the white man's *Debrett*, his genealogical claim to birth and privilege. For the coloured man and his descendants it is the instrument of permanent bastardization.

(2) *From Politics to Administration*

The establishment and maintenance of unequal-status contact depend on a monopoly of power. The model for this monopoly is the removal of non-white affairs from politics to administration.

Parliamentary representation conformed substantially to the apartheid political model when the present Government took office, though there were two important deviations, viz. the representation of natives and the coloured vote. The relegation to administration was most fully developed in the field of native affairs,[7] and the Government has extended this principle further. The Bantu Authorities Act, passed in 1951, provides additional administrative machinery in the form of tribal, regional, and territorial authorities. The recent removal of native education from the Union Education Department to

[5] *Hansard, House of Assembly Debates,* Vol. 70-73, p. 2,521.
[6] The Minister of the Interior, *ibid.,* pp. 2,498-9.
[7] See Leo Marquard, *The People and Policies of South Africa* (London, Oxford University Press, 1952), pp. 108ff.

the Department of Native Affairs is designed to extend the administrative centralization of native affairs as well as to ensure a more efficient education policy, in keeping with apartheid ideology. But the representation of Natives in the legislature – by three white members of the House of Assembly out of a total of one hundred and fifty-nine, and by four elected and five appointed Senators of the forty-eight white Senators – though negligible, is in conflict with the principle of removing native affairs from politics, and its abolition, particularly in the House of Assembly, has been threatened by Government spokesmen.

More serious is the vote of the Coloureds in the Cape Province, since the inclusion of Coloureds on a common electoral roll in contrast to the communal representation of the Natives is an equal-status contact. Moreover, the Coloureds disturb white politics by the effect they may have on the outcome of elections in certain constituencies and more particularly by a direct influence on party programmes shaped to entrap their vote, which is potentially a substantial factor although the actual number of registered coloured voters in the Cape Province at the present time does not exceed 40,000. Finally, from the point of view of the Government, many Coloureds so misconceive their true interests as to vote against apartheid policies. The steps which the Government has taken to remodel the coloured vote along the lines of native representation in the Cape Province have enriched the literature of constitutional law, but the coloured vote on the common roll still remains a thorn in the martyrdom of the Afrikaner apostles of apartheid.[8]

The clearest working out of the principle of removing

[8] The coloured vote on a common roll is entrenched against modification by the requirement in the South Africa Act of a two-thirds majority of both Houses sitting together. The penultimate stage in the removal of this vote to a separate roll has apparently now been reached by the reconstitution of the Senate so as to provide the Government with the necessary two-thirds majority. The effect is to render the Senate an adjunct of the party in power. The Government has also enlarged the quorum for the Appellate Division, whenever the validity of an Act of Parliament is in issue.

non-white affairs from politics to administration, from direct participation to bureaucratic files, is to be found in the Native Labour (Settlement of Disputes) Act, No. 48 of 1953. In place of Native trade unions,[9] the Act provides machinery for the establishment of Native Labour Committees at the regional level and a Central Native Labour Board at the national level. Although Natives appointed by the Minister serve on the regional committees, they negotiate with employers through their European chairman and an inspector of labour. Should the negotiations prove unsuccessful, then the dispute is referred to a Central Native Labour Board, exclusively European. This Board in turn negotiates with the employers and contacts the Industrial Council, which has no Native members. If the representatives of the Central Native Labour Board are dissatisfied with the recommendations of the Industrial Council, they can report to the Minister of Labour for Wage Board procedures.

Layer upon layer of white administrators thus prevent the Natives from directly promoting their own interests in industrial employment and bringing organizational pressure to bear on the employers. Control of the conditions of native employment is firmly secured to the whites in so far as this can be achieved by administrative procedures. Decision-making is an all-white affair, and the Natives have only a means of calling the attention of the administrators to their grievances. The relationship is that of petitioning subject to authoritarian ruler; concessions are by grace of the master and not by right.

[9] *Hansard, House of Assembly Debates*, August 4th, 1953, p. 873. The Minister of Labour was opposed to the recognition of Native trade unions, which, he declared would be used as a political weapon: 'We would probably be committing race suicide. . . . It might result in raising the standard of living of the Native worker, but inevitably it will result in a lowering of the standard of living of the European worker.' He was also opposed to allowing the Natives separate, specially-designed procedures for collective bargaining, which he declared would be to their disadvantage because of their general inability to present a case in terms of industrial law, *ibid.*, pp. 870-2. This is the conventional double-pronged settler logic: if opportunities are extended to the Native he will understand his interests so well as to advance them *vis-à-vis* the whites; on the other hand, he has so little understanding of his interests that the opportunity of advancing them would in fact prove detrimental to him.

(3) *Monopoly of Social Change*

The exclusion of non-whites from effective political participation is the basis of the Government's monopoly of constitutional social change. Nevertheless there remain a number of channels, both legal and illegal, for non-white action in initiating social change, and the control of these forms of action is necessary for the secure maintenance of white domination.

The possibilities of legal action narrow down to the boycott (in cases where no obligation is imposed to act or abstain from acting in a particular manner) and to the legal enforcement of civil rights; illegal action can take a constitutional form as in the passive resistance movement, or an unconstitutional revolutionary form.

The boycott, in the form advocated by the Non-European Unity Movement, is an attempt to defeat the Government's policy of removing non-white affairs from politics to administration. The main targets of the boycott are 'those political institutions that are created for our own enslavement'.[10] Tabata, spokesman of the Unity Movement, argues that the choice of weapon in a liberatory struggle must be related to the objective conditions of the society, that the subordination of the non-whites in South Africa rests on the collaboration of quislings, both chiefs and intellectuals, in working the machinery of oppression; and that, in the circumstances, the most effective weapon at the present time is non-collaboration. In essence, therefore, the boycott is designed to make the administration of non-white affairs unworkable by withholding the non-white administrative agents whom the Government requires both to handle the sheer volume of administration and to secure a measure of consent from its subjects.

It is difficult to estimate the possibilities of the boycott. The leaders of the two main non-white organizations, the African National Congress and the South African Indian Congress, vacillate between the rejection of the boycott and its

[10] I. B. Tabata, *The Boycott as Weapon of Struggle* (Cape Town, The All African Convention Committee, 1952, p. 19).

acceptance.[11] Such campaigns as have been conducted in South Africa (for example, non-collaboration in the recent elections of native representatives or in the Van Riebeeck Tercentenary celebrations) were only partially successful, which is to say that they failed substantially. Unless there already exists strong solidarity, it seems inherent in the boycott that it should split the subordinate groups, particularly in the field of collaborative administration where the Government has the highest rewards to offer. The net result may be to deflect the struggle for improved status into bitter internal dissension. In South Africa there is not yet sufficient non-white solidarity for the successful boycott of political institutions and, in any event, the Government has the necessary power to counter a boycott by the suppression of both leaders and organizations.

The second mode of legal action, the enforcement of civil rights, has been effective in the United States, where equality under the constitution provides a basis for the advancement of the Negro. In contrast, the inferior status of the South African non-white is embedded in the constitution and in legislative policy. Yet the possibility of legal action has been opened up also by two circumstances in South Africa. First, there are basic inconsistencies in the South African legal system, which derives from its sources in Roman Dutch law and English law many liberal equalitarian principles in conflict with the racially stratified structure of South African society. Second, the legislature often uses the technique of oblique rather than direct race discrimination. Thus many inequalities in the access to public amenities are not specifically enacted but are established by delegating Government departments a general power to provide separate facilities. While this technique enables the rulers to maintain a public façade of equity and

[11] During the discussion of Central African Federation, there was the same vacillation among African leaders in Nyassaland, where indirect rule would seem to provide more favourable conditions for the boycott than in South Africa. One of the reasons for this indecision in South Africa is the failure of the leaders to distinguish between types of boycott. Some types of boycott, such as an economic boycott, can be effective if supported by a small proportion of the population; others – for example, the boycott of elections – require solid support.

justice, it gives the non-whites the opportunity of challenging the exercise of the delegated power.

The combination of these circumstances to provide a cause of action is illustrated in the case of Regina *v.* Lusu, heard by the Appellate Division in 1953. Lusu was acquitted of a charge of entering a railway waiting-room reserved for Europeans on the ground that there was partial and unequal treatment to a substantial degree as between the races. The Court did not assert that where separate facilities are supplied for the different races these facilities must be equal, as is the case in the United States, but simply that, if the legislature had intended substantial inequality, it would have made express provision to that effect. In the absence of such provision, it must be assumed that the legislature could not have intended to delegate wide and arbitrary powers of discrimination to a government department.[12] The Court relied on a principle derived from English law which protects the individual from arbitrary administrative acts, a principle clearly at variance with the facts of race relations in South Africa.

The Government's response to Lusu's case and to the many similar actions challenging race inequality in the provision of public amenities was simple and direct. With its characteristic rational systematization of a non-rational ideology, it made explicit what had hitherto been largely implicit, viz. the legality of substantial inequality in the reservation of public amenities. Instead of dealing singly with the issues as they arose, the Government passed an omnibus statute, the Reservation of Separate Amenities Act, No. 49 of 1953, which provides that any person may reserve, under penal sanctions, public premises or public vehicles for the exclusive use of a particular race, and

[12] See Julius Lewin, 'Apartheid Comes to Court', *The Forum*, December 1952. He points out that since the close of the nineteenth century, it has been a principle of English common law – which is the basis of South African law in public affairs – that discrimination on the basis of race or colour is unreasonable. The effect, in South African law, is that discrimination can only be introduced if there is explicit statutory authority. In Rex *v.* Rasool (A.D. 1934) the Appellate Division accepted the legitimacy of 'separate but equal' facilities in post offices, notwithstanding the absence of clear legislative authority.

that, furthermore, no such reservations may be invalidated by reason of a substantial inequality in the facilities provided for the races or by reason of the fact that no facilities whatsoever are provided for a particular race.

Superficially, there appears to be little change, since, in cases where the legislature did not expressly delegate authority to discriminate, the right of the non-whites to separate but equal facilities was dependent on their not exercising the right and on their acceptance of substantially inferior facilities. But, in fact, the position of the non-whites has deteriorated. Traditionally, discrimination is camouflaged in social hypocrisy,[13] expressed in the claim that discrimination is *altruistically* imposed by the whites *in the interests of the groups discriminated against* and hence morally justified. Social hypocrisy has the function not only of securing some measure of acceptance by the subordinate groups but, more important, of keeping alive a different system of values – in this instance, a recognition of the rights of subject peoples. The significance of such statutes as the Reservation of Separate Amenities Act is that they are a rejection of more equalitarian values, a denial of moral obligation, and a naked assertion of self-interest. They have the effect of hardening apartheid sentiment.

The real threat to the stability of race domination lies in illegal action. The legal mechanisms of change are so effectively controlled by the Government's monopoly of power that the hard-won gains of years of effort can be swept aside from time to time by a simple legislative enactment. There is no need to anticipate the steps which will be taken by the non-whites or to deny them a measure of initiative. In the case of the more serious challenge of illegal action, however, the Government took early preventive measures in the Suppression of Communism Act, No. 44 of 1950, which creates the new and major offence of promoting communism.

[13] *The Torch* (August 11th, 1953) uses the term '*politikolo*' for what it describes as the political abuse of language: ' "Land" Acts take away land, "Representation" Acts disenfranchise, "Education" Commissions are violently opposed to education, and Labour "Settlement" Bills are calculated to unsettle labour.'

The crime of promoting communism not only includes the advocacy or use of unconstitutional techniques for the complete transformation of the social structure; its statutory meaning has been extended in South Africa to cover gradual non-revolutionary change within the constitutional framework if furthered by illegal acts. Communism is defined generally in the act as Marxian socialism and, in particular, as any doctrine or scheme which aims at the dictatorship of the proletariat, or *'which aims at bringing about any political, industrial, social or economic change* [my italics] within the Union by the promotion of disturbance or disorder, by unlawful acts or omissions or by the threat of such acts or omissions or by means which include the promotion of disturbance or disorder, or such acts or omissions or threats.' Hence, a rising would fall into the same category as a purely local strike by Natives for improved conditions of work in a particular industry (i.e. economic change), or as the passive resistance movement, which is in effect a dramatic way of petitioning the legislature itself to ameliorate the lot of the non-whites (i.e. social change).[14]

This curious extension of the meaning of communism is in fact logical if interpreted against the background of South African social structure. The common element in the definitions of communism is the modification of the structure of race relations: communism is the symbol of any threat to white domination. That this is the correct interpretation of the 'Red' Act appears from the further statutory particularization of communism as any doctrine or scheme *which aims at the encouragement of feelings of hostility between the European and non-European races of the Union,* the consequences of which are calculated to advance the achievement of the objectives of communism.

The 'Red' Act thus provided machinery for the suppression

[14] Indeed, the action of white residents in Bloemfontein who defied a ban on Sunday fishing is also communism, as was the action of the Government in passing the invalid High Court of Parliament Act as a preliminary to the removal of the coloured voters from the common roll. But clearly the purpose of the statute is not to prosecute cabinet ministers or the ordinary white voter.

of the passive resistance movement prior to its inception, and the leaders were immediately convicted of communism. But the machinery was in a sense too elaborate for the prosecution of the rank and file who refused to carry curfew passes, for example, or who trespassed on an amenity reserved for whites, while the existing legal penalties of short-term imprisonment did not act as a sufficient deterrent. The need for more drastic punishment, easily invoked, was met by the Criminal Law Amendment Act, No. 8 of 1953, which provides that:

'Whenever any person is convicted of an offence which is proved to have been committed by way of protest or in support of any campaign against any law or in support of any campaign for the repeal or modification of any law or the variation or limitation of the application or administration of any law, the court convicting him may, *notwithstanding anything to the contrary in any other law contained* [my italics] sentence him to

'(*a*) a fine not exceeding three hundred pounds; or
'(*b*) imprisonment for a period not exceeding three years; or
'(*c*) a whipping not exceeding ten strokes; or
'(*d*) both such fine and such imprisonment; or
'(*e*) both such fine and such whipping; or
'(*f*) both such imprisonment and such a whipping.'

The penalties are even more drastic in the case of a person who advises, encourages, incites, commands, aids, or procures any person to commit an offence by way of protest against any law, or who uses any language calculated to cause a person to commit an offence in protest, or who solicits, accepts, receives, or offers any funds in support of such a protest campaign.

The Criminal Law Amendment Act expresses the essential character of white domination in South Africa. Since domination rests on legislation, the sanctity of the law is vital to its maintenance. If the laws do not command the voluntary acceptance of the non-whites – because they are so easily deceived by agitators, communists, Indians, liberals, Anglican pastors, or the United Nations, and thus fail to appreciate the beneficent dispensations of their rulers – then conformity must be compelled. Civil disobedience, no matter how trivial the form in which it is expressed, becomes a major criminal offence, analogous to treasonable activity. In the Criminal Law Amendment Act there is the clear avowal that the basis of order in South African society is not the consent of the governed but a code of penal sanctions – or, more simply, force.

The remaining weapons in the control of illegal action are the Public Safety Act, No. 3 of 1953, which provides the machinery for the assumption of wide emergency powers; the reorganization of the police to facilitate the efficient mustering of force; and a change in the functions of the police. One of the problems in police action is that of specifying the conditions under which violence may be used and the extent and nature of police violence in relation to the threatened disturbance. These justifying conditions have been redefined, in the words of the Minister of Justice, as follows: 'The days are past when the police officer was like a rainbow; now he comes before the storm.'[15] The symbolism of the police preceding the storm, which suggests the role of the storm trooper, is as yet only partly appropriate in the field of race relations.

Paradoxically, the present relationship between the Government and the non-whites is such as to mobilize even non-white assistance, albeit involuntary, in perfecting the machinery of white domination. The enforcement by the non-whites of rights to equal public facilities focused the Government's attention on defects in its legislation with a consequent improvement in the machinery of apartheid. Similarly, although the Suppression of Communism Act anticipated the deliberate breach of laws as an instrument of change, the subsequent passive resistance campaign served to streamline its provisions by stimulating the innovations of the Criminal Law Amendment

[15] Translated from report in *Die Burger*, July 20th, 1953.

Act. The relationship between Government and non-white is like that of spider and fly. Under present conditions, each movement of the non-whites merely increases their helpless entanglement in the web of apartheid.

Apartheid and Profit

Whether the South African experiment will have the results anticipated by the Government depends on the compatibility of the Government's objectives and the appropriateness of the means for their realization. Given the Government's objectives and its ideological commitments, it is difficult to see what more effective machinery could have been devised. Unequal-status contact reinforces sentiments of superiority in the white group and stimulates the desire for more extreme inequality. The substantial relegation of non-white affairs to administration secures to the whites the control of legal change, while the branding of illegal action against domination as communist serves to mobilize the force of the State and the sentiments of the ruling group.

The Government's objectives are to maximize profit as well as apartheid; indeed, profit is a major incentive for its version of apartheid. In so far as they are compatible, there is no problem for the Government. Thus the Group Areas Act is an effective solution, since it provides machinery for the conversion of apartheid into profit by a redistribution of wealth. Similarly apartheid (discrimination) in public services (amenities, education, welfare) secures a highly privileged position for the whites in the sharing of public funds and rewards.

However, difficulties in reconciling apartheid and profit arise in the industrial field. The substantial reservation of skilled work for the whites and the wide gap between skilled and unskilled wages are highly rewarding for the dominant group. But there is already industrial pressure to open up more semi-skilled and skilled occupations to the non-whites, to employ workers in terms of their value to the organization rather than on the basis of race, and to rationalize industry by the impersonal criterion of efficiency. This pressure will increase as labour shortages and competition create the need for the more efficient use of native labour, while at the same time the problems of developing a skilled non-migrant labour force and of providing adequate incentives – higher wages and opportunities for occupational and social advancement and for consumption, such as home ownership – will become more acute.

In these circumstances, it is significant that the Government has delayed the implementation of industrial apartheid. Apart from the reservation to the whites of additional employment opportunities in Government departments and the opening up of some types of work to non-whites in their own areas, the first major act of industrial apartheid, the Native Labour (Settlement of Disputes) Act, was passed only toward the end of the 1953 parliamentary session. The classification of employment categories as white and non-white is still projected. Even the physical separation of employees of different races is not fully enforced.[16] The explanation of this tardiness lies, of course, in the conflict between the consistent application of apartheid and the maximizing of profit. The dynamic factor in the South African situation and the challenge to Government policy is that while apartheid is an instrument of Mammon, the ecstatic worship of Mammon threatens the sanctity of apartheid.

Hence the question arises whether the Government will modify apartheid for the sake of profit or forgo profit for the sake

[16] Morroe Berger, in his discussion of the use of legislation to secure equality, comments: 'It has become evident that the relationship of employer to worker is so devoid of personal sentiment under present conditions of large commercial and manufacturing enterprises, has become so purely an economic tie, that it becomes a fit subject for legal control.' *Equality by Statute* (New York: Columbia University Press, 1952), p. 168. If the impersonality of industrial organization makes it a proper field for legislation against discriminatory practices, then presumably the argument is equally strong that industrial relations are a fit subject for discriminatory practices. It is all the more remarkable therefore that the Government has not fully enforced employee segregation in industry, though the Factories, Machinery and Building Works Act of 1941 provides the necessary machinery to impose segregation in respect of accommodation and conveniences.

of apartheid. Both motivations are deeply rooted. The strength of the economic incentive is clearly expressed in the growth of Afrikaner nationalist organizations designed to wrest an increasing share of the economic wealth of the country from the English (suggestive, in some manifestations, of a continuation of the Boer war); in the rapid entry of Afrikaners into commerce and industry; and in the use of non-legitimate techniques for amassing wealth (such as white-collar crimes), presumably a most efficient index of the strength of the economic incentive and, in the past, largely the prerogative of other groups.

Similarly, apartheid sentiment is deeply rooted. It developed as a defence against the loss of privilege which would follow upon absorption by a numerically preponderant but conquered and despised people. It was also a defence against the wayward libidinous tendencies which are the necessary mechanisms of this absorption. With the passage of time, however, apartheid has come to assume the sanctity of a law of God. And it received a curious reinforcement.

The psychology implicit in apartheid legislation is the psychology of the coloured man who has successfully 'passed' into the white group. Over the generations, there would have been inculcated into the successful 'passer' the dominant value that 'whiteness is all': the importance of looking white, of acting white, of living white; and, at the same time, there is the fear of exposure and of contact with the coloured group.[17] It is these values which apartheid legislation expresses, and these fears which apartheid legislation allays, by a certificate of whiteness, ensuring membership in the dominant group in perpetuity, notwithstanding appearance or ancestry, and interposing a barrier between white and coloured which is a permanent assurance against the possibility of a relapse. Indeed, the psychology of the successful 'passer' seems to set

---

[17] The observation commonly made in South Africa that it is the coloured-looking white who behaves with special brutality to the non-white is relevant to the psychology of successful 'passing'.

the level of apartheid sentiment and to give it a high intensity.

The circumstances in which many Afrikaners find themselves serve as a further reinforcement of apartheid sentiment. In process of adaptation to Western industrial society, and in the uncertainty of a strange environment, they seek security in rigid adherence to the familiar pattern of domination and of race discrimination.

Inherent in apartheid is the dynamic tendency to develop to ever higher levels of intensity. First, there is the familiar phenomenon of the vicious circle arising from the relationship between interaction and sentiment.[18] Race hostility is expressed in apartheid, in the avoidance of contact; this in turn increases suspicion and hostility between the races and gives rise to further measures for apartheid, so that there is a continuous development of apartheid to greater and greater extremes.

Second, race hatred, of which apartheid is the overt expression, provokes a counteraction by the non-whites in the form of organization, programmes for civil rights, and passive resistance movements. The resultant insecurity emphasizes the need for white solidarity and an authoritarian form of government. Hence there arises the curious anomaly: the greater the conflict created by the Government's apartheid policies, the more secure is its position with the white voter and the wider is the acceptance of these policies. In consequence, the official opposition finds itself obliged to assimilate its non-white policies and indeed its leadership with that of the Government, so that national parliamentary politics tend to take the form of personal rivalry between Afrikaner leaders substantially agreed on the broad principles of apartheid, though differing on points of detail.

Third, the dramatic ritualization of apartheid in Parliament, preceded by a wide-scale whipping up of fear, has the effect of heightening apartheid sentiment. The consequences extend also to the white opponents of Government policy. They cannot

[18] See George C. Homans, *The Human Group*, (London) Routledge and Kegan Paul, 1951, pp. 110-13, for a discussion of this relationship.

fail to be affected by the apartheid ritual and by the increasing range of new crimes and penal sanctions. If, as Durkheim argues, repressive law is a measure of the collective conscience, then it seems reasonable to assume that repressive law is also an instrument for deliberately modifying the state of the collective conscience. Inevitably the imposition of penal sanctions on interracial intercourse, for example, influences the attitudes of even those who regarded it in the past as a purely private matter.

Clearly, apartheid has a momentum of its own and the Government is no longer in full control. The so-called 'pig-headed obstinacy' of the Government, and the abortive non-rational attempts to circumvent the constitution, are not entirely matters of free choice; hence there is little likelihood that the Government will modify apartheid. The probability is rather that it will persist in its present experiment of economic expansion and race domination, though there may be a change in the direction of economic expansion. This would take the form of a reversal of the present trend toward secondary manufacturing industry and a return to the traditional bases of the economy, mining and agriculture. The objective would be to maintain and develop the economic institutions most compatible with apartheid, since the mines rely on an unskilled native labour force.

The opportunity to change economic policy by diverting resources from secondary manufacturing industry to mining arises from the growing exploitation of uranium. The effect of such a change in policy would be to produce a re-alignment of forces within the white group. Many Afrikaner industrialists, conscious of the conflict between profit and apartheid, and valuing profit more than dedication to an ideological relic, would combine with their English-speaking counterparts who are so largely responsible for the present economic development of the country. But the Government could look for support to many mining groups, to farmers dependent on State assistance for the supply of native labour, and to the large numbers of

Afrikaner workers on the lowest rungs of industrial and state employment. The latter are especially staunch protagonists of apartheid since it helps them to satisfy their ambitions for social mobility, partly by the reservation of educational and employment opportunities and partly by advancing their position *vis-à-vis* the non-whites. Since social position is relative, it may be raised either by advance along the social scale or by depressing lower strata.

The first threat to Government policy lies, therefore, in the incompatibility of its objectives. This is particularly marked in the case of secondary manufacturing industry. Yet even in mining the competition for labour among mining groups themselves, and between the mining industry and manufacturing industry, will exert pressure to raise the status of the non-whites. Moreover, in the event of the Government subordinating the interests of secondary industry to mining, the industrialists themselves will seek to secure a modification of apartheid policy.

The second threat to the success of the Government's experiment will be made by the non-whites themselves, though it is customary in South African political circles to regard the non-whites as objects of administration rather than as a political factor.

Self-fulfilling Prophecy?

Ideologically, apartheid has little to offer the non-whites since it is based on permanent inferiority; and the Government will not succeed in indoctrinating a general acceptance of apartheid by control of native education. It is inevitable that a system of education designed to train Africans for subordinate roles should fail. Over the generations, exposure to an ideology of trusteeship and to the currents of western civilization, the developments in Africa, and, more particularly, participation in industry, have shaped aspirations to equality. The practical applications of apartheid, stripped of the ideological camouflage, are even less likely to modify these aspirations. Since apartheid is an instrument of policy in a capitalist economy motivated by the pursuit of unlimited gain, opportunities to the Africans for development of their own rural areas will be kept to the minimum. In the cities, moreover, the pattern is already established. African industrial workers are denied the right to acquire freehold property or to organize for improvements of working conditions; they are rigidly limited in their expectations by the overriding interests of the dominant group. At the same time, the goal of almost unlimited occupational and social mobility is held out to white workers. There is no reason to suppose that the non-white will prefer the more restrictive of these two systems of rewards available to workers in the same industries. Nor does apartheid offer sufficient opportunities of personal advancement in administrative service to attract more than a section of the educated and potentially mobile non-whites.

The form and ideological content of the non-white rejection of apartheid will be shaped by the means which the Government has devised for the control of social change. These means render futile any non-white legal action for progressive social change, and muster the force of the State against illegal action. Overt illegal action calls down the heavy penalties of the 'Red' Act and the Criminal Law Amendment Act as well as the proscription of the leaders. Notwithstanding these heavy penalties and the difficulty of effective organization in the absence of a strong trade-union movement, strike action seems likely since it is precisely in the industrial sphere that the major tensions will arise. However, the more probable long-term response of the non-whites can only be an underground movement. The very efficiency of the Government's control of social change will dictate this reaction.

Similarly, the ideological content of the movement will be shaped by the Government's policies. It may include nationalism and racialism. These are the culture patterns which the Government has most effectively presented to the non-whites, the immediate rewards are clearly demonstrated, and the

Africans are a vast majority of the population. Moreover, apartheid stimulates nationalism and racialism by emphasizing the unity of the segregated groups and confining social contact as far as possible within each group.

Communism is, however, a likely rival ideology for the underground movement, since Government policy is also an effective demonstration of the fact that the race conflict is a class conflict, with wealth and privilege concentrated in the white group, and the non-white substantially an industrial proletariat and an impoverished peasantry. Proscription under the 'Red' Act has the effect of driving some moderates to a more radical position, while the hardened cohorts needed for a communist revolution are being trained by the brutalizing sanctions of white domination. The Government's fear of communism, its monopoly of legal change, and the characterization of the illegal mechanisms as communism, must suggest to the non-whites that communism is the effective response to apartheid and cause them to identify their advancement with communism. May not the Government achieve what the communists themselves failed to achieve, the recruitment of large numbers of non-whites to communism? May not the results of the Government's experiment be the very antithesis of its objectives – revolutionary social change in the form the Government most fears and which it has falsely defined as communism?

Indeed, it seems probable that the Government's false definition of communism will generate traditional communism.

III

THE SOCIOLOGICAL NATURE OF
PASSIVE RESISTANCE

THE form of non-white reaction, whether it is to be violent or non-violent, is as significant as its ideological content. Passive resistance and Mau Mau are very different forms of resistance adopted, in recent years, by the indigenous peoples of Africa against the domination of white settler groups. The response of the dominant group in Kenya to the primitive violence of Mau Mau is the counterviolence of modern warfare, while in South Africa the white rulers have responded to passive resistance, not directly by violence, but by the establishment of the necessary machinery for violent action. Superficially it would seem that violence is evoked by both forms of resistance.

General Characteristics of Passive Resistance

The term 'passive resistance' is misleading. The plain implication of the words is that the resistance is initiated by acts of omission, such as the non-payment of taxes, and that the resister submits to the consequences, which are determined by the actions of others. In fact, however, passive resistance campaigns have also been initiated by acts of commission, such as Mahatma Gandhi's march in protest against the salt tax in India, or the deliberate breach of curfew laws in South Africa.

The common factor in all these movements is obviously, in the first place, that of resistance. Thus, neither the present Bhoodan Yajna (Land-gift) movement launched by Vinoba

Bhave in Bihar nor his Sampattidan Yajna (Sacrifice of Wealth) movement is a resistance movement, since both are based on co-operation, on the voluntary redistribution of wealth as a religious duty. They lack the element of a conflict of interest between groups in opposition.

The second common factor is the renunciation of the use of force as an instrument of change. The resistance is passive in the suffering of violence, rather than its infliction. Passive resistance may be described with greater accuracy as non-violent resistance.

Passive resistance arises when petitions, humble submission to the will of the master, and patient waiting for the carrying out of promises and for a change of heart, have been ineffective. The aim of the resisters is to change the current system of interaction in which domination is expressed, and to bring about a new phase of interaction in which modifications will be carried out co-operatively.

The means used for this purpose fall broadly into two classes; non-co-operation and civil disobedience. Submission to the laws is clearly co-operation, and hence civil disobedience is logically a form of non-co-operation. It is, however, usually treated as a separate category in resistance literature, and we will follow this usage, since civil disobedience works in a some-what different way from other forms of non-co-operation.

In the case of most forms of non-co-operation, the objective is to reduce interaction to the level at which the dominant group will be obliged to negotiate. Mahatma Gandhi, in the non-co-operation campaign against the Rowlatt Act (India, 1919), advocated initially the giving up of titles and honorary posts – thus attacking the shared system of values on which stable interaction depends – and, in later stages, the resignation of Civil Servants, police and soldiers, thus undermining the whole basis of government. Similarly, the Non-European Unity Movement in South Africa now campaigns against participation in government and administration, against working the 'machinery of oppression'. Indeed, this technique is indicated wherever government rests on the participation of a subordinate group which has a high degree of solidarity, as may be the case under indirect rule in some colonial territories.

Civil disobedience works in the opposite way by heightening interaction. It provides a means for the dramatic presentation of demands, compels a response by the dominant group, transforms the routine, relatively unconscious pattern of interaction by an infusion of emotion, moral fervour and conflict, thus providing a stimulus for reconsideration of the relations between the dominant and subordinate groups. The result of this reconsideration may, of course, be a perfecting rather than a relaxation of domination.

Types of Passive Resistance

Mahatma Gandhi distinguished passive resistance movements on the basis of the *motives of the resisters*. On the one hand, there is passive resistance 'in the orthodox English sense', which 'has been conceived and is regarded as a weapon of the weak. Whilst it avoids violence, being not open to the weak, it does not exclude its use if, in the opinion of a passive resister, the occasion demands it.' (*Satyagraha*: Ahmedabad, Navajivan Press, 1951, pp. 3 *et seq.*) In other words, the resister is not in possession of equal or superior force, and violence would not pay; the overriding consideration is not non-violence, but expedience. In the second type of passive resistance, the Satyagraha evolved by Mahatma Gandhi himself, non-violence is regarded as an expression of strength. The passive resister is motivated by a moral conviction that violence is sinful under all circumstances and relies on the moral superiority of the soul, and soul-force as against body-force.

The difficulty in applying this distinction is that it involves an analysis of motive, always difficult, and more especially so in the case of research into a passive resistance movement. Moreover, the motives of the resisters are likely to vary, as Gandhi himself found among his own *Satyagrahis*.

74

Although some analysis of motive is unavoidable, a more concrete distinction may be made between passive resistance movements in terms of *the mechanisms by which change is to be effected*. These mechanisms work either by making the system of domination in its present form embarrassing to the rulers, or by conversion of the rulers through a change of heart. The particular mechanism employed can be deduced to a large extent from the actual conduct of the campaign. There are difficulties, however, since the means used are substantially the same, and resistance movements are often of a mixed type. Nevertheless, theoretically the two forms have very different sociological characteristics, and empirically the distinction between them is useful.

(a) Change by Embarrassment of the Rulers

The norms for the selection of means in this type of passive resistance are non-violence, and effectiveness for the purpose in view. These norms are linked through the means. Some types of means, though effective – as, for example, processions, strikes, picketing – have such an emotional charge as to stimulate the possibility of acts of violence by the resisters themselves, unless the movement is strongly disciplined. Other means, again, may be of a type which will almost certainly precipitate immediate acts of violence by the dominant group. The tendency is for passive resisters to accept responsibility for their own acts of violence, but not for the violent counteraction of the dominant group; indeed, the violence of the rulers may be claimed as a moral victory by the resisters. Nevertheless, the possibility that the rulers will use force in response to a form of resistance, and the probable extent of that force, are necessary considerations in assessing the effectiveness of the proposed means.

The means are significant in this type of resistance movement not in themselves, but as effective techniques for initiating specific changes in the social structure. Since the selection of means is governed by considerations of effectiveness, the means themselves will depend on the conditions which prevail in the society. Choice of means, that is to say, is relative to particular circumstances, and not based on absolute values, on assumptions as to validity in all societies and under all conditions.

Specifically, the selection of means will depend on the economic organization of the society, the system of domination, the extent of the force available to the rulers and their willingness to use it, the numerical relations between the groups, the degree of solidarity in the subordinate group as well as in the dominant group, and, above all, the assessment of these factors by the leaders of the resistance movement. Thus, in a society based on the labour of the subordinate groups, as in many parts of Africa, the obvious target for the resistance movement is the economic system, and such action as the withholding of labour is indicated. At the same time, this course of action is likely to be hazardous, since the subordinates are economically dependent on the dominant group, and since the rulers may be expected to react with special violence against any threat to their material interests.

Again, in the absence of solidarity within the subordinate group, the boycott of administrative positions, such as posts in segregated departments, is not likely to be effective, since if even a small proportion of the subordinates are attracted to the relatively high rewards of administration, not only does the boycott fail, but dissension within the subordinate group is inevitable. On the other hand, the boycott of commodities may influence policies even if it is only partially effective.

Or, again, the resisters' assessment of the effects of violent counteraction by the dominant group will depend on the numbers of the rulers and the forces at their command. Where, as in South Africa, there is a very large settler population with well-equipped police and military, forceful measures by the rulers in the initial phase of the resistance may have the effect of crushing it completely. In vast territories with a small settler group and a numerous subordinate group, the settlers may be obliged to call in an outside power in order to suppress resistance. This may have the effect of ultimately advancing the position of the subordinate group, if the outside power is less involved in the local issues and hence more ready to make concessions.[1]

The relationship between ends and means, in this type of passive resistance, is direct and observable. A necessary qualification is that the ends may not, in fact, be those announced by the resisters. Thus, the subordinate group may be so poorly organized that it cannot attempt immediate effective action for a change in the more important aspects of domination, and is obliged to select quite trivial incidents of domination. The ends are the building up of self-respect in the resisters, of a strong determination to resist, and of an effective mass organization; they are not the removal of the incidental stigmata of domination, as announced by the resisters, but basic changes in the attitude of the subordinate group and ultimately in the structure of domination itself.

Where the resisters are not in a position to challenge domination, the means may take the form of a planned gradation of activities, from occasional local strikes to a national strike, from civil disobedience by selected individuals to mass civil disobedience. The course of the campaign, from stage to stage, will be moulded by the reactions of the dominant group and the responses of the subordinate group, and in some respects resemble a cat-and-mouse manœuvring. At the stage in which effective mass resistance can be organized, the need for it may have disappeared; the subordinates' ability to organize may so clearly demonstrate a change in the power relations of the groups as to open up the possibility of negotiation, the breakdown of which rendered passive resistance necessary in the first instance.

In the form of resistance movement which we are considering, the success of civil disobedience and of non-co-operation generally depends on the extent of mass participation, and of

[1] Some of the Kenya settlers, for example, suggested the use of South African troops against the Mau Mau. South Africa, they must have felt, could be relied upon to introduce a more compatible approach to race relations than the British.

consequent embarrassment to the rulers. This distinguishes our first type of passive resistance from Satyagraha, which in theory is independent of mass support.

(b) Satyagraha – Conversion by Suffering

Satyagraha (insistence on truth), as developed by Mahatma Gandhi, is a universal religious ethic governing all social relations – between father and son, kin, neighbours, groups and nations. Its main values are expressed in the vows required of the Satyagrahi,[2] which include:

Truth – the quest for God, 'Truth is God';

Ahimsa – non-violence, non-aggression in thought, speech or deed, but having also the more positive connotation of universal love;

Bramacharya – perfect chastity in thought, word and deed, including complete celibacy, and involving not only control of sex, but of all organs of sense;

Non-possession – or non-attachment, linked with the vow of poverty; reduction of possessions to the minimum necessary for the maintenance of life, and the extinction of desire for the things of this life; and

Fearlessness – freedom from fear, whether as to possessions, false honour, relatives, government, bodily injuries or death.

When applied to resistance, Satyagraha may be defined as a method of securing rights by personal suffering. The suffering must be that of the resister, not of the persons resisted. This is a necessary requirement. For Mahatma Gandhi, specific laws did not impose an obligation to act in a particular manner, but an obligation willingly to undergo the penalty for failing to act in the prescribed manner. The resister does not submit to specific laws, but to law and order; indeed Gandhi contended

[2] M. K. Gandhi, *Satyagraha, op. cit.*, pp. 37 and following, and H. S. L. Polak and others, *Mahatma Gandhi*, London, Odhams Press, 1949, Chapter IX (by H. N. Brailsford).

that only those who scrupulously observed the laws of the country from inner conviction had the right to practise civil disobedience. The resister is therefore free to disobey particular laws in accordance with the dictates of his conscience or the Satyagraha ethic. Since the conscience of the resister is set above the laws of the State, a safeguard against arbitrary acts of resistance is the restriction of suffering to the Satyagrahi himself.

Looking at the vows of the Satyagrahi from the point of view of a materialist and sensual culture, it would seem that the passive resister who has achieved *Bramacharya* and non-attachment has little to lose. The tyrant cannot readily hurt the resister through his possessions, or through intense personal attachments. There remains, however, as a weapon of the dominant group, the infliction of suffering by physical deprivation beyond the threshold of the resister's training, or by violence. Here emerges the importance of the role of suffering in Gandhi's philosophy. It is a positive value; it is actively sought. Mortification of the flesh is regarded as a condition of spiritual progress; self-purification is to be achieved through suffering. The amount of suffering willingly undergone serves as a measure of progress: the purer the suffering, the greater the progress. Hence, suffering being positively desired by the resisters becomes an armour against the tyrant rather than a weapon in his hands.

The effect of Satyagraha is thus to set both oppressive laws and force at nought. The force behind domination is normally translated into laws, the sanctity of which is emphasized by the dominant group. Satyagraha strips this sanctity from the laws, and compels the application of sanctions, thus converting domination again to naked force. In relation to this force, the passive resister has so subjected himself to ascetic discipline that the range of effective sanctions is greatly reduced, and the hurt he sustains is a means toward the much desired self-purification.

The mechanism of change in Satyagraha is not the embarrassment or coercion of the government, as in the first type of passive resistance, but a change of heart in the rulers, their conversion through the suffering of the subordinates. The inherent goodness of the rulers and their searching of conscience are activated through sympathetic understanding of this suffering, and change is made voluntarily by the rulers in consultation with the resisters.

From the emphasis on conversion by suffering flow a number of consequences which give Satyagraha its characteristic and often enigmatic form.

The means are substantially the same as in the first type of resistance, non-co-operation and civil disobedience, but they operate at very different levels. Embarrassment of the rulers works directly at the level of power relations, while, in Satyagraha, the conflict is essentially at the level of moral values. The picture of social relations implicit in Satyagraha, the insistence on the independent force of ideas in social change, is the very antithesis of the Marxist emphasis on the role of material factors.

The preferred technique in Satyagraha is civil disobedience in the sense of a breach of laws not involving moral turpitude, the ready submission to sanctions, and motivation by civility or love. The reason for this preference is that many forms of non-co-operation, such as for example, the rejection of foreign cloth, may bring little suffering, whereas civil disobedience is a guarantee of suffering. It is 'a terrifying synonym for suffering'.[3]

A new technique, perhaps an aspect of non-co-operation, becomes important, the individual act of suffering, as in Gandhi's fast in disapproval of untouchability. The late Field-Marshal Smuts describes this technique as Gandhi's distinctive contribution to political method,[4] based, as in the Aristotelian theory of tragedy, on the principle of the purifying effect of vicarious suffering on the emotions of others. Smuts felt that

[3] M. K. Gandhi, *op. cit.*, p. 69.
[4] 'Gandhi's Political Method', in *Mahatma Gandhi*, edited by S. Radhakrishnan, London, George Allen and Unwin, 1949, pp. 280-5.

the success of the technique depended on an appeal to the emotions and on coercion, whereas Gandhi claimed that the appeal was to reason through the heart and denied the possibility of coercion, unless the fast was for purely personal ends.

Since the mechanism of change is conversion by suffering, there need be no direct relationship between ends and means. It is sufficient to stir the conscience of the rulers by suffering which is quite remote from the circumstances which gave rise to the resistance. Thus, in protest against a decision of the Cape Supreme Court invalidating marriage according to Indian religious rites, the Mahatma's wife, Kasturbai, challenged the laws against the entry of Indians into the Transvaal without a permit, by crossing the border between Natal and the Transvaal.[5] In the same way, the agitation in India for the removal of the statue of General Neill was interpreted by Gandhi as pointing the way to reach the disease of unjust rule itself, though the statue was only a symptom.[6]

Linked with the relative independence of ends and means is the emphasis on the means themselves. They are no longer auxiliary, but assume a dominant position. This has two aspects. First, the Satyagrahi is enjoined to look after the means and the end will take care of itself. He must be 'unattached' to the attainment of the object of Satyagraha; otherwise his desire for the realization of the goal may lead him to compromise the means by considerations of expediency. 'A Satyagrahi has nothing to do with victory. He is sure of it, but he has also to know that it comes from God. His is but to suffer.'[7] The second aspect is that the Satyagrahi does not regard himself as responsible for the consequences of the means used, if the means themselves are pure and undefiled. Indeed, the assumption is that the consequences themselves cannot but be right. Thus, in the resistance movement against the British in 1930, symbolized by opposition to the Salt Tax, Gandhi declared that

---

[5] Polak, *op. cit.*, pp. 83-4.   [6] M. K. Gandhi, *op. cit.*, pp. 73-4.
[7] *Ibid.*, p. 73.

'if in spite of such repeated warnings people will resort to violence, I must disown responsibility save such as inevitably attaches to every human being for the acts of every other human being'.[8] Conduct in Satyagraha is thus oriented to an ethic of ultimate ends rather than an ethic of responsibility.[9]

In contrast to our first type of resistance, a degree of co-operation is necessary in Satyagraha. In the case of civil disobedience, the suffering depends on the act of the opponent himself, who must therefore co-operate in imposing the punishment. This led to the curious development in South Africa where the Natal resisters carefully notified the police of the time and place of acts of civil disobedience. Indeed, on one occasion, they paraded the streets and the entrance to the police station in an attempt to secure arrest, when the Durban police were experimenting with non-co-operation in the form of non-arrest. In any event, whatever the form of the resistance, knowledge of the suffering, if it is to act as a catalyst, must be brought home to the rulers. Hence, the act of resistance should be attention-compelling and public. This is assisted by press publicity and open trial; the resister uses the court as a forum to make known his motives in opposing the rulers. Here, too, a measure of co-operation from the rulers is necessary. Where, however, rule is tyrannical, the act of resistance may be completely muted by secret arrest and trial, and thus partly fail in its purpose.

The co-operative nature of the relationship between the rulers and the resisters limits the lengths to which resistance may be carried. It must stop short of the breakdown of the social order. Indeed, the Satyagrahi shows a readiness to agree as far as possible with the rulers on other than fundamental issues and to explore solutions of the basic conflict. Conversion of the opponent by a change of heart is, of necessity, non-revolutionary.

---

[8] M. K. Gandhi, *op. cit.*, p. 275.
[9] See Gerth and Mills, *From Max Weber*, Oxford University Press, 1946, p. 120.

No bitterness, among either the resisters or the rulers, must attend the resistance campaign, since this would militate against conversion of the rulers and a co-operative solution. For this reason, the resister may select a relatively trivial issue, in which emotions will not be heavily involved; the recent South African acts of resistance directly attacked incidental aspects of domination, and in such a way as to minimize the annoyance of the Europeans. For the same reason – the avoidance of bitterness – the resistance campaign must not lead to the humiliation of the rulers, and should be conducted with love, with civility. Gandhi declared that incivility would spoil Satyagraha like a drop of arsenic in milk, though he realized the difficulty of combining civility to the rulers with an emancipation from fear of them. Such principles as hating the sin and not the sinner provide a basis for resolute action against oppression without bitterness against the oppressor. The resistance acts must be in a spiritually satisfying form and end gracefully, while the suffering itself should be of such a nature as not to repel or horrify the rulers.

In practice the pure form of Satyagraha is rare, and perhaps best exemplified in Gandhi's fasts. Even Gandhi's major campaigns did not conform strictly to Satyagraha. While Gandhi insisted that numbers were irrelevant, that a single man's voice could make itself heard, that quality not quantity was decisive, nevertheless, he confessed in 1939 that he had not yet found with certainty how a handful can act effectively.[10] Gandhi did, in fact, often rely on mass following and weighed such factors as the mobilization of public opinion and large-scale organization of resistance with an impairment of pure Satyagraha in two aspects: an impurity of motive among some of his followers, serving personal ends and not dedicated to non-violence; and coercion of the rulers by embarrassment. Empirically, Satyagraha tends to be influenced by considerations of expediency. Conversely, the prestige of Gandhi's Satyagraha colours the expedient use of passive resistance by

[10] M. K. Gandhi, *op. cit.*, p. 296.

the introduction of values not strictly relevant to the selection of means in terms of effectiveness.

Social Change by Suffering

The Effect on the Rulers

The first type of passive resistance makes use of conventional political techniques – dependent on the conditions within the society – in a direct struggle for advancement, while the new element in Satyagraha is suffering. If the emphasis on suffering is stripped away. the distinction between the two types of passive resistance largely disappears. Looking at passive resistance purely as a technique of social change in a situation of race domination by white settlers or by a colonial power, the problem is whether voluntary suffering is justified by its effectiveness as a means for converting the rulers.

There is no historical warrant for the basic assumption in Satyagraha 'that the sight of suffering on the part of multitudes of people will melt the heart of the aggressor and induce him to desist from his course of violence', as Mahatma Gandhi himself admitted.[11] In fact, the assumption is not subject to scientific proof. Satyagraha is based on faith; it is a closed system. If it fails, then the suffering was not pure; and indeed, one cannot say with certainty whether Satyagraha has failed in a particular campaign, since it works at a highly complex psychological level, one among many factors, and its observable effects may be delayed. At another level, too, the belief in the efficacy of suffering is not readily amenable to research, namely, where suffering lies at the root of the religious inspiration of a great spiritual leader. We will therefore take the problem at the relatively mundane level of the impure suffering of ordinary people seeking to advance their political rights.

Evidently, in general, people do not create suffering for themselves, unless indeed they are already suffering intolerably, though societies do, of course, vary in their cultural emphasis on the avoidance of pain. If, then, suffering is implicit in the

[11] M. K. Gandhi, *op. cit.*, pp. 362-3.

system of domination, part of the routine of being adminis-
tered, why should additional suffering, voluntarily undertaken,
move the rulers? For example, in South Africa, if half a million
non-whites were convicted of minor statutory offences in 1951,
what difference can it make to the rulers that an additional
8,000 resisters were convicted in 1952 for some of these same
statutory offences? Or, again, if 50,000 strokes are given in the
gaols in one year, will another 1,000 flay the conscience of the
rulers? If indeed, there is a difference, then it can only be
because the suffering is voluntarily undergone, raises a moral
issue, and involves people of higher status than the general run
of offenders.

Voluntary suffering in Western European society, and among
the ruling settler and administrative groups deriving from
Western Europe, is an arresting phenomenon, since to take
pleasure in suffering is regarded as a perversion. The assumption is that individuals maximize pleasure, not pain. At a
sophisticated level, the motives of the sufferer may be attacked,
as for example, in ascribing Gandhi's fasts to masochism, and
thus interpretimg his suffering not as vicarious but as self-
interested. Or, again, the act of suffering may be interpreted as
an exploitation of the rulers' good-natured reluctance to allow
unnecessary suffering, and not as expressive of personal courage
or virtue in the sufferer. Indeed, in societies where aggression
and violence are admired, there may be contempt for the
voluntary submission to pain; the whole process may seem
entirely ridiculous against the background of the dominant
group's system of values, more particularly when there is no
lack of space in the gaols and no lack of work for the convicts.
But, whatever the response, the unusual nature of the act
makes it, in theory, a fitting means for stirring up ferment.

The initial reaction of the rulers, under the social conditions
we are considering, may be violence, not apparently a moral
conflict, though perhaps violence is a way of expressing moral
conflict. Thus in the raid on the salt-pans in 1930 as a protest
against the Indian government's salt-tax, the police might

easily have arrested the resisters, since the duty of the Satyagrahis was to surrender themselves willingly in their thousands
to an unarmed policeman. Instead, 'the enraged police' fell
upon the resisters as they sat, 'beat them on the head and kicked
them in the abdomen or the testicles. Some were dragged along
the ground and thrown into the ditches. Hour after hour this
went on, while stretcher-bearers removed the inert, bleeding
bodies.'[12] Manilal Gandhi, who led this raid, told me that
the police used special knobbed, iron-spiked sticks against the
resisters. In South Africa, the campaign of 1952 led to the
stepping up of penalties for minor statutory offences from a
short term of imprisonment with the option of a fine to maximum penalties of three years' imprisonment and ten strokes,
where the offences were committed in protest against any law.

The explanation of this violence lies in the nature of the
domination itself. Since the naked force of conquest has been
translated into a series of laws, and now rests on the sanctity of
law, a challenge by the subordinate group of any law, no matter
how trivial, is interpreted by the rulers as rebellion. The fact
that the particular law has no special significance for the
dominant group by no means eliminates bitterness. Because the
amount of force currently in use is not sufficient to suppress
the rebellion, the rulers may apply more force. An unwillingness
of the resisters to submit to the increased suffering spells the end
of the campaign, as was the case in the recent South African
resistance. Manilal Gandhi's criticism is valid, that the resisters
were told that all they needed to do was to submit to imprisonment for a period of three to six weeks; they were prepared only
for a limited amount of suffering, and not for continuous
suffering, to death if necessary, as Mahatma Gandhi required
from Satyagrahis. 'The greater the repression and lawlessness
on the part of authority, the greater should be the suffering
courted by the victims.'[13]

[12] Account of an eyewitness, as reported by Brailsford, in H. S. L. Polak and
others, *op. cit.*, p. 178.
[13] *Op. cit.*, p. 275.

Violence may also be expected to arise in a different way. In certain circumstances, the rulers may incite the resisters to violence, by use of *agents provocateurs* and of extreme provocation, for two reasons. First, force is more readily mobilized against violence,[14] and there is a lack of experience in handling non-violence, though this experience is now steadily accumulating. Second, the severe repressive measures, which the ruler may wish to use and is organized to use, require some justification. The violence of the resisters themselves is the best justification for violent counteraction; this explains the tendency of the ruling groups in South Africa to identify the passive resistance campaign with Mau Mau. There is some likelihood of success in the incitement to violence, since the resisters are in a state of fervour heightened by their privations. In India, Gandhi temporarily suspended passive resistance precisely because of violent reactions by the resisters, and not on account of any reluctance on their part to undergo suffering.

The problem we are considering may now be taken to a different level, the conversion of the rulers by the intensification of suffering in the later stages of resistance. The suffering has now passed beyond the ordinary routine of subordination and is expressed in exceptional form. Will there be a conversion of the rulers because of a revulsion of feeling, a satiation with suffering, a swing from the sadistic to the masochistic component of the authoritarian personality? The answer is clear from the Nazi extermination of the Jews that there is no inevitable revulsion of feeling on the part of the rulers. To be sure, the Jews did not practise Satyagraha as recommended to them by Gandhi, and there may be a decisive difference in the consequences of suffering which is only passive and suffering in the more positive spirit of Satyagraha. In any event, there is no doubt that the threshold of indifference to extreme forms of suffering may be very high indeed. We must therefore

---

[14] *Ibid.*, p. 57. Mahatma Gandhi writes: 'Non-violence laughs at the might of the tyrant and stultifies him by non-retaliation and non-retiral. . . . The might of the tyrant recoils upon himself when it meets with no response, even as an arm violently waved in the air suffers dislocation.'

question Gandhi's belief that conversion by the suffering of others is universally effective, and look at the particular circumstances which favour conversion.

Simmel demonstrates that among the relevant circumstances is the structure of the social system, namely whether the dominant and subordinate statuses are held by individuals or collectivities.[15]

In the case where the rulers are a collectivity, the collective behaviour assists the individual to suspend certain norms by which he ordinarily governs his behaviour, and to soothe his conscience by hiding behind the decision of the group.[16] The suffering tends to be institutionalized; it takes a relatively impersonal form – administration in terms of law or of an ideology, such as apartheid or the race theories of the Nazis. The more brutalized, sadistic elements, who may be expected to relish the suffering, are the agents of the collectivity. The insulating barrier of institutional procedures protects the average citizen from emotional involvement. This process may be assisted, too, by rationalizations justifying the infliction of more extreme forms of suffering, as for example, rationalizations which debase the Mau Mau adherents in Kenya to the level of wild animals.

Where the subordinates are a collectivity,[17] Simmel comments that the psychological re-creation of suffering – the essential vehicle of compassion and tenderness – fails easily if the sufferer is not a nameable or visible individual, but only a totality. If this is correct, it offers some confirmation of Mahatma Gandhi's belief in the effectiveness of individual suffering, and the irrelevance of the numbers who submit to suffering. It also may explain the general indifference of South African whites to the civil disobedience of men of high status in the non-white communities. They are perceived, not

[15] Kurt H. Wolff, *The Sociology of Georg Simmel*, Glencoe, The Free Press, 1950, 'Subordination under a Plurality', pp. 224-49.

[16] *Ibid.*, p. 226.

[17] *Ibid.* The relevant question is not the objective structure of the subordinates, but the rulers' social definition of the subordinates as a collectivity.

individually as highly-respected professional men, but generically as Indians and Natives. The reaction to the few white resisters, in contrast, was in terms of their individual personalities; photographs, biographical details, and interviews appeared in the newspapers.

The fact that the sufferers are defined as a collectivity is not decisive for determining the reactions of the dominant group, as Simmel shows. Other factors are relevant, and their influence can be seen in the very different reactions of rulers to events affecting the subordinates as collectivities.

The cause of the suffering is relevant. Thus, the average privileged member of the dominant group can place himself in the position of people suffering through an Act of God, such as a cyclone or a flood, to which we are all subject. He finds it difficult, however, to identify himself with subordinates in the ordinary routine of a life quite remote from his own, more especially since he is trained to regard the subordinates as objects of action rather than as purposive beings. In the case of an Act of God, where suffering arises from agencies outside human control, sympathy – the feeling of a common humanity and of a duty to assist others – is readily evoked; moreover, the bringing of relief is consistent with, and indeed strengthens, the domination. On the other hand, where the suffering is caused by passive resistance against routine subordination, sympathetic understanding is limited in the first instance and, indeed, the fact that the resisters have originated their own suffering actually alienates sympathy in two ways. First, there is a quality of impudence about it, of status-usurpation, when looked at from the point of view of the dominant group, since it is one of the prerogatives and symbols of domination to inflict suffering arbitrarily on the subordinate group. And second, because domination is often justified as being in the interests of the subordinates, the self-infliction of suffering is interpreted as the result of viciousness or error or subversive foreign influence.

The degree of intolerance for the subordinate group, as, for example, the extreme intolerance of the Nazis for the Jews, is also relevant to the effects which the suffering has on the dominant group. In South Africa, though the whites respond to both Africans and Indians as collectivities, and for many purposes treat them as a wider collectivity – that of non-Europeans – nevertheless the specific attitude to these two groups is different. The whites are dependent on the Africans and tolerate them in subordinate roles, whereas in the case of the Indians there is neither such dependence nor toleration. On the contrary, the Indians are economic rivals; they offer a leadership in place of white leadership and their complete removal from the society is strongly desired by most whites. Hence, the suffering of Indians and of Africans may be expected to have different consequences.

Finally, the reaction of the dominant group to the subordinate collectivity will be influenced by the extent to which values are shared. The South African Government would no doubt have responded immediately to passive resistance by Cape Malays for segregation from other coloured people, since this movement would have been consistent with its own values. Similarly, the sympathetic response of the outside world to the South African resistance movement, and of liberals and English-speaking Christian leaders within South Africa, reflects the extent to which the resisters appealed to a system of shared values – a higher tribunal, standing above the parties.[18]

In contrast, the passive resistance movement in South Africa ran counter to the values generally held by the dominant group, and the reaction was, for the most part, not only indifference to the suffering of the resisters, but determination to increase the amount of their suffering. For the suffering of the resisters to move the whites in South Africa, it must of necessity penetrate beyond the values of apartheid, and appeal to certain shared values – in this case of Christianity and of democracy. Even if we accept with Gandhi that God resides in the breasts of us all, or if we believe that there is a basic common humanity

[18] Kurt H. Wolff, *The Sociology of Georg Simmel*, pp. 195-7.

which is stirred by suffering, we must nevertheless recognize that the ideologies of domination interpose formidable barriers. To penetrate beyond apartheid and the rationalizations identifying passive resistance with Mau Mau, Russian Communism and Indian Imperialism, and to reach the Christian conscience of white South Africans, is a major task, not readily achieved by suffering.

It is difficult, therefore, to accept Gandhi's belief in the efficacy of extreme suffering as a universal means of conversion, where the ruler is a collectivity and responds to the subordinate as a collectivity, and where the suffering is a challenge to the ruler's ideology of domination. Nevertheless, there are other consequences of resistance by suffering, effects within the subordinate group, such as the enhancing of self-respect and solidarity, which may influence the selection of this method.

The Effect on the Subordinates

To the extent that the resister has risen above the fear of suffering, and indeed welcomes it, he is emancipated from domination. He takes the initiative in originating his suffering, and by becoming the active agent of suffering rather than a passive recipient, he subtly alters the relationship. The resister is strengthened by the experience and the conviction of his own inner strength. Those who have suffered become in a sense an élite, a seasoned brotherhood, exchanging stories of their experiences and their deprivations. It is a mark of distinction to be an old gaol bird.

The humiliation of subordination, the sense of inferiority, are replaced by a feeling of self-respect and of worth. Brailsford writes that the Indians 'had freed their own minds. They had won independence in their hearts. . . . By these acts [of resistance] they broke the paralysis, the consciousness of a pre-destined inferiority, that had oppressed them from their childhood. They shed their servility and thought henceforward as free men. This was true of the vast majority, who accepted non-violence only as a tactic; the few who practised it as a faith won something more, a marvellous self-control.'[19] There are, of course, techniques developed in totalitarian countries which will break the spirit of any resister. The ability of the resister to gain strength from suffering is dependent on the ruler accepting certain self-imposed limits on his power to inflict suffering.

Where the subordinate group is very numerous in relation to the dominant group, Satyagraha arises because of a lack of unity among the subordinates. In these circumstances, the example of the resisters and the inspiration of their suffering may promote solidarity in the subordinate group, as in India where conditions were specially favourable for the wide acceptance of Gandhi's philosophy of suffering, and his mass following made British rule increasingly unworkable. Whether or not solidarity will follow on the use of Satyagraha depends on its compatibility with the culture of the subordinate group, and on the structure of the subordinate group.

Purification by voluntary suffering is an integral part of Hindu culture, in contrast to Bantu culture. Though suffering among the Bantu may be ascribed to a breach of a taboo or some other duty, in much the same way as in Hindu culture, the explanation is generally sought in witchcraft. Suffering is regarded as an ill, and the self-infliction of suffering is a concept foreign to peoples who emphasize the sensual satisfactions of the lusty dance, the feast celebrated with meat, and physical prowess. It is no doubt for this reason that some observers have assumed that passive resistance could have no appeal for the Bantu peoples and that, if they did embark on a resistance campaign, it would inevitably become violent. Berry states quite categorically that 'passive resistance comes readily to the Hindu mind, whereas it would be incomprehensible to a Zulu or a Sioux.'[20] Yet Zulus did in fact participate in a disciplined way in the 1952 South African resistance campaign.

[19] Polak and others, *op. cit.*, p. 188.
[20] *Race Relations*, Boston, Houghton Miflin Co., 1951, p. 414.

Without detailed investigation into the background of the resisters, we do not know whether the Bantu who took part in civil disobedience were representative of the broad mass of the people. The indications are that it was largely the Christians among the Bantu who volunteered, and that Christianity gave meaning to passive resistance, to the doctrine of conversion by vicarious suffering. Some of the leaders are most devout Christians. Prayer meetings, the singing of hymns, the drawing of inspiration from the Bible, were a marked feature of the campaign, more particularly in the Eastern Cape where the resistance movement was strongest, and where there is least contact with Indians.

The structure of the subordinate group, the extent to which there have developed revolutionary cadres on the one hand and vested interests in the *status quo* on the other hand, will also influence the effects of Satyagraha in promoting solidarity. Passive resistance is essentially non-revolutionary, Satyagraha, in particular, being based on collaboration with the rulers. The issues do not affect in any fundamental way the economic structure of society. The trained leaders spend their time in gaol, the physical force of the ruler is rendered more effective by the voluntary submission of the subordinates, and belief in the possibility of converting the rulers blunts the militancy of the subordinates. Nevertheless, the Marxists may go along with the movement up to a point in the hope of organizational gains and the embarrassment of the Government. In the 1946 South African campaign by Indians, the Communist Party allowed members to make a personal decision, and both in the 1946 and in the 1952 campaigns individual communists participated. Ultimately, however, the Marxists may be expected to oppose passive resistance. Again, those among the subordinates who have vested interests in the society, such as the wealthy merchants, will tend to feel that there is still room for conciliation when other sections are ready for passive resistance, but will give their support to passive resistance in a revolutionary situation.

Violence or Non-violence

The consequences of passive resistance are so complex that it is difficult to draw any clear-cut conclusions. Under the conditions which prevail in South Africa, it is doubtful whether the Satyagraha form of resistance could command a sufficient following to make it an effective mass movement. Nor does it seem likely, either, that the rulers will be converted by extreme suffering when they are so strongly confirmed in the ideologies of white domination, or that the subordinate peoples will submit peaceably to violence.

If this analysis has substance, the leaders of the 'liberation movements' would not be justified in subjecting their followers to Satyagraha, save for the effect on the outside world. In the expedient use of passive resistance there is sufficient room for a wide range of experiments which minimize suffering. For the leaders, the problem is whether change can indeed be effected without violence, and they will compare the results of the non-violent resistance campaign in South Africa with those of Mau Mau in Kenya. At the present time there is both less bitterness in the ruling group in South Africa and at the same time less indication of willingness to make concessions to the non-whites. It is a crucial issue in Africa whether Mau Mau or other forms of violence pay better than passive resistance.

THE STORY OF
PASSIVE RESISTANCE

IV

PRELUDE TO PASSIVE RESISTANCE

THE passive resistance movement is deeply rooted in the history of white domination. The Nationalist Party stimulated its growth, but did not sow the seed.

Disillusionment, or political sophistication, of even moderate African leaders was already far advanced under the United Party Government of the late Field-Marshal Smuts, a Government which loudly proclaimed a trusteeship which its policies patently denied. In 1947, for example, African leaders rejected proposals designed to extend the scope and powers of the Natives' Representative Council, as being a mere tinkering with the main defects of current policies. These defects they defined as the lack of safeguards for the legitimate rights of the African people; the denial of hope for the future; the principle of permanent separatism, creating hostility and racial bitterness between black and white; and finally, the undermining of confidence in the Government.[1]

Indian disillusionment was even further advanced. In 1946, the Indians launched a passive resistance campaign[2] against the Asiatic Land Tenure and Indian Representation Act, which offered communal representation as recompense for the restriction of Indian rights to landed property. The prisons of

[1] Julius Lewin, 'The Rise of Congress in South Africa', *The Political Quarterly* (July 1953), p. 296. The Natives' Representative Council consisted of European officials and African members. It was set up to advise the government on legislation affecting Africans and was later abolished by the Nationalist Government.

[2] The resistance leaders usually refer to the 1952 campaign as the 'defiance' campaign to distinguish it from the 'passive resistance' campaign of 1946.

the Union Government had already seasoned some 2,000 Indian resisters before the Nationalist Party came to power in 1948.

The Nationalist Government therefore found among the non-whites a developed political consciousness. This it proceeded to heighten by providing a high-pressure finishing school for the training of non-white leaders, and some rapid-results courses for the broad masses. Apartheid demonstrates the plain meaning of white domination, and spreads political consciousness among ever-widening circles. It shatters the illusion that the white man will ever willingly allow the non-whites to take their place as equals in a common society, and drives home the lesson that liberation can be achieved only by their own efforts.

During the three years between the coming to power of the Nationalist Party and the passive resistance campaign in 1952, the political organizations of the non-whites experimented with the boycott and large-scale demonstrations. The 1949 Conference of the African National Congress accepted generally the policy of uncompromising non-collaboration with the Government and agreed specifically to boycott Advisory Boards, the Natives' Representative Council, and indirect parliamentary representation. Dr A. B. Xuma, the President-General of the African National Congress, opposed this policy on the grounds that there were sufficient collaborators to ensure the perfect working of these institutions, and therefore urged that Congress should use the available machinery for its own purposes. He was overruled, and replaced, as President-General, by Dr James S. Moroka, who firmly pledged himself to the boycott.

Three major demonstrations were held in 1950. The first, a Freedom of Speech Convention, was opened by Dr Moroka in Johannesburg. This was followed by May Day or Freedom Day demonstrations against discrimination, in which the Communist Party played an active, sponsoring role. Africans, Indians and Coloureds took part, and many children stayed away from school. Disturbances broke out in the late afternoon and evening, and the demonstrators suffered heavy casualties. The third demonstration, called by Dr Moroka, was a National Day of Protest against the Group Areas Bill and the Suppression of Communism Bill, and a day of mourning for Africans who had lost their lives in the struggle for liberation. This was observed on June 26th, again on an interracial basis, and with the participation of school children. The urban areas of Durban, Port Elizabeth and the Witwatersrand gave the most active support.

In the following year, 1951, the proposed removal of coloured voters from the common roll by the Separate Representation of Voters Bill spread the struggle further. Coloureds formed the Franchise Action Council to oppose the Bill, and on May 7th staged an effective strike in Port Elizabeth and the Cape Peninsula, with some support from Africans and Indians; again, many children stayed away from school.

The broadening of the struggle, and mounting apartheid legislation, provided a favourable setting for concerted action. A conference of the national executives of the African National Congress and the South African Indian Congress, with representatives of the Franchise Action Council, met in July 1951, and appointed a Joint Planning Council. It was given the task of co-ordinating the efforts of the national organizations of the African, Indian and Coloured peoples in a mass campaign for the repeal of the Pass Laws, the Group Areas Act, the Separate Representation of Voters Act, and the Bantu Authorities Act, and for the withdrawal of the 'so-called' rural rehabilitation scheme, including the policy of stock-limitation. The plan submitted by this Council, as amended by the African National Congress, forms the basis of the passive resistance campaign.

Blue-print for Resistance[3]

The Joint Planning Council, reporting in November 1951, recommended that the African National Congress, supported by the South African Indian Congress and other democratic

[3] See Appendix C for the Joint Planning Council's report, as amended by the African National Congress.

99

organizations, should call upon the Government to take steps for the repeal of the offending laws and policies. Failing repeal, the two Congresses should embark 'upon mass action for a redress of the just and legitimate grievances of the majority of the South African people'.

Two alternative dates, April 6th and June 26th, 1952, were suggested for the commencement of the struggle. April 6th was chosen because it was the day set aside by the white population for the tercentenary celebrations of Van Riebeeck's landing at the Cape. From the point of view of the Joint Planning Council, it marked

> 'one of the greatest turning points in South African history by the advent of European settlers in the country, followed by colonial and imperialist exploitation which has degraded, humiliated and kept in bondage the vast masses of the non-white people'

Equal significance attached to June 26th,

> 'as it also ranks as one of the greatest turning points in South African history. On this day we commemorate the National Day of Protest held on 26th June, 1950, the day on which, on the call of the President-General of the African National Congress, Dr J. S. Moroka, this country witnessed the greatest demonstration of fraternal solidarity and unity of purpose on the part of all sections of the non-European people in the national protest against unjust laws. The 26th June was one of the first steps towards freedom.'

The preference of the Joint Council for the earlier date reflects a sense of urgency.

The Council recommended that the struggle should take the form of defiance of unjust laws, that is, the deliberate breach 'of certain selected laws and regulations which are undemocratic, unjust, racially discriminatory and repugnant to the natural rights of man'. Three stages of defiance were suggested:

first, selected and trained persons to go into action in the big centres, such as Johannesburg, Cape Town, Bloemfontein, Port Elizabeth and Durban; second, an increase in the number of volunteer corps and centres of operation; and, third, mass action on a country-wide scale, embracing both urban and rural areas.

Two factors, the degree of obnoxiousness of the law and the possibility of defying it, determined the selection of specific acts of resistance. Africans are not vitally affected by the Group Areas Act; their obvious targets are the many deeply resented restrictions on freedom of movement imposed by the Pass Laws, which lend themselves easily to defiance. The very existence of Indians is threatened by the Group Areas Act, which can only be defied when steps are taken to impose racial separation; Indians are not restricted by the Pass Laws, though they are denied free movement across provincial borders. The Coloureds are not so adversely affected by the plans for racial segregation as the Indians, and enjoy a freedom of movement denied the Africans. All three groups suffer more or less equally under discrimination in public services and amenities.

These considerations explain the recommendations of the Joint Planning Council in regard to acts of resistance. Defiance of the Pass Laws was suggested for the African National Congress. For the South African Indian Congress, the planners recommended action against provincial barriers, apartheid laws such as train, post-office and railway station segregation, and the Group Areas Act, *if and when possible*, while general apartheid segregation and the Group Areas Act, *if and when possible*, were held out as targets for the Franchise Action Council.

Similarly, differences in the type of discrimination against the various sections of the non-white peoples influenced the organization of volunteers. The plan called for a number of volunteer corps, each in charge of a leader, responsible for the maintenance of order and discipline and for leading the corps into action when called upon to do so. The membership of each volunteer corps was restricted to the members of a particular racial group (to the members of the African National Congress, or of the South African Indian Congress, or of the Franchise Action Council or other organization of Coloureds). Only in cases where the law or regulation applied 'commonly to all groups' would racially mixed units be allowed.

The effective organization of the campaign posed the problem of finding a focus of resistance which would involve the rural African population in struggles initiated by the politically more sophisticated urban dwellers. This was all the more urgent, since the ready reserve of labour in the rural areas and the migrant-labour system place the urban passive resisters at the mercy of their white employers. Mahatma Gandhi found a focus of mass resistance in the apparently trivial issue of the Indian salt tax. Pandit Nehru certainly did not anticipate the success of the struggle against the salt tax, unrelated as it was to the movement for national independence.[4] The task of the Joint Planning Council was to select targets of resistance which would serve as a South African counterpart to the salt tax, and carry resistance to the masses.

The planners sought these targets in the Government policy of stock-limitation, and in the Population Registration Act. They recommended that during the struggle against the Pass Laws the rural Africans should be asked not to co-operate with the authorities in culling cattle or limiting livestock; and they suggested, as a possible means for carrying the struggle from the second to the mass phase, the organized resistance of all sections against registration under the Population Registration Act. Stock-limitation must have seemed a most appropriate focus for resistance, since cattle are a source of prestige among rural Africans, a symbol of wealth, and intimately connected

[4] *Nehru on Gandhi*, New York, John Day and Company, 1948, p. 54. 'Salt suddenly became a mysterious word, a word of power. The salt tax was to be attacked, the salt laws were to be broken. We were quite bewildered and could not quite fit in a national struggle with common salt. . . . What was the point of making a list of some political and social reforms – good in themselves no doubt – when we were talking in terms of independence?'

with the rights and obligations of families. Yet the salt tax fired the imagination of rural Indians, while stock-limitation has indeed given rise to bitterness, but only to sporadic resistance. The explanation of these different reactions would seem to lie partly in the spiritual inspiration of Mahatma Gandhi, and partly in the fact that the South African Government has not prosecuted its stock-limitation policy with vigour. Similarly, the Population Registration Act must have seemed a likely target; it imposes a general duty to register, and lends itself readily to passive resistance on a mass scale. Again, hopes of a mass response have not been realized. Registration proceeds with no sign of resistance.

The choice of passive resistance as a form of struggle appears to have been governed by considerations of expediency rather than by the ethic of Satyagraha. The planning of the campaign in three stages, culminating in mass action, indicates that we are dealing with a tactical use of passive resistance. A mass movement is clearly aimed at the embarrassment of the rulers, and not at their conversion by a change of heart. Moreover, the given historical conditions weighed with the Joint Planning Council, and not the assumed universal efficacy of voluntary suffering, as appears clearly from the report:

'With regard to the form of struggle best suited to our conditions we have been constrained to bear in mind the political and economic set-up of our country, the relationship of the rural to the urban population, the development of the trade union movement with particular reference to the disabilities and state of organization of the non-white workers, the economic status of the various sections of the non-white people and the level of organization of the National Liberatory movements. We are therefore of the opinion that in these given historical conditions the forms of struggle for obtaining the repeal of unjust laws which should be considered are (a) defiance of unjust laws and (b) industrial action.'

As between these alternatives, the planners recognized 'that industrial action is second to none, the best and most important weapon in the struggle of the people for the repeal of the unjust laws, and that it is inevitable that this method of struggle has to be undertaken at one time or another during the course of the struggle'. Nevertheless, they opposed, though they did not positively exclude, industrial action in the initial phase of the struggle.

The postponement of industrial action, and indeed the absence of any economic programme whatsoever, are remarkable features of the planning report for two reasons. First, the non-whites are, in general, an impoverished group without property, and live under great economic pressure. Second, the political views of the members of the Planning Council are such that the importance of economic struggle must have been emphasized in the discussions. The chairman of the Joint Planning Council, Dr James Moroka, described by the Crown in a list of accused under the Suppression of Communism Act, as a 'Native Male, 60 years, Medical Practitioner', is a conservative, profoundly disillusioned with white rule, as is indicated by his analysis of the role of Christianity in the subjection of the African people.[5] The representatives of the African National Congress, John Joseph Marks, 'Coloured Male, 49 years', and Walter Max Sisulu, 'Coloured Male, 40 years, Secretary', are on the left wing of the African political top-flight leaders. Dr Yusuf Mahomed Dadoo, 'Indian Male, 43 years, Medical Practitioner', President of the South African Indian Congress, is also left-wing, as is the second representative of the Indian Congress, Yusuf Ahmed Cachalia, 'Indian Male, 37 years, Secretary', member of a family dedicated to social service and linked with the work of Mahatma Gandhi. Hence, at least four of the five planners must have been keenly conscious of the role of economic factors in the subjection of the non-whites.

The reason for the postponement of industrial action lies partly in the Council's terms of reference, which did not specify

[5] See Chapter II, p. 52.

economic change among the issues raised. This was to be expected since the members of the two Congresses are not agreed on economic policy, and the non-white leaders, apart from the left-wing political leaders, do not picture the struggle as a conflict between economic classes. They emphasize, instead, colour as the basis of their subordination, and for the good reason that it is the criterion for discrimination and for the limiting of economic opportunity. Nevertheless, it is clear that the planners considered a broad economic struggle to be the most effective form of action, and deferred its use to a later stage, because of their assessment of the given historical conditions. In particular, the weakness of non-white trade union organization, the political immaturity of the rural African, and the need to strengthen the two Congresses, must have influenced the planners in favour of civil disobedience.

The members of the Joint Planning Council would be well aware of the danger that their liberation movement might be blunted if the struggle were directed against specific incidents of discrimination, instead of against the principle of discrimination as such. Hence, they related the campaign to the broad principles of democracy on the following terms:

All people irrespective of the national groups they may belong to, and irrespective of the colour of their skin, are entitled to live a full and free life on the basis of the fullest equality. Full democratic rights with a direct say in the affairs of the Government are the inalienable rights of every man – a right which in South Africa must be realized now if the country is to be saved from social chaos and tyranny and from the evils arising out of the existing denial of franchise to vast masses of the population on grounds of race and colour. The struggle which the national organizations of the non-European people are conducting is not directed against any race or national group, but against the unjust laws which keep in perpetual subjection and misery vast sections of the population. It is for the creation of conditions which will restore human dignity, equality and freedom to every South African.

At the same time, the planners drew a distinction between these final objectives of the struggle for freedom and the immediate objectives of the resistance movement, which they declared to be the repeal of the unjust laws mentioned in their terms of reference. They conceived the campaign as a first step in the progressive extension of democratic rights to the non-whites.

An Exchange of Letters[6]

The African National Congress, at its annual meeting in December 1951, adopted the report of the Joint Planning Council and selected April 6th, 1952, for the beginning of the struggle. The South African Indian Congress resolved to support the African National Congress; and the third partner, the Franchise Action Council, pledged its support of the demonstrations scheduled for April 6th.

In accordance with the blue-print for passive resistance, prepared by the Joint Planning Council, the African National Congress sent a letter (undated) to the Prime Minister, Dr D. F. Malan. It was signed by Dr J. S. Moroka and Mr W. M. Sisulu, the President-General and Secretary-General, and took the form of a legal demand: '. . . Conference unanimously resolved to call upon your Government, as we hereby do, to repeal the aforementioned Acts,[7] by NOT LATER THAN THE 29TH DAY OF FEBRUARY 1952, failing which the African National Congress will hold protest demonstrations and meetings on the 6th day of April 1952, as a prelude to the implementation of the plan for the defiance of unjust laws.'

The preamble to the demand drew attention to the founding of the African National Congress in 1912,

'to protect and advance the interests of the African people in all matters affecting them and to attain their freedom from all discriminatory laws whatsoever. To this end, the

[6] See Appendix B, pp. 233-47.
[7] Pass Laws, Stock Limitation, the Suppression of Communism Act of 1950, the Group Areas Act of 1950, the Bantu Authorities Act of 1951 and the Separate Representation of Voters Act of 1951.

African National Congress has, since its establishment, endeavoured by every constitutional method to bring to the notice of the Government the legitimate demands of the African people and has repeatedly pressed, in particular, their inherent right to be directly represented in Parliament, Provincial and Municipal Councils and in all councils of state.' The Government, 'through its repressive policy of trusteeship, segregation and apartheid,[8] and through legislation that continues to insult and degrade the African people by depriving them of fundamental human rights enjoyed in all democratic communities, have categorically rejected our offer of co-operation'. In consequence, there has been a gradual worsening of the social, economic and political position of the African people, aggravated by recent legislation. 'The African National Congress as the National Organization of the African people cannot remain quiet on an issue that is a matter of life and death to the people; to do so would be a betrayal of the trust and confidence placed upon it by the African people.'

In further explanation of Congress Policy, the writers assert their firm belief that 'the freedom of the African people, the elimination of the exploitation of man by man, and the restitution of democracy, liberty and harmony in South Africa are such vital and fundamental matters that the Government and the public must know that we are fully resolved to achieve them in our life-time'. The struggle, however, would not be directed against any racial or national group, 'but against the unjust laws which keep in perpetual subjection and misery vast sections of the population'. The letter concludes with an expression of confidence in the support of 'enlightened' men and women, and of posterity.

[8] It is an indication of the political outlook of the writers that trusteeship, segregation and apartheid are treated as different labels for the same commodity – race domination.

Presumably Dr Malan does not belong among the band of 'enlightened' men and women. His rejection of Congress demands, dated January 29th, 1952, starts by rebuking Congress for being so presumptuous as to communicate direct with him; their letter should have been sent to, and dealt with by, the Minister of Native Affairs and his department. This is in accordance with the general principle of relegating native affairs to administration, and insulating the Africans from political participation. However, the Prime Minister waives this point and proceeds to deal with the issues.

The limited demand for the repeal of specific laws is re-interpreted as a demand for the abolition of all differentiating laws, as well as for direct representation in Government. This claim to be treated in the same way as the whites is self-contradictory, since the Africans are racially different. Under no circumstances would the Government entertain the idea of giving to non-Europeans administrative or executive or legis-lative powers over Europeans, or within a European com-munity.[9] The Government, therefore, had no intention of repealing the long existing laws differentiating between Euro-pean and Bantu.

Further, according to the Prime Minister, the demands of the Congress are not a genuine offer of co-operation, but a first step toward supplanting European rule. Racial harmony can only be secured by apartheid. The acceptance of apartheid would be 'co-operation in the real sense of the word'. More-over, the differentiating laws themselves are not at all of an oppressive and degrading nature; on the contrary, they are largely protective. 'Even those laws which are regarded as particularly irksome by the Bantu people have not been made in order to persecute them, but for the purpose of training them in the performance of those duties which must be fully observed by all who wish to claim rights.' The Government was only too willing to encourage Bantu initiative, services and administration within the Bantu community.

[9] See the discussion of this point in Chapter II, pp. 57ff.

In conclusion, the Prime Minister threatened drastic reprisals if Congress persisted in the campaign. '. . . The Government will make full use of the machinery at its disposal to quell any disturbances, and thereafter deal adequately with those responsible for initiating subversive activities of any nature whatsoever.'

There was a clear failure of communication between Congress and the Government, a fundamental conflict between the world outlook of these two bodies. Congress proceeds on the basis of a liberal humanitarian creed, which asserts the dignity of the human personality, the belief that all men are born equal, the conviction that the human being is educable, and the assumption that history is the story of the unfolding of freedom. In contrast Dr Malan, and many supporters of the Nationalist as well as the opposition United Party, refuse to draw a distinction between race and culture; both are God-given or, at any rate, biological. Because of racial and cultural differences, the claim to equal rights is contradictory. Rights are not universal, but dependent on biological, that is permanent, racial-cultural, characteristics. In the case of the Africans, whatever they receive from the rulers is a revocable privilege, not an acknowledgement of rights. An authoritarian government determines the scope of these privileges, and the only possible form of co-operation consists in grateful appreciation of the rulers' benevolence. Agitation for the extension of privileges, and more particularly for rights, is not merely ingratitude, but subversion, and justifies severe punitive action.

The final letter in this correspondence, dated February 11th, 1952, could not possibly bridge the difference in outlook. Congress attempted to explain to the Prime Minister the distinction between culture and race, and to demonstrate that the differentiating laws were not intended to protect the Africans, but to advance the interests of the Europeans, nor were they designed to preserve the racial identity of the Europeans, but to perpetuate the systematic exploitation of the African people. In reply to the Prime Minister's threat to use the full machinery of the State to quell any disturbances, Congress expressed its fear that the Government would itself create the disturbances and emphasized, in contrast, its own determination to conduct the campaign peacefully.

On February 20th, 1952, the South African Indian Congress added to this correspondence a letter to the Prime Minister. In content, this follows the original letter of the African National Congress, but there is a broader approach to the differentiating laws passed by the Nationalist Government. Whereas the African representatives dealt specifically with the position of the African people, the Indian Congress analysed the effect of recent legislation on non-whites generally, the African and Coloured population, as well as the Indian. This was to be expected in the case of the small Indian minority, powerless in itself to achieve basic social changes, and hence obliged to identify itself with the numerically powerful groups. It is understandable, too, that the letter from the Indian Congress should have been less restrained and more aggressive in tone. The policy of apartheid is described as reactionary, only capable of being imposed by Fascist tyranny and unrestrained dictatorship: there are accusations of unbridled incitement of race animosity and prejudice, of the use of violence and intimidation by the police: of continuous impoverishment of the people and of the further enslavement of the urban African population. The letter from the African National Congress gives an impression of strength, while the Indian Congress letter speaks of the condition of a people desperately seeking to defend itself against the implacable enmity expressed in the election manifesto of the Nationalist party, which its representatives quote:

'The Party holds the view that Indians are a foreign and outlandish element which is unassimilable. They can never become part of the country and must therefore be treated as an immigrant community. The Party accepts as a basis of its policy the repatriation of as many Indians as possible and proposes a proper investigation into the practicability of such a policy on a large scale in co-operation with India and other countries.'

The letter from the Indian Congress was apparently not deemed worthy of a reply and the stage was now set for the demonstrations on April 6th. These were heralded by a series of public meetings at which the Congresses made their plans known to the African, Coloured and Indian peoples. The demonstrations, held on the same day as the celebrations of the Van Riebeeck tercentenary, took the form of mass meetings and prayer meetings. At Freedom Square, Johannesburg, an estimated 5,000 Africans, Coloureds and Indians, with a sprinkling of white University students wearing Congress colours, attended a meeting at which Dr Dadoo presented Dr Moroka with a mantle of freedom. In Cape Town, thousands of Non-whites 'pledged relentless struggle against unjust laws'. In Port Elizabeth, some 10,000 were said to have gathered on a hillside overlooking the town and the sea, the mighty voice of their songs sweeping across the city. Kimberley observed a day of prayer, while two mass meetings were held in the East Bank Location of East London. About 10,000 met at a number of meetings in the Pretoria location, and special services were held in many of the Native churches. The correspondent of the *Star* reported that 'there were no incidents, although squads of police and C.I.D. [Criminal Investigation Department] men attended the meetings'. (The *Star*, April 7th, 1952.) The Durban attendances were smaller than in the other large cities and Africans and Indians met separately; the wounds of the African-Indian riots in 1949 had not yet healed and co-operation was still uncertain.

All in all, this was a convincing demonstration of the growing strength of the non-white organizations. It was not sufficient to elicit from the Government any concessions, nor even any indication of a willingness to discuss concessions. Accordingly, on June 1st, at a Unity Conference, the Congresses scheduled

June 26th, anniversary of the National Day of Protest, as the date for the commencement of the defiance of laws. Indeed, the civil disobedience campaign may be said to have started earlier, when some of the resistance leaders defied a ban on their addressing public meetings. The recruiting of volunteers was speeded up, the goal being a National Volunteer Corps of 10,000, organized on the model of a peaceful army, with commanders-in-chief and their deputies, volunteers-in-chief, and local units with their leaders.

Resistance Themes

During the many public meetings held in the first half of 1952, the police took verbatim notes of the speeches of the resistance leaders. These notes were used in the course of prosecutions under the Suppression of Communism Act. The illiteracy of many of the police recorders, and their unfamiliarity with the English language, so marred some of the records as to render them almost unintelligible. Others make good sense and seem more reliable; and I have used them in the form in which they were quoted during the preparatory examination of 'W. M. Sisulu and 19 Others' (Magistrate's Court, Johannesburg, Case L.134/52), correcting, however, the more blatant grammatical errors. They provide a source for the analysis of resistance themes, though they may contain many gross misstatements.

A dominant and recurrent theme in the speeches of the resistance leaders is that of despair, frustration, endless suffering and humiliation:

'I know you will be called upon to make many sacrifices and you may have to undergo many sufferings. But what are these sufferings compared with the sufferings of other people in this country to-day, who are suffering under these laws and who are dying in their hundreds of thousands because of starvation and our babies are dying because there is no food. We die of tuberculosis. How are we going to prevent it? We must have better housing conditions. Our people suffer every day, and it is all wasted. What we say is, suffer, but for a cause, and let us rather die for a good cause.' (Dr Yusuf Dadoo, January 27th, 1952, p. 62 of the preparatory examination.)

'Life in South Africa, as far as the non-European people are concerned, is hell! We are insulted on every corner, in every train, and in every walk of life. We are degraded, we are humiliated by the people, by the authorities. (Applause.) There is no respect for man, there is no respect for our mothers, for our daughters, for our wives, for our sisters, for our brothers.' (Mr Yusuf Cachalia, February 24th, 1952, p. 195.)

'We too are made of flesh and blood, we too are the sons and daughters of Almighty God, we too feel the pains that are inflicted on us, we are not any longer prepared to stand this pain, we are not any longer prepared to stand these indignities and insults, we are no longer prepared to be called "Kaffir" and "Koelie" and Hotnot". From now on you call every black man "Mister". [Applause.] And not "Boy". Friends, yesterday they took a friend away. His name is Ismail Bhoola. He is the secretary of the Transvaal Indian Youth Congress. They took him away because the Minister had served a banning notice on him and they say he defied the ban. . . . I went to the gaol, Marshall Square, and I said I want to see Bhoola, and I went up and they said "*Koelie, kom uit jong . . .*" [*Voices:* Shame!] "'*n ander Koelie wil jou sien.*" [Coolie, come out, boy, another coolie wants to see you.] Friends, we know that calling us koelies and kaffirs does not make us small. It only boils up the indignation, it only boils up our resistance to this government.' (Mr Rissik H. Desai, June 19th, 1952, p. 250.) 'And the fact that you are not supposed to walk on the same bridge as a white man – the *same bridge* of all things! I am so full up.' (Mr Moses Kotane, March 9th, 1952, p. 226.)

Interwoven with this frustration and despair are the contrast between the wealth of the white man and the poverty of the non-white, and the perception that this contrast is not a divine dispensation but rooted in the very human motive of greed.

'This occasion is even bigger than the occasion when Jan van Riebeeck landed in South Africa. The reason for that is that for the last three hundred years we have seen here things happening in our country. The rivers that flowed in this country now flow only for a few. The landscape and mountains have been snatched for a few, a small group of people. . . . When we brought the Government a message from the people we got bullets. When we ask for bread we get atomic bombs. We are called kaffirs, coolies and hot-nots, and we are told that we have no right to be in this country, that it is a country for white people . . . Recently we have seen that white civilization is trying to extermin-ate the non-European population of South Africa, accord-ing to the law of the jungle.' (Mr David Wilcox Bopape, January 27th, 1952, pp. 54-5.)

'The time has come for action. For too long have we been talking to the white man. For three hundred years they have oppressed us. They have ruined our country. Our country, it was peaceful; our country, it was happy; our country, where there was no starvation, has been ruined by the white man. And, friends, after three hundred years I say that the time has come when we will talk to the white man in the only language he understands; the language of struggle. [Applause.] Friends, let's look around our country to-day. Our chairman has asked you who grows the food in this country. It is our little children ten years, fifteen years, who work and starve and die on the farm for the white man. *They* grow the food so that the white man can eat and get fat. But yet thousands and thousands of our little children can't get that food that he grows. In the Transkei, the Ciskei, thousands and

thousands of our children die every year because they can't
eat that food. And a lot of that food is sent away overseas.
Yesterday I read that many shiploads of oranges have
been sent by Dr Malan to feed the white people of New
Zealand.' [*Voices:* Shame!] 'I ask, man: those oranges
belong to us and our country. Why didn't our little
children get those oranges? We look around to Parktown,
to Norwood and Houghton and all the nice, beautiful
areas where the white men live in beautiful homes. Who
built those homes? Wasn't it our black people who
sweated and toiled day and night for two pounds a week
with their children dying at home of starvation? Didn't
those black people build those homes? Yes! And those
people have to live in the shanty towns of Moroka where
the white man is afraid to keep his dog. Yes, friends, and
we are not free to move about as we like in the country of
our birth.' (Mr Ahmed Kathrada, June 19th, 1952,
pp. 244-5.)

'Three hundred years ago Jan van Riebeeck landed upon
the shores of this land. Since that day many things have
happened. Today South Africa is reminding herself of those
events which make the pattern of her story of three
centuries ago. In Capetown today the van Riebeeck celebrations have reached an unprecedented climax in the splend-
our and the pomp, the pageantry and the ceremony that
mark the occasion. The white man's cup of joy is overflowing. The Europeans have every reason to feel happy
and to display their joy upon this colossal scale. They have
spread themselves upon this vast expanse of land. They
have found a land rich with minerals. They have exploited
and are still tapping the mineral wealth of South Africa.
The soil has yielded abundantly. Their factories, their
warehouses and their commercial undertakings show
the measure of their prosperity. Taken man for man, the
Europeans of this land are some of the richest people in
the world. World statistics show that they are some of the

healthiest people of the world. But we Africans also look back over that period of three hundred years. We see a record of sadness. We know that three hundred years ago van Riebeeck was sent specifically by the Dutch East India Company to trade with the aborigines of this land. We know how he and his Christian European compatriots obtained the land from the unsophisticated non-Christian non-European. We remember the cattle deals of those early days. We know that the institution of slavery – by which the Europeans in this land held the non-Europeans of this land in bondage nearly two hundred out of the three hundred years – came with van Riebeeck. . . . Today we should all be rejoicing after three hundred years of living together. But everybody knows that we are not all happy. I wish to remind the Europeans of this country that in taking stock of the past three hundred years they cannot escape the fact that whatever page they turn to in the history of South Africa, they find it red with the blood of the fallen, they find ill-will and insecurity written plainly across the pages. I appeal to them to weigh and consider and say if a different course of events over the past three hundred years could not have paid them and us better dividends.' (Dr James Moroka, April 6th, 1952, pp. 318-22.)

'And you who today work in the mines, you today who work on the farms, you today who build a beautiful road for the motor cars, you are the people who are hungry, you are the people who have no clothes, you are the people who must live under pass laws; you are the people who are oppressed in this country [Applause] . . . If they put you in gaol, I ask you: is your condition better outside?' (Mr Yusuf Cachalia, March 9th, 1952, pp. 215 and 220.)

Distrust of the white man is expressed very clearly in the ambivalent attitude to Christianity. Many of the demonstrations took the form of Christian prayer meetings. At the political gatherings, speakers stressed the affinity between non-violent resistance and the ethic of Christianity. Yet, at the same time, they voiced suspicion as to the role of Christianity in the subordination of the non-whites, and indeed outright rejection of the white man's Christianity.

'We looked up to God while the European looked down and collected our gold and our women.' (Mr Isaiah Mac-Donald Maseko, June 13th, 1952, p. 103.)

'Once upon a time I said that one king was told that he had been weighed and found wanting. Now that saying is in the Bible. Today we are living under three hundred years of European domination of this land. Now they came here three hundred years ago and within that period they have been weighed and we are now judging and we find them wanting . . . A lion, you know, will never eat another lion. . . . These people are Christians, but they eat people . . . If they represent God then they represent a false God. And if God is like that, then God is no good for Africa. [Applause.] But if he is like that they represent him, then he is no good for us. If God says my children must be looked after and your children must starve, then. . . . Now the fact that you can't use the same bridge, the fact that you can't use the same post-office, the fact that you can't use the same subway – and then you remember that the God of these people, he can't be our God at all.' (Mr Moses Kotane, March 9th, 1952, pp. 222-7.)

English-speaking white South Africans generally plead innocence of responsibility for race conflict, and complacently shift the guilt to the Afrikaner Nationalist. This is not the view of the resistance leaders, who see white domination in the broad perspective of three hundred years of exploitation, though some speakers blame the Nationalist Government for the present deterioration in race relations and the trend towards fascism. Nor do the leaders give voice to hatred of the white man, as we would expect. On the contrary, they go out of their way to bridge the gap between white and non-white. They assure their own followers and white South Africans that they are opposed to racialism, that the Africa which is wanted by the African National Congress is Africa of the African, who accepts any man of any colour willing to work with the African people. They emphasize that they bear no man a grudge, that their struggle is directed against unjust laws, not against any racial group. Yet occasionally a speaker pours out the banked-up resentment against the white man, and the emotion and intensity of these tirades give some measure of the forces which the resistance leaders are seeking to control.

'I know that you are tired of seeing your motherland raped by foreigners from Europe; your mothers, your fathers wakened in the middle of the night by stupid Dutchmen of the platteland. . . . It is within you to end this system. And your National Congress has said the first step is to defy unjust laws, to loosen the stranglehold of the white leeches. It is within you to get rid of these leeches who are sucking our blood. [Applause.] To rid ourselves of human parasites. . . . We are tired of having this white serpent. [Applause.] Down with white oppression. [*Many voices:* Down with white oppression.] Down with the Nats.' [*Many voices:* Down with the Nats.] (An African speaker, June 19th, 1952, pp. 241-2.)

In relation to the police, however, as distinct from other whites, many speakers freely expressed their antagonism. The contact of the urban African with the Government is essentially a contact with the police, and with the police, not as protectors, not as the cherubim and seraphim of justice, but in their punitive role. There was an occasional voice to suggest that the enemies of the people are not the police, but an oppressive system of which they are the paid agents, and that the police themselves, drawn from the poorest sections of the Afrikaners, are also victims of exploitation.

'The police do not care whether you are a B.A. or a Minister. They ask your pass. They want the women to carry passes so that they can sleep with them in the police cells when arrested, as in a case which happened in Springs when a European raped two African girls.' (An African speaker, June 12th, 1952, p. 94.)

'They [the volunteers] must behave well as the police will provoke them. Tomorrow the police will say, "*Ek het 'n kaffer geskiet, hy het my met 'n klip gegooi.*" ("I've shot a kaffir. He threw a stone at me.") But that policeman has never been injured. But what will they say now? "*Hoe gaan ons werk, kerels, die mense baklei nie:*" ("What shall we do, chaps? These people don't fight.") You must give them that headache. Even if the police kick you out of the trams you must just say, please take me to the other side.' (An African speaker, June 22nd, 1952, p. 131.)

'They can bring their machine guns, as they did on the 1st of May, and shoot us down – innocent men – without provocation. And what will happen to you if you die? I ask you. My friend let me tell you that when you die they must take that chain off you and you will be free in your death.' [Applause.] (An Indian speaker, March 9th, 1952, p. 220.)

'And the police who are supposed to uphold order, but who only start riots, shot down a hundred at Bellhoek, May the 1st, 1951! I don't need to remind you that in many African townships the police started riots. If Africans will not fight, the police make them fight. At the City Hall. Only this year! Another riot!' (An African speaker, June 19th, 1952, p. 239.)

Yet notwithstanding the expectation of deliberate violence from the police, the resistance leaders stressed again and again that their own campaign was to be peaceful. Both types of approach to passive resistance are represented in their speeches. Thus Mr Nana Sita, a disciple of Mahatma Gandhi, expresses the pure type of Satyagraha:

119

'The weapons we are to use will be stronger than the atomic bomb. I hope you understand that weapon. A just and righteous rule will be established. By suffering we shall march forward with this weapon.' (June 22nd, 1952, p. 135.)

The African speaker quoted below is clearly swayed by considerations of expedience, and not by a moral repudiation of violence as such:

'If in this country violence is to come we shall not allow the white man to tell us where the battlefield will be. [*Voices:* Afrika!] The white man will not choose the time. I say if violence must come, the African will choose the time and the battlefield. But I repeat, violence is not contemplated. We say this campaign is going to be peaceful.' (June 19th, 1952, p. 240.)

Throughout these demonstrations, the leaders inspired their followers with belief in ultimate victory, springing, no doubt, from their own inner convictions. This belief is many-faceted. The racial composition of Africa, and the trend of world opinion, provide a solid basis for confidence.

'I want to tell the white man that there are a hundred and fifty million of us in the continent of Africa. And in the continent of Africa there are only three million white people. And when the army of freedom marches forward it will brush aside those three million white people.' (Mr Ahmed Kathrada, June 19th, 1952, p. 245-6.)

'And the whole of the East, India, China, Japan and all the other parts, Europe, America and the northern part of Africa – all have their eyes on the African National Congress. [Applause.] Many of them have written to Dr Moroka and his secretary to say, "Congress, you are going to lead the millions into action. Tell us how you want us to help you".' (Mr Joseph Marks, February 24th, 1952, p. 207.)

More tenuous is the conviction that good will triumph over evil, whether the good consists in non-violent means or in just ends:

'Friends, what is this machinery of the government? The machinery of the government is the police. [Applause.] The police who were responsible for killing innocent men in this location on the 1st of May, 1950. And what have they got? They have got guns, they have got machine guns and they have got those big lorries and they have nasty Nazi-minded memories and, my friends, this is no joke – their power is great. But are we going to be frightened of that power? . . . The power of man is greater than the power of machine guns. The determination of one black man, whether he be an Indian or a Coloured or an African, is greater than the determination of any other man. And if justice and truth is on our side, no machine [guns], no police, no power can stop us from marching onwards.' (Mr Yusuf Cachalia, March 9th, 1952, p. 219.)

Finally, most tenuous of all grounds for faith in the future is the promise of history conceived as the inevitable unfolding of freedom. In the belief that history favours the oppressed, the leaders called on the resisters to sacrifice themselves in the cause of non-white liberation.

V

THE CAMPAIGN

HERALDED by a day of prayer in many locations throughout the Union, the campaign was launched on June 26th, 1952. Disciplined volunteer corps, pledged to the aims of the resistance movement and under the control of trained leaders, deliberately committed acts of civil disobedience. These acts, in general, took one or other of the following forms:

Entering a location without a permit.
Being out at night without a curfew pass.
Sitting on railway seats marked 'Europeans only'.
Entering the European waiting-room on railway stations.
Travelling in railway coaches reserved for Europeans.
Entering the European section of the post office.

In other words, the only law directly challenged was the Pass Law, symbol of domination for the whites, and of subjection for the Africans. For the rest, the resisters' acts attacked apartheid regulations, mainly on the railways.

The movement developed in the main urban centres, as recommended by the Joint Planning Council for the first phase of the struggle. The Witwatersrand area and Port Elizabeth entered the campaign on the opening date, and they were followed by the major South African cities. Two of these, Cape Town and Durban, delayed their entry, and there was an uneven pattern of participation in the different regions. In the provinces of Natal and the Orange Free State, the only active centres were Durban and Bloemfontein, each contributing a small quota of resisters. The whole of the Cape Western area was relatively inactive, and even the Transvaal, the industrial core of the Union with an immense urban African proletariat, did not participate as fully as might have been expected. In contrast, the Eastern Cape, which includes the port cities of East London and Port Elizabeth, provided the main body of support. This appears from the following figures showing the regional distribution of resisters:

Eastern Cape	5,719
Western Cape, Mafeking, Kimberley . .	423
Transvaal	1,911
Natal	246
Free State	258
	8,557

(The Secretarial Report to the 21st Conference of the South African Indian Congress, July 9th-11th, 1954.)

The reasons for these differences are not at all clear. The level of participation in Natal was exceedingly low, when compared with the extent of Indian resistance in the 1946 campaign. This is all the more remarkable, since Indian life in Natal is seriously threatened by the Group Areas Act. The explanation is possibly that the Indian Congress, as junior partner in the campaign, did not wish to take the lead, that the Natal branch of the African National Congress was poorly organized, and that strong nationalist and anti-Indian sentiment dampened African enthusiasm for the campaign. Yet Africans participated fully and in great numbers in the resistance meetings.

In the Free State, Dr Moroka declared, it was deliberate policy not to prosecute the campaign vigorously, presumably so as to conserve energy for more promising areas. The limited response in the Western Cape no doubt reflects the lack of organization among the African migrants, newly arrived in this area, and the apathy of the Coloureds, who are concentrated there. For the most part, the Coloureds fear identification with other non-whites and still tend to pin their hopes on the paternalism of their white overlords, though the Government is steadily shattering this simple faith. It is as if the Coloureds were paralysed by the danger of losing their few privileges, and firmly anchored to the *status quo* by their legal superiority over the Africans and Indians.

The difference in the participation of the highly industrialized Transvaal Province as compared with the more rural Cape Eastern Province is very marked, a ratio of one to three, and puzzling. Many explanations of the greater strength of resistance in the Eastern Cape have been advanced: the longer period of contact with Europeans; the extent of conversion to Christianity;[1] the strength of the trade unions; the relatively more liberal policies and hence the sharper reactions to the deprivations of apartheid; political training acquired in the exercise of a limited franchise; the greater stability of family life; and the more homogeneous character of the African population. In any event, whatever the explanation, the large and small towns of the Eastern Cape were the core of the resistance movement.

The months of August, September and October mark the peak periods of resistance. In the last five days of June, 146 volunteered, in July, 1,504, in August, 2,015, in September, 2,258, in October, 2,354, and in November and December only 280. (Secretarial Report to the South African Indian Congress.) The first stage of the resistance movement was completed in October; selected groups of volunteers had defied the laws in the main centres, and resistance had, indeed, already spread to some of the smaller towns. Thereafter, resistance, far from developing in the rural areas according to plan, declined precipitately.

[1] See Chapter IV, pp. 116-17.

Conduct of the Campaign

While the plan of the Joint Planning Council was shaped by tactical considerations, the Satyagraha form of passive resistance clearly influenced the actual conduct of the campaign.

The activities were open and public. No attempt was made to conceal intentions or to deceive the authorities. On the contrary, the resisters co-operated fully with the police and the Government. Thus, Mr Nelson Mandela, a lawyer and one of the leaders of the African National Congress, handed the following letter to the Magistrate at Boksburg on the date of the commencement of the campaign:

> SIR,—We have been directed by the Joint Action Committee of the African National Congress, Transvaal, and the Transvaal Indian Congress, to advise you that in terms of the decision of the Congresses the persons in the list attached herein will defy the permit regulations and deliberately court imprisonment by entering Boksburg Location today at 2.30 p.m. without obtaining the necessary permits. Mr Nana Sita, President of the Transvaal Indian Congress, will lead the batch.
>
> Yours faithfully,
>
> N. THANDRAY, Secretary, Transvaal Indian Congress.
> S. SELLO, Secretary, African National Congress (Transvaal.)
> (Preparatory Examination of W. M. Sisulu and 19 others, p. 286.)

From a purely expedient point of view, the resisters might have elected not to notify the authorities of their plans, nor to invite arrest. It would have been sufficient, for example, that more and more Africans should cease to carry their passes. Nor would the refusal of the police to effect an arrest have created a problem. But, in terms of Satyagraha, the courting of arrest and the willing submission to punishment are the essential means for conversion of the rulers.

Because of this influence of the Satyagraha type of resistance, the resisters cheerfully lined up for arrest, and sought to sustain arrest, trial and imprisonment with good humour. Hence, too, when the police made no arrest, the resisters offered themselves again and again. Mr Ismail Meer's batch was obliged to repeat its attempt to enter the European section of the Berea Road railway station, and Dr Wilson Conco, Chairman of the African National Congress (Natal), with his group of volunteers, paraded the streets for two nights, soliciting arrest.

Flash of November 5th and 6th, 1952, carried an account of Dr Conco's defiance. On Sunday night, Dr Conco with his batch of twenty-three men and women defied the curfew law, informing the police well in advance, but the police declined to effect an arrest on the ground that they were 'busy with more important matters'. *Flash* commented that this could hardly have been the true explanation, because over twenty African non-defiers were sentenced in the Durban Courts on Monday morning for breach of the same curfew regulations. Again, on Monday night, Dr Conco and his batch 'marched past the Charge Office under the very nose of the District Commandant's Headquarters. Policemen saw the resisters, looked the other way (one bowed his head down shamefully) and passed on their way.' On Tuesday morning, 'Dr Conco and his gallant band were not to be denied the pleasure of arrest and imprisonment for long!' They entered the railway cloak-room and booking-hall reserved for Europeans, were arrested by the police, and 'pushed and prodded into the van, though they were most willing. . . . Like a lot of sheep or cattle, they were driven off – but they were neither sheep nor cattle – these men and women with a purpose. They left jubilantly, all the time giving out the *"Afrika"* salute from the inside of the van.'

Another batch, this time in Mafeking, suffered the curious frustration of conviction without imprisonment, a frustration only intelligible in terms of Satyagraha. As the gaol was overcrowded, the magistrate declined to punish the resisters. After the trial, Dr S. M. Molema, brother of one of the accused and a prominent member of the African National Congress, said that the magistrate's leniency had surprised them and temporarily upset their plans, but that the campaign would continue in Mafeking. (*Press Digest*, No. 42, October 7th, 1952, p. 417.)

Again, under the inspiration of Satyagraha, the resisters generally sought to minimize bitterness by their selection of defiance acts. The Berea Road railway station in Durban and the New Brighton railway station in Port Elizabeth are largely used by non-whites; entry into the waiting-room reserved for Europeans at these stations would directly affect few white passengers. Walking the streets without a curfew pass and going into an African location without a permit are acts purely domestic to the non-whites themselves; were it not for police action and the newspapers, the ruling group would be completely unaware of any change in the pattern of South African life.

When sentenced, the resisters, with few exceptions, chose imprisonment, rejecting the tempting option of a fine. Nor did they plead in mitigation. Instead, following precedent in India, the resisters used the court as a platform from which they might reach out to the conscience of the ruling class. *Flash* (November 6th, 1952) describes the court scene when Dr Conco and his batch were sentenced.

The resisters pleaded guilty, and Dr Conco, through his attorney, asked for permission to make a statement. The magistrate replied abruptly that he was not concerned with explanations of motives with political reasons; the Court was not a political arena. The statement, however, might be handed in. *Flash* comments that if it was a bad statement to be read, it was surely also a bad statement to be 'filed on record'. Thereafter, the defending lawyers argued that it was the duty of the Courts to refuse to administer unjust laws, to which the magistrate responded by imposing the maximum sentence and addressing the following homily to the accused: 'The laws of the country are there to be obeyed. . . . The legislature has seen fit to pass these laws. It behoves all citizens to obey them. You have all transgressed the laws in the full knowledge that you were doing so. I am not concerned with your motive for breaking the law. There has been far too much of this deliberate transgression. It is high time you obeyed the laws of the country. My advice to you is to obey and respect the laws of the country before you ask for other privileges.' Again, *Flash* had the last word, though not to the magistrate. 'How mistaken was the magistrate! These men and women did not ask for any "privileges". They only fought for their rights.'

It is not difficult to understand the magistrate's impatient reaction to protests against the laws which he is obliged to administer. Many of these protests took the almost routine form of a direct indictment of unjust laws, and gave reasoned explanations of the motives for deliberate defiance and the voluntary submission to punishment. Others touched deeper chords of emotion and of the yearning for freedom. The statement read by Mr. S. Mokoena, Bloemfontein Volunteer-in-Chief, to the Bloemfontein magistrate is a moving example of the court literature of the resistance movement:

'We have decided voluntarily, and without any form of compulsion having been exerted upon us, to defy the laws which not only we non-Europeans regard as extremely unjust, but also a growing number of Europeans in this country.

'It has been suggested by our European administrators, Your Worship included, that we should ventilate our grievances through the "proper channels", and that, as it is now, the law needs must take its course against us. Some there are who have even gone so far as to suggest that, as these laws were passed by Parliament, we should see to it that the same Parliament repealed or amended them. You will be the first to agree, Your Worship, that we have exhausted all attempts to air our genuine sufferings through the so-called "proper channels".

'The history of our struggle for liberation is a sad story of unfulfilled or broken promises by our White administrators. It is a history characterized by obsequious representations and cap-in-hand deputations. The Natives' Representative Council was a "proper channel" – albeit an ineffective one – through which we could draw the attention of the Government to our sorry lot. The Council is now no more. The Location Advisory Boards and the Bungas, toy telephones that they actually are, are also some of the oft-spoken "proper channels".

'Theirs is an ineffectual voice. Our so-called European Native representatives in Parliament are yet other "proper channels". These representatives were the first to admit that theirs was a voice in the wilderness as they were battling against "a stone wall of colour prejudice" in Parliament. Is there any wonder therefore that we have decided to throw caution to the winds – in so far as personal consequences are concerned – and embark upon this painful method of airing our grievances? To suggest that we should bring pressure to bear upon Parliament to repeal or amend these unjust laws is to make mockery of our sufferings. It is common knowledge that, because of our colour, we are a voteless and voiceless majority.

'It is interesting to speculate, Your Worship, what the reaction of the European would be, were he, just by sheer miracle, to discover himself an African just overnight and thus be subjected to the thousand and one irksome discriminatory laws that our people have borne for centuries with Christian-like fortitude. This I say, because just recently two South African Members of Parliament protested strongly against alleged discrimination, real or imaginary, to which, so they said, they were subjected in India; discrimination which by mere comparison with what is our daily dose of this satanic doctrine is not worthy of the name. And, to come nearer home, Europeans are up in arms in South Africa against the introduction of the population registration measure which they regard as the extension of the pass system to them.

'The local curfew regulation which is one of our targets of defiance is extremely unfair. Hitherto, our movements in town were limited up to 10 p.m. But recently the Minister of Native Affairs, with the approval of the City Council, brought down the time to 9 p.m., and this notwithstanding the protestations of the "proper channel", the local Native Advisory Board, that is. The majority of trains leave the station long after 9 p.m., and many an African man or woman has been arrested for the "crime" of having gone to see somebody off at the station after 9 p.m.

'It has been our painful observation that, whenever apartheid is practised, we are always the sufferers. The endless queues at the ticket office during public holidays or week-ends, and the equally long queues in the local post office, will convince any one that it is being taken as a matter of course that we must ever be satisfied with unequal and inadequate facilities.

'Even in a location that is supposed to be our own; in a location where we are left "to develop along our own lines", we have no freedom whatever. Your parent, wife or relative needs must get a permit before he can sojourn with you. Indeed, Your Worship, when you stop to think how painful, how humiliating some of these restrictions are to people that are living in a supposedly free and democratic country, the wonder will not be that we have embarked upon this resistance campaign at all, but that it has taken us so long a time to do so.

'We do not quarrel with Your Worship when you say you have no alternative but to punish us for deliberately breaking the unjust laws; that is the unenviable duty you are bound to carry out. But, with due respect to Your Worship, we wish to state that punishment, no matter how severe, can be no deterrent to us. We have undertaken this campaign fully expecting such punishment. We have steeled and braced ourselves up to bear whatever punishment may come our way. And, happily, we derive encouragement and inspiration from the knowledge that practically the whole of the African population in Bloemfontein is four-square behind us, if not actively, then at least morally.' (The *Bantu World*, November 15th, 1952.)

But the Courts were not an effective forum for reaching the great white public. Only brief depersonalized accounts of the proceedings appeared in the newspapers circulating among white readers. The protest statements were rarely mentioned; laconic news items, 40 ARRESTED FOR DEFYING APARTHEID LAWS, 88 MORE ARRESTS, engulfed the individual strivings and aspirations, inevitably perhaps in view of the many resistance acts and consequent decline in news value.

The resisters were therefore thrown back on their own resources to make known the sacrifices of the resistance movement, and for the most part reached only sections of the non-whites themselves. Mimeographed news-sheets, such as *Afrika* and *Flash*, filled in the skeleton outlines provided by the national Press. More effective were the meetings associated with different stages of civil disobedience acts; the dispatch of the volunteers (as when Mr J. N. Singh's batch left the public meeting at Durban to defy railway apartheid regulations), the trial and the return from gaol.

Thus, in July at Uitenhage, during the trial of ten resisters, hundreds knelt and prayed, led by an old African woman in a red shawl. At East London, some 250 singing and praying Africans gathered outside the Magistrate's Court while eighty-five of their fellow campaigners were charged with not being in possession of night passes. (The *Star*, July 23rd, 1952.) According to an account in the *Eastern Province Herald* of July 18th, 1952, about 1,000 Africans gathered outside the courtroom in Port Elizabeth, and sang hymns and prayed for the accused. In August, again at Port Elizabeth, some 5,000 Africans prayed for the success of the campaign, after welcoming 250 volunteers released from prison. (*Press Digest*, No. 34, p. 334.) A week later, at the opening of the trial of Dr Moroka and other leaders of the resistance campaign, thousands of non-Europeans crammed the corridors of the Courts in Johannesburg singing defiance songs, and later moved to a vacant square, where meetings continued throughout the day. White University students and Indian schoolchildren were reported to have taken part in these demonstrations. (*Press Digest*, No. 35, p. 343.)

The prayer meetings, most marked in the Eastern Cape, the symbolism of flags and slogans, the resistance songs and the speeches, the vicarious participation in the suffering of the resisters, served to spread among non-whites the meaning of passive resistance, and to heighten its political and spiritual significance.

The resistance leaders might well feel that the campaign was a great success. Six thousand volunteers had defied the laws in the first hundred days of the campaign. A firm control by the leaders and discipline and good humour among the followers demonstrated the increasing strength of the non-white organizations. There were occasional outbursts of bitterness, but remarkably few incidents between the resisters and the police. The so-called U.N.O. batches had gone into action at a time when the United Nations General Assembly was about to discuss apartheid policy in South Africa. The Transvaal branch of the African National Congress, at its October Conference, felt sufficient confidence to plan the extension of the struggle into the rural areas. A correspondent of the *Star* reported on October 11th, 1952, that 'all over the township [of Lady Selborne in Pretoria, where the Conference met] Native children – including those only just old enough to speak – give the sign and beamingly call out the resistance slogan: "*Mayibuye Afrika*" '. (As reported in *Afrika*, October 21st, 1952.) A news reporter of the *Pretoria News*, impressed by the spirit of the Conference, posed the question whether there was 'not some truth in the passionate declaration by Dr Nkomo, when welcoming delegates on Friday "that to-day we witness the turning point in the history of South Africa".' (October 13, 1952.)

It was precisely at this stage, at the high peak of a successful campaign, at a time most inauspicious for the aspirations of the non-whites and most convenient for the Government, that a series of riots broke out.

The Riots

The immediate causes of the riots are by no means clear. The Government refused to hold a commission of inquiry; not that a Government commission would necessarily add to our understanding. Facts vary with the political viewpoint, especially in Government commissions.

A mass of documentary evidence has accumulated in newspaper reports, in the records of trials and inquests, and in a number of investigations by local authorities and private individuals. Sifting these sources is a major research project in itself, and falls outside the scope of this study, since there is no evidence to connect the resistance movement with the disturbances, nor was violence at any time advocated by the resisters as a means of struggle. The reactions of the resistance leaders and of the whites, and the way in which the Government made use of the riots to suppress the resistance movement, are relevant to this history, rather than the riots as such.

The police and official versions of the riots were given prominence in the national Press. The first disturbance was at Port Elizabeth, on the afternoon of October 18th, 1952, when a railway constable at New Brighton station attempted to arrest two Africans suspected of stealing a drum of paint. According to the constable's account, the men resisted arrest and other Africans came to their assistance. In the immediate and ensuing struggle, the constable shot one of the suspected men who attacked him with a long knife, hit another assailant in the right breast, fired a shot which glanced off the temple of a third assailant, wounded in the arm a woman attempting to set the ticket office alight, and thereafter fired other shots at different groups, who were stoning the station. All told, he admitted to firing twenty-one shots. (Evidence at the Preparatory Examination of William Gova and 126 Others,

Magistrate's Court, Port Elizabeth, pp. 3-7. At the subsequent trial of some of the accused, in the case of Regina *v.* William Gova and 10 Others, the Judge commended the constable for his great courage and devotion to duty in the midst of large numbers of hostile Africans and in the face of a serious threat to life and property.)

Police reinforcements arrived to find a crowd of between 2,000 and 3,000 Africans throwing stones at the railway station. They fired a few warning shots in the direction of the crowd, since verbal warnings would have been useless because of the noise. The crowd diminished: some of its members left; others took refuge behind buildings, running out to hurl stones at the police. The latter, a small force, fired on their attackers, action which the Judge held was well within the rights of the police. When there was a lull, the police divided into two bands, one returning to the police station in case it should be attacked, and the other moving on to the railway station. About an hour later, in response to a message, the police entered New Brighton Location. A big crowd was throwing stones at some buildings and burning an overturned lorry. The police fired a few shots at the foremost of the stone-throwers, causing the crowd to scatter, and then discovered the first white fatality, a man with head battered in, clothing torn and covered with blood. There were no further attacks; the police officer went back to the police station with most of his men, and re-entered New Brighton some two hours later in time to rescue a white woman. The cinema was burning, and three white men lay dead on the other side of the road. (Preparatory Examination, pp. 23-9, and Judgment in Regina *v.* William Gova and 10 Others.)

One company of police fired some fifty shots, the second company about forty shots. The African casualties were seven dead and twenty-seven injured, according to official accounts. No doubt the casualties were higher, since the police demanded explanations from those wounded of the circumstances under which they had sustained their injuries, with the result that the people would tend to hide their wounded. The only serious injury to a European policeman was a stone injury on the shin. (Preparatory Examination, pp. 28-9.) Much damage was done to property.

The second incident was at the Denver Native Hostel on November 3rd, 1952, when the residents, who had resolved not to pay an increase in rental from eleven shillings to one pound per month, rushed at a tenant who tendered the rental, shouting that he should be 'hit' and 'killed'. The municipal police took the tenant into the administrative offices, and the crowd threw stones through the windows. Police arrived; the crowd severely damaged a car belonging to the acting superintendent of the hostel and stoned police vehicles and the hostel building. The police fired some shots outside the building, but apparently without injuring the rioters. Later they fired again, this time into the hostel, from the protection of a tunnel or portico and from behind a double iron gate. The regional magistrate, in his judgment at the trial of Moathludi and others on a charge of public violence, held that the first shootings were justified, since there was real danger to life. He was, however, not prepared to take the same view of the later shootings into the hostel, which caused the casualties. He failed to see how anyone who stood behind the gates could have been in danger of life or limb from missiles. (This account of the events is taken from the magistrate's reasons for judgment in Regina v. Moathludi and Others, Case No. M.6/53, in the Court of the Regional Magistrate, Southern Transvaal.)

Three Africans were shot dead and four were wounded. One constable received an injury from a missile which struck his collar bone. In evidence, a police constable stated that 'our instructions are to shoot to hit where stones are being thrown. This was done with a view to injure us.' (P. 108 of the Preparatory Examination.) Other constables told the Court that they were instructed to, and did, shoot to kill; the officer-in-charge, on the other hand, contended that his instructions were to wound and not to kill. (See the magistrate's reasons for judgment.)

On November 8th, 1952, at No. 2 Location, Kimberley,

three young Africans bought beer at the municipal beer hall, and when they had finished drinking, stood up, shouted '*Afrika!*', threw the beer mugs in the air, and tramped on them. When they were ordered out, most of the other beer-drinkers followed them. A crowd gathered and started to stone the building. Members of the Municipal police, who attempted to drive them off, were obliged to take refuge in the hall, where they were trapped. (Evidence of a beer-hall employee, and summing up of the magistrate at the inquest proceedings on the African dead; *Natal Daily News*, November 26th, 1952, and December 3rd, 1952.) A small police contingent arrived, were stoned, and opened fire under instructions 'not to shoot women and children if this could be avoided and to shoot only those actually stoning the bus or police'. The mob scattered, reformed, continued throwing stones, and the police withdrew when ammunition ran low. 'Attacks were repelled only by shooting. Warnings had no effect.' (Police account, the *Natal Mercury*, November 26th, 1952.)

The beer hall and administrative block were now on fire. The police returned with a force of seventy men, and, under a heavy rain of stones, fired only at selected targets. They refrained from killing a youth of between twelve and fifteen years, leading a frenzied attack, with a solid mass of women behind him. The police searched houses and yards for stone-throwers without success, and then 'decided to fire at whoever were stoning us from behind a galvanized iron fence'. Firearms were only used 'to protect ourselves from death or serious injury'. A baton charge would have been inviting extermination. Tear gas had proved ineffective. (Police account, *Natal Daily News*, November 26th, 1952.)

The magistrate came to the conclusion that the police on all occasions had fired in self-defence; that if they had not done so, all who entered the location would have been killed by the crowds; and that the small death roll indicated that there had been no indiscriminate shooting by the police. (*Natal Daily News*, December 3rd, 1952.) African casualties were twelve or thirteen dead, seventy-eight injured.

Volunteers assembling to get a final 'briefing' before 'defying' the law

They are taken away under police escort. Some of the supporters raise their hands in the 'Afrika' salute

Above: Three thousand non-whites gather at 'Red' Square, Durban, on August 31st, 1952

Left: Indian Congress leaders give the 'Afrika' salute on their release from Durban gaol

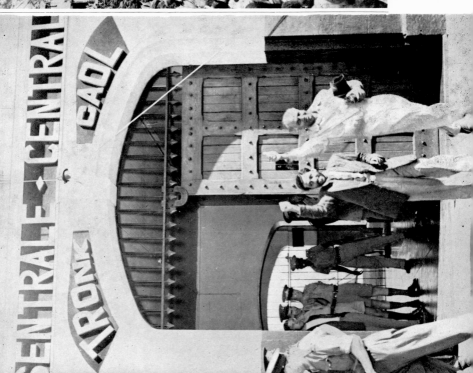

The fourth riot broke out in East London. On November 7th the Government prohibited public meetings of non-Europeans in five districts, including East London. Permission was granted for the holding of an open-air prayer meeting of Africans in East Bank Location, East London, on November 9th. Fifteen hundred people came to the meeting. The police decided that the meeting was not religious and ordered its dispersal. (*Rand Daily Mail*, November 8th and November 11th, 1952.) A police captain stated that as the crowd clearly showed it would not disperse, he issued a warning and then ordered a baton charge. Later a second baton charge was ordered. The crowd withdrew, but did not leave the square. The police captain shouted that sterner methods would be used. He then heard two shots ring out from the crowd, stones began to fall, and he ordered his men to fire. After about thirty shots, the stoning ceased, the crowd dispersed behind buildings and more stones were thrown. The police fired at the people who were stoning them. They then returned to the police station because the crowd had dispersed. 'On the way we were stoned again and shots were fired at these Natives.' About a half-hour later, a police patrol was sent out and found a burning motor-car and the body of a nun, a white missionary doctor, who had been brutally murdered. Then a report was received that a European man had been murdered. The police patrol, sent to recover the body, was stoned and fired in retaliation. One constable was wounded by a shot from a revolver 'fired by a Native'. After this, various buildings were set alight by Native gangs. 'At no time was indiscriminate firing resorted to. We only resorted to our fire-arms as a last resort in protecting ourselves from serious bodily injury and possible death.' (Police captain's account, *Natal Daily News*, March 28th, 1953.)

The circumstances of the missionary doctor's death, and the spoliation of her body, horrified the nation, more particularly since she was a devoted servant of the African people. Added to this were the death of an innocent European man and the

destruction of many buildings, including the Roman Catholic
Mission and a wood-and-iron Anglican Mission church. The
non-white casualties were eleven dead and more than fifty
injured. Some unofficial sources gave appreciably higher
estimates of both the dead and the injured.

In contrast to the official versions, little has been heard of
the views of the Africans as to the immediate causes of the riots.
Some laid responsibility on *agents provocateurs*. (For example,
Dr W. F. Nkomo, as quoted in the *Bantu World*, November
29th, 1952.) In this connection, a comment of the director of
the South African Institute of Race Relations has some relevance. 'In both Port Elizabeth and Kimberley, Europeans stated
that strangers had come into the neighbourhood previously to
the riots. The implication is that strangers to the cities concerned might have been deliberate immediate causes – "not
our own Natives".' (Report by the Director on visits to Port
Elizabeth, East London and Kimberley in connection with the
riots, R.R.9/53, January 12th, 1953.)

Others commented on the fact that anti-social elements,
and more particularly *tsotsis*, took advantage of the situation to
express their destructive proclivities, and that the Government,
by its suppression of responsible African leaders, was handing
over the leadership of the Africans to the *tsotsis*. These *tsotsis*
are maladjusted juveniles, frustrated by the general conditions
of urban African life and the lack of facilities for schooling and
employment. Some evidence of the extent to which juveniles
were thought to be involved in the East London riots is given
by the numbers charged before the Courts – forty-eight of a
total of ninety-one. (W. B. Ngakane, *Investigation into Case
Histories of African Juveniles involved in the East London Riots*.
Report by the South African Institute of Race Relations,
R.R.41/53, April 21st, 1953.)

Another source lays responsibility squarely on the police,
emphasizing the way in which the role of the police had been
re-defined by the Minister of Justice, and seeking to demonstrate that the readiness of the police to shoot precipitated the

riots. According to this source, the people in East London location were holding a *bona-fide* prayer meeting. While the preacher was reading about the oppression of the Israelites, a police officer in charge of two lorry-loads of armed police decided that he could not permit such subversive theology and ordered the crowd to disperse within five minutes. The meeting immediately broke up. In less than two minutes, while people were walking away, the police officer is said to have ordered a charge, a second charge, then shots were fired, and a man was killed. The police thereupon climbed into their lorries and drove up and down the main streets of the location firing at people and into houses. Nobody had attacked the police – it would have been suicide to do so. There are reported to be bullet holes all over the location, many far from the scene of the disturbances.[2]

Similarly, this source finds the immediate cause of the Port Elizabeth riots in the actions of the railway policemen at New Brighton station, and the subsequent actions of police reinforcements in firing into the crowd outside the station. In Kimberley, the disturbances were said to have ceased on the arrival of the police, who nevertheless fired into the crowd and then shot their way through the streets of the location. At Denver, again according to the same source, stone-throwing stopped on the arrival of the police, there was a pause for some time, then suddenly a burst of firing and, after that, sniping at residents in the hostel.

The deeper causes of the riots are to be found in the social and economic conditions of the African people and in the policy and application of white domination. The immediate causes will never be known, but it seems reasonably clear that in Port Elizabeth and East London the taking of the lives of innocent white people, the destruction and the brutality were a mob reaction of a type all too familiar throughout the world,

[2] I cannot take the matter any further than the presentation of the official version and an unofficial counterversion. Alexander Campbell, in *The Heart of Africa* (London, Longmans, Green & Co., 1954), Chapter IV, gives an account of his own inquiries into the events of the East London riots.

and a retaliation for the police shooting of their own people; that this retaliation was anti-white, directed against the few white people in the locations, and the buildings which symbolized the white man's world; and that the relationship between the police and the African people is one of deep antagonism and a threat to the peace of the country. There can be no doubt of the violence of the mobs, once aroused, and of the need for firm police action. But I find it difficult to understand how the police themselves escaped with so few injuries if the threat to life was dangerous enough to justify the drastic measures they used.[3] It is disturbing to recall the words of one of the African speakers on June 22nd, 1952, four months before the riots (see p. 119), when he warned against police provocation. 'To-morrow the police will say, "I've shot a kaffir. He threw a stone at me." But that policeman has never been injured.'

Suspension of the Campaign

Though the immediate causes of the riots are obscure, their effects were to damp down the spirit of resistance. It is, of course, conceivable that the campaign had reached its peak prior to the riots, and was, in any event, in process of decline.

The resistance leaders vigorously denied the charge that they were responsible for the riots, and their conduct was entirely consistent with innocence. Dr Moroka immediately issued a statement on behalf of the African National Congress and the African people, strongly condemning the violent disturbances at Port Elizabeth. Both Congresses demanded an impartial commission of inquiry. They showed no anxiety whatever that the findings might possibly be against them and they could not have known that the Government would refuse to set up the usual routine public investigations, after events of such magnitude.

Nor did the Congresses hesitate to charge the Government

[3] The Minister of Justice is reported to have said that it was significant that in the recent disturbances not one policeman had been murdered or hurt. He said it must never happen and had, therefore, instructed that there must be sufficient men and sufficient weapons and the police should shoot before they themselves were killed. (The *Natal Mercury*, November 29th, 1952).

and police with responsibility for the riots. Dr J. L. Z. Njongwe, President of the African National Congress (Cape), emphasized that the seven Africans shot dead at Port Elizabeth were killed before a single European had been harmed, and demanded an inquiry so that the facts could be brought into the open. (*Press Digest*, No. 45, October 30th, 1952, p. 451.) The Natal branches of the Congresses called upon the Ministers of Justice and of Lands to stop creating social tension by talking about batons, guns and blood. 'No matter what Nationalist spokesmen say about the Defiance Campaign, the fact remains that our campaign is based on the noble ethics of non-violence and peace. We challenge the Government to prove the contrary. . . . The concept of violence and bloodshed is being spread by the Nationalists and nobody else. (*Advance*, November 20th, 1952.)

In the same issue, *Advance* reported the contents of a leaflet distributed by the National Action Committee of the two Congresses. The shootings at Kimberley, East London and Denver were described as part of the Government's plot to weaken the defiance campaign and to ruthlessly oppress the non-European people.

'The Government wants –
'to create race riots between European and non-European, Indian and African, and African and Coloured;
'to use the riots and general disturbances to cause panic among the Europeans so as to drive them into the arms of the Nationalists;
'to declare a state of national emergency, to seize absolute power, to cut off the leaders from the people and to impose a fascist dictatorship on the country.

'Its methods are –
'to send out agents among the people to provoke incidents which can be used by the police as a pretext for shooting and to incite and preach race hatred; to accuse the Indians, blame the Africans and praise the Coloureds;
'to use the police for the purpose of inciting racial strife

between the Africans and Indians and for the distribution of literature propagating apartheid.'

Non-Europeans were warned not to be provoked, not to 'listen to those who talk against any section of our population – anyone who speaks against the Indian, the Coloured, the Chinese, the African or European is an enemy of the people and an agent of the Government'.

Challenging the Government to hold an inquiry into the recent disturbances, the National Action Committee of the African National Congress and the South African Indian Congress stated that authentic reports strongly suggested that the disturbances were engineered by *provocateurs* and that the 'shooting order' of the Minister of Justice played a major part; failure to hold an inquiry indicated that these riots and disturbances were deliberately incited and provoked by the Government. (*Advance*, November 20th, 1952.)

Apart from the repudiation of responsibility for the riots, and counter-attacks on the Government, the resistance leaders firmly declared their intention of continuing the campaign in a peaceful, disciplined and non-violent manner. And the campaign did continue after the Port Elizabeth riots. Even during the period between the Port Elizabeth and East London riots, resisters took part in civil disobedience. Moreover, the leaders still planned the extension of the campaign to the rural areas. On October 27th, 1952, the Press reported a statement by Dr Njongwe that 'if you hear one day that the Ciskei has also gone into action, you will know that the victory will be achieved within five weeks'. (*Press Digest*, No. 45, p. 449.) Shortly after, at the opening of the Provincial Conference of the African National Congress (Natal), Dr Njongwe further developed this theme:

'Your duty now is to go and spread the message of Freedom to the people who live in the reserves. They know what oppression is, what it is to have their cattle culled. They know what has been done to their Chiefs, and they are ready. They have been ready for years, waiting for you. Even your trade union movement in the towns becomes futile because of the scab labour they can get any time from the reserves. Organize the reserves, and there will never be any scab labour. There must be deputations to the people. Go and put the standpoint of the African people all over the country. Get every African, man, woman, and child into the struggle. Those are the kind of deputations that we want. We do not want deputations to Dr Verwoerd. DEMOCRACY CANNOT MEET ON THE SAME TABLE AS FASCISM. WE HATE FASCISM.' (*Afrika*, November 7th, 1952.)

Indeed, so little abashed was the African National Congress at allegations of complicity in the riots, and so little intimidated by threats of drastic action, that on November 10th, 1952, it organized in Port Elizabeth a one-day strike against the imposition of a curfew. The Coloureds did not participate, but as far as the Africans were concerned, 'the strike was 96% successful and brought to Port Elizabeth industrialists the realization that the African community had a power of organization which they could not afford to ignore, particularly in such a vulnerable industrial port as Port Elizabeth'. (Report of the South African Institute of Race Relations, R.R.9/53.)

Yet notwithstanding all these activities after the Port Elizabeth riots, and the determination of the leaders, the resistance movement was tailing off into suspension. In October the movement was still in full vigour. The number of resisters was the highest sent into action – 2,354, according to the figures given in the report by the Joint Secretaries of the South African Indian Congress. Probably as many as 1,000 defied the laws in the latter half of October. In November and December, however, the number of resisters fell to 280. Nor did the introduction of white resisters check the decline.

On December 8th, a mixed group consisting of three white men, four white women, thirteen Indian men, six Indian women, ten African men and two African women entered

Germiston Location in the Witwatersrand area without permits. They were arrested, and later charged; first, with contravention of a Government proclamation by inciting Natives to resist, break or obstruct the administration of any law; second, with entering the location without permits; and third, with not being in possession of proper passes, a charge preferred against the African men only. The participation of white resisters, two of them, Mr Patrick Duncan and Miss Freda Troup, with aristocratic connections; the inclusion of Mr Manilal Gandhi; the high proportion of professionals, of University graduates and undergraduates; made this an unusual, a 'bumper batch'.

The following day, in Cape Town, four white resisters, three of them University students, marched into the non-European booths of the General Post Office, and began writing telegrams to Dr Malan. They were arrested and removed by the police. A week later, a white trade union organizer defied the apartheid regulations in a Johannesburg post office; presumably his telegram to the Minister of Justice, calling for the abolition of colour discrimination, has not yet been dispatched.

Congress leaders welcomed this participation of white resisters, partly as a demonstration to their own followers that all whites are not oppressors, and partly as a means of placing the struggle on the clear basis of principle, rather than of race conflict. As long as the movement embraced only non-whites, they sensed the danger that it might take a racial form. They must have hoped, too, that the sacrifice of the white resisters would stir the conscience of white South Africans; it is certainly easier for so colour-conscious a group to identify itself with the sufferings of people of the same pigment. Whatever the effects on the conscience of the whites, they were not stirred to further acts of defiance, and for all practical purposes the resistance campaign was at an end.

Possibly the impending general elections were a factor in the final suspension of the movement. While the resistance leaders did not distinguish between the election programmes of the Government and opposition parties – the non-European policies of the two parties were not fundamentally different – they nevertheless did not wish to do anything which would ensure the return of the Nationalist Party to power. Thus they refrained from taking advantage of the Appellate Court decision in the case of Regina v. Lusu (March 1953), when they might have flooded, with impunity, many of the amenities reserved for whites.

Certainly, the arrest of the leaders must have contributed to the decline of the campaign. The new laws were also an important factor, as stated by Chief Albert Luthuli, the recently elected President-General of the African National Congress. 'Round about November,' he said, 'there was a Government Proclamation which made certain things illegal. Parliament later passed the Public Safety and the Criminal Law Amendment Acts. In the light of that, it was necessary for the organization to take stock of the situation. It meant studying our programme and the new situation to adapt our plans and to see what we could do.' (The Leader, April 24th, 1953.) Clearly the riots played a decisive role. Quite apart from their effect on the resisters, the riots provided the opportunity for the Government to take over the initiative and to assume far-reaching powers with some measure of justification.

June 26th, 1953, the first anniversary of the launching of the campaign, was observed as a day of commemoration and rededication. In a message to Africans and their allies, Chief Luthuli appealed for the lighting of bonfires or candles or lanterns outside their homes, 'as a symbol of the spark of freedom which we are determined to keep alive in our hearts, and as a sign to freedom-lovers that we are keeping the vigil on that night'. Older members of each household should tell the younger 'the story, so far as they know it, of the struggle of the African people in particular, and the non-Europeans in general, for their liberation'. (The Leader, June 26th, 1953.)

The passive resistance campaign was already passing into the history of the liberation movement.

VI

REACTION

BOTH the Nationalist Party and the United Party sought to canalize reactions to passive resistance through the Press, virtually the only link between the mass of the white electorate and the resistance movement. In contrast, the reactions of the non-whites themselves received little publicity. The views of the non-whites were used mainly as ammunition in a vigorous battle for public opinion, and the variety of their reactions provided scope for the political propagandists.

Non-white Reactions

The Congresses received support in their campaign from large numbers of persons participating not as members of organizations, but as individuals. The extent of this support is indicated by the thousands who attended the many mass meetings and demonstrations, the wide diffusion of the resistance songs and symbols, and the growth of the paid-up membership of the African National Congress during the campaign from 7,000 to 100,000 (according to a report of Chief Luthuli, *Press Digest*, No. 15, April 21st, 1953, p. 16).

Among the organized groups, the Transvaal Council of Non-European Trade Unions decided to support the campaign (*Press Digest*, No. 48, November 21st, 1952, p. 490); and observers ascribe the strength of the movement in the Cape Eastern areas partly to local trade union participation. The Churches also gave a measure of support. The link between the Churches and the resisters is shown in the many prayer meetings, and in the role of prayer generally during the campaign. In addition, a number of Church leaders publicly pledged their support.

The Ministers and Elders of the Bantu Presbyterian Church of South Africa, acknowledging the Word of God to be the supreme rule of faith and life, were convinced that the demand which God made in ancient time, and the demand which He is still making, is a demand for justice between men in their various groupings. Of old, God's spokesman cried, 'Let my people go', and they, the Ministers and Elders, could renew, in their own day, that simple demand for justice and release. The present non-violent campaign of disobedience to unjust laws found its source, not in the lower nature of men, but in their partial grasp of the truth that they, too, are people of God and sons of the Highest. Passive resistance was the only course open to people who were denied the political instruments that make for peaceful change, and the Ministers and Elders could not therefore withhold moral and spiritual help, though they warned against incitement and bitterness as the campaign intensified. (*South African Outlook*, November 1952.)

The Secretary of the Port Elizabeth African Ministers' Council and of the Cape Midlands Non-Denominational African Ministers' Association, both affiliated organizations of the Interdenominational African Ministers' Federation, declared, according to a report in the *Star* on September 4th, 1952, that African Churches in the Eastern Cape would take their stand in support of the resistance movement. The parent body, the Interdenominational African Ministers' Federation, whose members include African ministers from separatist Churches as well as from most of the European-controlled missions, published a statement absolving the African National Congress from responsibility for the riots, and asked for an impartial commission of inquiry. The Federation announced that it was not against the resistance campaign, but, as an organization, it did not wish to become involved in the resistance activities. It therefore left members a free choice. 'The supporters of the Campaign to our knowledge have not been confined to any particular Church denomination and we are not aware of any members who are opposed to it.' (Statement by the General-President, Reverend J. A. Calata, Church of the Province, i.e. Anglican, and the Secretary-General, Reverend A. L. Mncube, Methodist Church of South Africa, the *Bantu World*, November 29th, 1952.)

A subsequent statement by the African Ministers' Federation (the *Bantu World*, May 16th, 1953), calling for the observance of an African National Day of Prayer on Sunday, May 31st, 1953, gave more open support for the campaign:

'Though we should not be carried away by emotion and use this day to give way to our political feelings, yet on this day we should ask God to intervene. Many sons and daughters of Africa are at present undergoing some persecution because conscience has led them to refuse to obey unjust laws, and as human beings we must submit to the dictates of our conscience. All pathways to resent oppression are being closed to the Africans by laws which carry very heavy penalties. To-day it is a crime for an African to complain that he is oppressed. Prayer alone has remained the only avenue open to us, and an avenue which will never be closed even by the two-thirds majority of Parliament, because it was entrenched on Mount Calvary. So, friends, it is meet to ask God to intervene especially at the present moment, because the African has reached the breaking-point. We should not at all interfere with the Will of God but let us ask God to intervene as He intervened among the Israelites of old. Finally, let us pray that God Almighty may create in us a new heart and give us a new spirit to drive away from us petty differences and become an African united front against all evils – persecution, oppression and all kinds of discrimination because of colour; these are evils in the sight of God. Only a united effort will be effective enough before God. Let us all be in sackcloth in our hearts and penitently come before our

God for forgiveness. Though we cannot all address meetings, yet can we pray all of us.'

For the most part, ministers of the separatist AfricanChurches refrained from issuing public statements. This was contrary to expectation, since the establishment of the separatist Churches arose partly from a desire for emancipation from white control. No doubt, the parlous position of many of these Churches, and their dependence on the Government, effectively muffled the free expression of support for the resistance movement. The ministers of the European-controlled Churches, on the other hand, were in a better position to pledge their support as individuals, though not on behalf of their congregations. The extent to which they gave their support to passive resistance poses a major problem for the Government. Christianity is an important source of those ideas of the worth of the human personality which underlie the aspirations of the African people. If the Government is to dissolve these aspirations, then it must reconvert African Christians to a form of Christianity which will give spiritual meaning to apartheid, or prevail on them to return to the 'heathen' fold.

The main organized non-white opposition to the campaign came from certain conservative or nationalist African groups, and from the radical Non-European Unity Movement. The so-called 'African National Congress (National Minded)', which broke off from the parent body after the adoption of the Joint Planning Council's report, decided not to take part in the defiance campaign, on the ground that their members were denied the opportunity of stating their case against ex-communist leadership in Congress. At the same time, their policy was one of non-interference with the campaign, 'because they realized that the African people were drowning in a sea of repressive laws, and therefore, like a drowning man, they would hold even on sharks in order to save themselves. There can be no doubt that the majority of those who took part or supported the "defiance campaign" did so not because they wanted the leadership of the ex-communists or Indians, but because of the intolerable conditions under which they are living and working.' (Statement of the Executive Committee, the *Bantu World*, April 11th, 1953.)

Anti-Indian sentiment links the conservative nationalism of the 'National Minded' group with the racialism of the Supreme Council for the Federation of Bantu Organizations. This Council and its affiliated organization, the Bantu National Congress, in their role as disciples of apartheid, served the Government and the Nationalist Party in two ways. First, they acted as a channel through which anti-Indian and anti-defiance propaganda passed to the non-whites; and second, they provided 'evidence' of anti-Indian sentiment among Africans, and of loyalty to the Government, reinforcing official propaganda to the whites.

The left-wing weekly paper, *Advance*, in its issue of April 22nd, 1954, published photographic copies of documents to demonstrate the association between Nationalist Party supporters and the Bantu National Congress. At the same time it announced the conviction of Mr Bhengu, President-General of the Bantu National Congress, on a number of charges of theft, fraud and forgery. An open letter from a minister of the Dutch Reformed Church declared that the bearer, S. S. Bhengu, merits all the support our people can give him, wherever they are fighting communism. A donation list showed the South African Bureau of Racial Affairs, the counterpart of the South African Institute of Race Relations and proponents of apartheid, as contributing £50 to the funds of the Bantu National Congress, and other support was cited as evidence of the acceptability of Congress policy to the Nationalist Party and to Civil Servants.

During the resistance campaign, that is, before Mr Bhengu was discredited, statements by him and by the Supreme Council provided grist for the Nationalist Party propaganda mill. It was convenient that the Supreme Council could be reported as alleging that Indians were behind the defiance movement and had organized the riots for personal profit, since they would suffer great financial losses if the Group Areas Act were implemented (*Press Digest*, No. 47, pp. 476-7) and it was also appropriate that Mr Bhengu should describe the Torch Commando, an ex-servicemen's group opposed to the Government, as an incitement to the Indians to agitate the Natives against the Europeans, on the ground that any white organization that makes propaganda against the Government is put forward as an example to the uneducated Natives. It harmonized well with Nationalist Party publicity that Mr Bhengu should solemnly declare that 'as God has said in his great book that an uneducated people must be guided by wiser counsellors, so must the Bantu people be guided by the Europeans'; or that he should assure the white population that, as a result of interviews with nearly every Bantu Chief in Natal, he had no doubt that none of them supported the resistance campaign. (As reported in *Press Digest*, No. 37, pp. 367-8.)

Mr Bhengu may have overstated the attitude of the Bantu Chiefs in Natal to the resistance movement. The present Paramount Chief of the Zulu nation, Chief Cyprian, was reported in the Press as having warned his people not to take part in the campaign; he himself would examine their grievances and place them before the proper authorities. This report was, however, later repudiated. The Government-appointed chief, Albert Luthuli, also in Natal, and now President-General of the African National Congress, participated actively and, as a result, lost his chieftainship. In general, the chiefs are conservative, making use of the traditional administrative channels. They hold their positions, even in the case of hereditary chiefs, by grace of the Government, and clearly subject to their carrying out official policy. They could not have supported passive resistance without endangering their positions. On the whole, they appear to have maintained neutrality, speaking neither for nor against the resistance movement. Similarly, conservative opinion among the Indians was silent for the most part, though the Natal Indian Organization, representing merchant interests, dissociated itself from the boycott of the Van Riebeeck tercentenary celebrations, on the ground that the event had nothing to do with discriminatory laws, but was purely historical.

The most consistent attacks were made by the Non-European Unity Movement through its weekly journal, *The Torch*. The Unity Movement opposed the campaign on the general ground that the co-operation between the African and Indian Congresses was based on expedience rather than principle—that is to say it did not reflect a true unity – and on the more specific ground that passive resistance was politically futile and a Quisling technique.[1]

The Torch presented arguments to demonstrate the political futility of the movement; it heaped scathing ridicule on the leaders. The Joint Planning Council proposed to send a letter 'in which the Government is formally given notice to liquidate itself by February 29th, 1952, or suffer the consequences'. (Editorial, January 15th, 1952.) When the Government failed to liquidate itself on the named date, the Joint Planning Council had postponed sentence from a Leap Year Day to a new April Fool's Day (the demonstrations of April 6th), 'presumably to give Dr Malan a chance to think things over . . . The Herrenvolk has made up its mind over 300 years not to climb off the backs of the Non-Europeans of its own accord and free will.' (March 25th, 1952.) When eight million Africans are used as beasts of burden, when half a million Indians toil in the coal mines and sugar plantations of Natal, when a million Coloured people live and die in the squalor of District Six and the *pondokkies* of the Platteland, then struggle and martyrdom on an individual basis become nonsensical and even criminal. To think that ten 'trained' persons could bring freedom: that crossing a provincial barrier or forcing their way into a white bar or breaking a train regulation could harm the Herrenvolk, was the height of political childishness. (Report of speech, March 4th, 1952.) 'There is no possibility of any of these laws being modified or repealed because the ruling class

[1] See the Discussion of the Unity Movement in Chapter II, pp. 57ff.

have had it brought to their notice that the non-Whites hate these laws. They are fascists, and they know that we hate them and their laws. There is only deception and self-deception in dealing with "Malanazis" as though they were "democrats" and "Christians" who will suffer pangs of conscience because certain non-white "leaders" are in gaol. The function of leaders is to lead; the gaols are there to hinder and not help the cause of freedom. It is the duty of everyone to keep out of gaol as long as possible and especially of leadership not to find freedom from responsibility in gaol.' (Editorial, June 10th, 1952.)

The arguments as to the political futility of passive resistance are convincing enough on the premise of the materialist determination of social relationships: the followers of Mahatma Gandhi and the theoreticians of the Unity Movement work on different assumptions as to the nature of man and society. Entirely unconvincing was the second line of attack – that African Quislings and Indian merchants were the driving force behind passive resistance, and that they had sponsored it in their own interests. The Unity Movement argued that the Congresses had restricted their demands to the repeal of specific laws, to peripheral issues, and were not engaged in a genuine struggle for democracy; and that the technique of civil disobedience by small selected bands excludes the masses and the possibility of a broad struggle for basic human rights. These limitations were deliberately planned, in the view of the Unity Movement, since the real objective of passive resistance was to bring about a round-table conference as a result of which African leaders would be rewarded with administrative posts, and Indian merchants would gain relief from the Group Areas Act.

The propaganda of the Unity Movement and of the Bantu National Congress, though proceeding from entirely different premises, nevertheless converged in the attack on the Indians and on the Indian and African Congresses. Both the class-struggle approach and the racialist approach led to the conclusion that responsibility attached to the Indians, in the one case to the Indian merchants and in the other to the Indians as a whole, which from the point of view of most white South Africans is precisely the same thing. Mr Bhengu was reported as finding the cause of the riots in the 1951 resolutions of the African National Congress and in the actions of the two Congresses. (*Press Digest*, No. 47, November 18th, 1952, p. 477.) So too Mr W. M. Tsotsi, President of the All-African Convention, affiliated to the Unity Movement, accused the leadership of the two Congresses of having contributed toward the criminal waste of human lives in the riots, though the initial responsibility rested with the Europeans. (*Natal Daily News*, December 17th, 1952.) The use to which Mr Tsotsi's statement was put in Press propaganda elicited the explanation that it was 'criticism of a member of the same family by another member of the family', and not a condemnation of Congress opposition to colour oppression. (*Press Digest*, No. 53, December 23rd, 1952, p. 534.)

Thus do the divisions between the non-whites contribute to the maintenance of the *status quo*. The Unity Movement is untiring in its propaganda for unity, but contributes a full measure to the practice of disunity.

White Reactions

The Government, and almost all the Afrikaans newspapers, maintained a consistent attitude through the course of the resistance campaign. They followed the lead given by the Prime Minister in his reply to the original demand of the African National Congress. Apartheid is sacrosanct, and co-operation can only take place within its framework; to incite the Bantu population to defy any law is subversion, and the full force of the State would be used to quell disturbances, and thereafter to punish those responsible for initiating the activities.

Since non-white defiance of any law whatsoever, no matter how trivial, constitutes subversion, the Nationalists interpreted the campaign as directed against white domination, and not against specific laws, a point of view which the Minister of the Interior crystallized in his description of passive resistance as 'mutiny'. (*Natal Daily News*, November 22nd, 1952.) The laws of the Government must be obeyed unquestioningly. Indeed, a Synodal Commission of the Dutch Reformed Church in the Transvaal, dealing with the conflict between the races, declared that all forms of violent action and defiance of the standing laws of the lawful authority of the land are to be judged as a struggle against the Word of God. (*Die Voorligter*, January, 1953.) This sanctity of law is enhanced by a mystical approach to Nationalist Party legislation as the embodiment of the *volkswil* (the people's will, i.e. the Nationalist Party vote).

The demands for repressive action flowed naturally from the interpretation of passive resistance as subversion; they were sounded by the Afrikaans newspapers immediately following the exchange of letters between the Prime Minister and the African National Congress, and became more insistent after the launching of the campaign on June 26th, 1952. *Die Oosterlig*, on July 11th, commented that the sentences on resisters were simply ludicrous and would certainly not act as a deterrent; for the great majority of the people, unemployed and without shelter, prison is nothing other than a pleasant abode; and the only language they would readily understand is the language of the cane and the lash, though the alternative penalty of deportation might be used. (*Press Digest*, No. 29, p. 284.)

The pressure for repressive action reached its climax after the riots, and the theme of Congress responsibility was taken up by the Government and the Afrikaans Press. *Die Transvaler* commented that the African National Congress could not easily disengage itself from the incident; the defiance campaign was strongest in the Port Elizabeth area, and anything could happen in the atmosphere of contempt for law and order and hostility towards the white man which such a movement creates. Unless it could be shown that the disturbances were only an exception, even the well-intentioned concessions of positive apartheid would be endangered. (*Press Digest*, No. 43, October 21st, 1952, pp. 425-6.) The Minister of Justice declared that the Port Elizabeth disturbances were one of the direct results of the defiance campaign, that the police had been instructed to take immediate and stern measures, and that the Govenment would not hesitate to pass new laws, if necessary. (*Press Digest*, No. 43, October 22nd, 1952, p. 424.)

Government-supporting papers carried a good deal of publicity on the Mau Mau movement in Kenya and likened it to the defiance campaign. The East London riots, in particular, because of the circumstances of the spoliation of Sister Aidan's body, provided the opportunity for exploiting this identification. *Die Burger* declared that it was not the spirit of the Mahatma which was at hand but that of the Mau Mau. (*Press Digest*, No. 46, November 12th, 1952, p. 460.) The Government made effective use of the South African Mau Mau theme and at the end of November the Minister of Justice announced that legislation would be introduced in the next session of Parliament to give the Government powers similar to those being employed in Kenya: you cannot fight the law of the jungle with the rule of law. (*Press Digest*, No. 49, p. 492.)[2] Early in 1953, the agitation for repressive action triumphed in the Public Safety Act and the Criminal Law Amendment Act.

The opposition United Party was obliged to condemn the resistance movement; any other reaction would have been interpreted as an incitement to the non-whites to break the law. But the condemnation was also consistent with its policy. The United Party, equally with the Nationalist Party, stands firmly for white domination, and for white control of social change. Thus, the opposition leader's condemnation of passive resistance, on the ground that the laws under attack had been passed constitutionally and could be repealed constitutionally, was mirrored in the statement attributed to the Nationalist Minister of Justice that, if the laws are bad, it is up to the people to elect a new Parliament and change the laws. (*Press Digest*, No. 35, p. 347, and *Rand Daily Mail*, September 27th, 1952.)

[2] The Minister of Justice was reported to have said that in Kenya it was all very well if sentences of twelve years' imprisonment and twenty-four lashes were imposed for being a member of the Mau Mau, but in South Africa there was an outcry when an Act was passed to provide for whipping for crimes of violence. (The *Natal Mercury*, November 29th, 1952.)

For neither of the parties did it seem crucial that the non-whites have no direct means of influencing legislation. The approach is essentially authoritarian; the white man is arbiter of the destiny of the non-whites and their interests are safe in his hands.

Yet there is a basic difference between the authoritarianism of the two parties. In contrast to a perfected apartheid enduring in perpetuity – a totalitarian ideology permitting of no deviation – the United Party adopts a less rigid approach. Within the fixed framework of white domination, United Party leaders are prepared to make concessions and to admit that the non-whites may have legitimate grievances. They were the more ready to recognize non-white grievances in the case of the resistance campaign because four of the five laws attacked had been passed by the Nationalist Government. Hence, the United Party, in its propaganda, interpreted passive resistance as a reaction to bad legislation and to the breakdown of consultative machinery between white and non-white, and not as a challenge to white domination.

The United Party therefore urged the Government to consult with non-white leaders. An editorial in the *Rand Daily Mail* described the 'concession' of consultation as the vital difference between Nationalist and United Party policy, and as a method which would safeguard the Europeans while opening a few safety valves through which a good deal of non-European hostility and resentment could escape. (As reported in *Press Digest*, No. 37, September 5th, 1952, p.364.) The English press and English churchmen and liberals voiced vigorous protests against repressive measures, and supported the United Party in its demand for consultation.

In itself, the pressure for consultation does not indicate any departure from traditional white policies. Consultative bodies, such as the Natives' Representative Council, had existed in the past, and consultation does not imply that steps will be taken to carry out recommendations. Indeed, the boycott of the Natives' Representative Council arose precisely because its advice was disregarded; the deliberations as such had ceased to act as a safety-valve. Moreover, some United Party supporters urged procedures which would emasculate even consultation: 'moderate' leaders should be consulted, the demands should be 'moderate' (that is, such as could be granted without any basic changes in social structure), and consultation should be directed to matters directly affecting the interests of non-whites, presumably such discriminatory legislation as Pass Laws. Broad national policies would fall outside the purview of consultation and of the legitimate scope of non-white interests. It is not surprising, therefore, that an editorial in Mr Manilal Gandhi's weekly journal, *Indian Opinion*, characterized the difference between the approach of the Afrikaans press and of the English press as the advocacy of the lash on the one hand, and the throwing of a few crumbs to the leaders on the other. (*Press Digest*, No. 33, August 8th, 1952, p. 326.)

While the United Party urged the Government to consult with the non-Europeans, it appealed to the resistance leaders for the suspension of their campaign. There is a widespread and apparently sincere belief among United Party supporters in their benevolent intentions towards the non-whites. It seemed reasonable enough, therefore, to call on the resistance leaders to leave their grievances in the hands of well-disposed Europeans and abandon their own efforts to secure relief. The *Star*, on January 30th, 1952, immediately after the exchange of letters between the Prime Minister and the resistance leaders, urged the African National Congress to return to the path of reason and prudence; the course it was taking would drown the voice of moderation, and would gravely embarrass those Europeans who had a right to call themselves the best friends of the native in his struggle for justice; strong forces were working unremittingly in order, in the fullness of time and by all constitutional means, to rid South Africa of the Nationalist régime. (*Press Digest*, No. 5, p. 40.) The Torch Commando, predominantly United Party, joined in this appeal; the non-Europeans should realize that many Europeans were vitally alive to their needs and were determined to see that they were treated with justice. (*Press Digest*, No. 11, March 10th, 1952, p. 100.) Impatience with the campaign intensified when the resisters finally launched civil disobedience; persistence, they were told, would alienate the well-disposed and harden the hearts of the reactionaries. It was as if United Party supporters reacted to passive resistance as a most unwarranted reflection on the high moral purpose of their leaders. 'It is a slight and an embarrassment to the large body of European opinion through whose efforts alone it should be possible in the long run to clear a way to a more hopeful future for the people of all races in South Africa.' (The *Star*, as quoted in *Press Digest*, No. 50, December 8th, 1952, p. 506.)

The riots sharpened the demand for the abandonment of the campaign. At the same time, the leader of the United Party called for an impartial judicial inquiry and charged the Nationalist Government 'with recklessness in their aimless and provocative non-European policy; with having failed to stop the defiance campaign against our laws and our leadership; with part responsibility for having provoked the recent outbursts of violence'. (*Press Digest*, No. 47, November 19th, 1952, p. 475.) The United Party Press supported the demand for an inquiry. There was no attempt to fix sole responsibility on the resisters, though some commentators did express the view that the atmosphere created by the campaign was a contributory factor in the disturbances. Throughout this period of heightened racial antagonism, of inflammatory proposals for arming of white women, the English press maintained a relatively calm perspective. But, in the end, the United Party accepted the principle of repressive action embodied in the Criminal Law Amendment Act and the Public Safety Act.

Only the small Labour Party and the Liberals persisted in their opposition to repressive action. For the Liberals, the passive resistance movement was a disciplined and highly principled response to oppressive legislation and the denial of basic human rights. To be sure, they did not express themselves unambiguously in these terms, since they could not lay themselves open to the charge of encouraging the breaking of laws. However, their statements implied, with greater or less circumlocution, that passive resistance was justified. Approaching race relations from the premises of a democratic ideology, Liberals reject the complacent authoritarian belief in the benevolent intentions of the white man, as clearly disproved by the extreme inequality between the races and the whole structure of legislation. They therefore repudiate the dogma that the monopoly of social change by the whites provides, in some mystic way, an adequate channel for the redress of non-white grievances, and they assert, as a matter of principle, that the non-whites have a right to share directly in political power.

In these circumstances, Liberals stressed that the laws attacked in the campaign were, in fact, unjust laws, and that the only channels open to the non-whites were demonstrations and passive resistance. They therefore appealed to the Union Government and to chief magistrates not to ban meetings; they warned against repressive action, and called for consultation with non-white leaders. At the same time, they recognized that consultation was an inadequate response to the passive resistance movement, and urged more constructive action.

Towards the end of September 1952, twenty-two Liberals issued a joint statement to the Press in which they declared that a constructive solution could be found in the revival of the old Cape Liberal tradition, based on the firm principle of equal rights for all civilized people and equal opportunities for all men and women to become civilized. Only the acceptance of this fundamental principle would provide, in their view, the moral basis which South African government now lacked. As an immediate short-term programme of reform, they urged the repeal of the most mischievous measures on the Statute book, such as the Group Areas Act, the Pass Laws, and the Suppression of Communism Act in its present form. The beginnings of the Liberal Party, established in 1953, can be traced to this declaration.

The English churches responded to the campaign by the issue of statements which ranged in political outlook from United Party policy to Liberalism, but tended towards the latter. The Annual Assembly of the Baptist Union of South Africa, in October 1952, appealed to the Government to meet with non-European leaders to discuss constructive measures for the future, and made specific recommendations in regard to housing, education, labour exchanges, and the wastage of man-power. (*Baptist Union Handbook*, 1952, pp. 94-5.) The Annual Assembly of the Congregational Union of South Africa urged the Government to call a national convention representative of all sections, protested against the increasing delegation of power to Cabinet Ministers, and affirmed that the African people must be regarded as an integral part of the South African social structure. (*Year Book, 1952-1953*, p. 38, October, 1952.) The General Assembly of the Presbyterian Church of South Africa expressed its deep sympathy and understanding with the African people and strongly condemned legislation which is unjust and repressive. At the same time, the Assembly could not approve, and deeply regretted, the emergence of the 'Defiance of Unjust Laws' campaign. (*Proceedings of the Fifty-first General Assembly*, p. 39, September, 1952.)

A more positive, liberal approach to passive resistance was adopted by the Methodists and the Quakers. The Annual Conference of the Methodist Church, meeting in October, 1952, pointed out that the non-European peoples, being almost entirely without the benefit of a common franchise and denied the opportunity to make effective representations, could respond to the discriminatory legislation under which they were suffering only by active resistance, passive resistance or submission. Since the Conference recorded its disapproval of violence, thus rejecting active resistance; and since apartheid was described as contrary to the interests of the country, which could best be served by a policy of integration with partnership and citizenship in view; the inference is reasonably clear that the Conference regarded passive resistance as justified in the circumstances.

The Quakers issued a statement in March, 1953, declaring that as a religious society they could not support the campaign. They were, however, united in a keen desire to express their deep sympathy with the non-European peoples in the frustration of their legitimate aspirations by unjust racial discrimination.

Means must be found quickly within the law whereby the voice of the non-European should be heard and heeded. All laws and regulations which prevented or hindered the free development of human personality towards the Father were immoral and detrimental to the good of the country.

A further reinforcement of the liberal attitude to passive resistance came from Anglican churchmen. In contrast to the Synodal Commission of the Transvaal Dutch Reformed Church, which identified obedience to secular law with obedience to God, the Anglican Archbishop of Cape Town emphasized that, while every churchman was under an obligation to be a law-abiding citizen, there were circumstances in which it was a man's duty as a Christian to refuse to obey a particular law. 'If a law were to be passed requiring you to do something which is in your belief contrary to the law of God, clearly your duty as a Christian is to obey God rather than men. Further than that, it has been the traditional teaching of the Christian Church that there is no obligation on a man as a Christian to obey unjust laws.' The decision to defy a particular law, if conscience forbids compliance, or if the law conflicts with fundamental human rights, is a matter for the individual conscience. The Church can neither authorize, nor rightly condemn, defiance of the law. (December archiepiscopal letter, as reported in the *Natal Mercury*, December 3rd, 1952.)

The Archbishop failed to see how anyone could avoid having some sympathy with the civil disobedience campaign. Nevertheless, he doubted its wisdom, since he thought it extremely likely that the movement would lead to violence and thus bring about greater evils than those against which it was a protest. Similarly, the Bishop of Johannesburg warned that the campaign was dangerous in its possible ultimate outcome, but was not the very existence of the campaign a judgment upon the Europeans in South Africa, a moral judgment underlining the injustices of discriminatory legislation passed in recent years? (*Rand Daily Mail*, October 21st, 1952.) And the Bishop of Bloemfontein declared that it was unchristian for rulers to impose upon those whom they rule laws which they have next to no share in making or reforming, laws which restrict and humiliate the dignity and liberty natural to man, laws whose chief effect was to fill jails to overflowing with non-criminal prisoners. It was cruel and dangerous for a Christian Government to impose such choices on its Christian subjects. (*Press Digest*, No. 44, October 27th, 1952, p. 442.)

The extent of agreement between the English churches, Nonconformist and Anglican, is reflected in the resolutions passed by the Executive Committee of the Christian Council of South Africa during January, 1953. The Committee expressed profound sympathy with the non-European Christians of South Africa living under racial discrimination without constitutional means for redress. It understood and sympathized with the motives of the resisters, but laid emphasis on the Christian duty of obedience to law unless it involved disobedience to the dictates of conscience, and advocated Government consultation with accredited representatives of the non-Europeans. (As reported in the *Proceedings of the Fifty-second General Assembly of the Presbyterian Church of South Africa*, p. 157.)

The Roman Catholic Church issued a general statement on race relations, dated July 14th, 1952. From the religious premises of Christian charity and justice, it derived the following conclusions among others: that discrimination based exclusively on grounds of colour is an offence against the right of non-Europeans to their natural dignity as human persons; and that justice demands that non-Europeans be permitted to evolve gradually towards full participation in the political, economic and cultural life of the country. These conclusions are fundamentally consistent with those of Liberalism.

In this way, the conscience of English churchmen spoke out against racial discrimination and repression, while the Government stood fast to its policy of forceful counteraction. Whatever the influence of the spiritual leaders of the English Churches, it did not affect the legislative outcome of the struggle for the control of public opinion.

VII

REACTION (*continued*)

The Battle for Opinion

THE main battle for public opinion between the Government and the United Party raged round three issues: the apportionment of blame; consultation as against repression; and the holding of a judicial inquiry into the riots. The end result of this battle was not a wider breach between the parties, as might have been expected, but increased solidarity in regard to the fundamentals of non-European policy.

The Government started at a disadvantage in this contest. The resistance movement was launched against laws which, with the exception of the Pass Laws, it had itself enacted. In his original letter to the Prime Minister, Dr Moroka described recent legislation as an aggravation of the position of the African people. For the first time, Africans, Indians and Coloureds had joined in passive resistance; the basis was being laid for non-white solidarity. In these circumstances, the United Party did not hesitate to draw, and make public, the obvious conclusion of Government responsibility for the deterioration in race relations.

Added to this, the outside world showered sympathy on the resisters, and expressed antagonism towards apartheid. The antagonism was directed specifically against the Nationalist Party, apartheid being interpreted as an Afrikaner ideology, rather than as a logical working out of traditional white domination.

World Critics

White South Africans might well be alarmed at the number and standing of these outside critics. The resistance leaders carried on an extensive propaganda campaign by letters and press statements, and received messages of sympathy, according to newspaper reports, from the Prime Ministers of China, the United Provinces of India, Persia, and of the Gold Coast, from the President of the Federal National Council of Nigeria, the All India Congress Committee, and the Secretary-General of the Arab League. These messages might be dismissed as coming from non-Europeans; and little or no publicity was given to letters of support from Negro organizations in the United States. But the Nationalist Party could not so lightly ignore the decision of India to raise the question of the passive resistance campaign before the United Nations General Assembly, and the appointment by the United Nations of a commission to study the effects of apartheid legislation; or the action of the British Trade Union Congress in condemning the South African Government for its complete denial of the United Nations Human Rights Declaration; or a letter in the London *Times* in October, 1952 asking for donations 'to give practical assistance where needed to families and the dependants of those who are imprisoned for conscience sake' and signed by English lords and ladies and other notables; or the many hostile accounts in the overseas press.

The following news item gives an impression of the deep hostility aroused in some outside observers by the Government's handling of passive resistance.

IN DARKEST AFRICA

(From the *New York Times*, August 22nd, 1952)

'Who among us can keep reading day after day the little news items from South Africa without a feeling of dismay? There is something degrading to humanity about these stories of Negroes being arrested – thirty, fifty, a hundred at a time – fined, jailed and now flogged. Their crime is to do things like sitting where only whites should sit, using entrances that are "For Europeans Only", refusing to carry special passes at night or, when they leave "African" reserves for the cities, getting in white men's queues. . . . Outsiders are watching the whole proceedings with a growing sense of dread, as well as disgust. At best the situation presents enormous difficulties for the small white minorities of Africa, and one always tries to be fair in appraising the problem. However, there is a pretty-well world-wide agreement that the apartheid policy as pursued by Malan's Nationalists is about the worst method that could have been devised to meet the problem. A solution that is based on pure racism, on the theory of perennial and innate superiority of one race over another, is false, immoral and repugnant.'

Criticism from overseas posed two problems for the Government, first that of winning over world opinion, and second, that of explaining away world-condemnation to South African whites.

The approach to world-persuasion was partly naïve, partly sophisticated. Believing, or pretending to believe, in the absolute morality of apartheid, Nationalist Party publicists took the line that world opinion was based on ignorance and that the task of the propagandist was merely to present the facts. The South African Bureau for Racial Affairs emphasized the need to spread accurate information overseas and requested the Government to investigate the improvement and intensification of overseas information services. (Resolution No. 13 taken at the Fourth Annual Congress.) Apparently Nationalist Party supporters do not realize that the Statute Books of the Union Government provide all too accurate an information service and that the problem is not one of *informing* the world, but of *converting* it to apartheid ideology. In any event, the Government sought to present its interpretation of the facts. *South African Survey*, for example, an official propaganda bulletin issued in London, paints, by judicious selection and blending of facts, a picture of the Government's benevolent care for the non-whites.

More subtly, South African propagandists exploited the conflict between East and West. As the South African Bureau for Racial Affairs expressed it: 'This Congress is convinced that Africa must remain an advance post of the Western world and civilization in the world struggle between East and West, and that steps must be taken to convince the outside world of this necessity.' (Resolution No. 22 of the Fourth Congress, translated from the Afrikaans.) A further propagandist line developed the theme that the outside world should not criticize South Africa adversely, since the effect would be to harden the attitudes of its white people. In relation to England, this theme was elaborated: South Africa might be driven to sever its ties with the British Empire and establish a republic. White Southern Rhodesians, of course, used a similar threat during the negotiations for Central African Federation, that British opposition might drive Southern Rhodesia into the arms of South Africa.

The task of explaining away world condemnation inside South Africa was relatively tractable in comparison with the Herculean task of winning over world opinion. It is not difficult to persuade white South Africans that the world is wrong and that they are right. Almost any argument will do, and the arguments were simple and direct. The propagandists relied on the theme that adverse criticism springs from sheer ignorance. Clearly, outside observers cannot have so intimate a knowledge of the non-whites as people who have spent their lives among them. The only experts on white-black relations are white South African adults. Thus the South African Bureau for Racial Affairs commented that, since most members of the United Nations Organization had insufficient knowledge of conditions in South Africa, their approach to South African problems must rest on prejudice and misconception; it therefore violates one of the most elementary human rights, namely that the judge should be unprejudiced and acquaint himself with all the facts before passing judgment on the accused. (Resolution No. 5 of the Fourth Congress.)

Added to ignorance, however, the propagandists asserted that there was downright malice, as shown by the fact that affairs in the home countries of the critics are no better than in South Africa. England has its slums and colour prejudice, India its caste system, America its race hostility, all carefully featured in both the Afrikaans and English newspapers, and used as conscience salves. Moreover, so runs the argument, since the attitude of white to non-white in Kenya and the Rhodesias is fundamentally the same as in South Africa, there cannot be anything wrong with South African policy: South Africa is a colonial power, and drastic dictatorial measures like those of Britain in Malaya and Kenya, and of France in North Africa and Indo-China, are accepted as necessary by the average Westerner. Indeed, white South Africans may well feel self-righteous when comparing British actions in Kenya with their own measures against the passive resistance movement and the riots. British policies in Kenya helped to justify repressive measures.

Local Critics

The Government and its supporters met the arguments of local critics, first, by the counter-argument that any criticism of the Government constituted an incitement of the non-whites to civil disobedience, and second, by the manipulation of the fears and aggressions of the whites.

Criticism and Incitement

The Nationalist Party publicists used this theme against the United Party in a curious propaganda war which was as unrelated to the problems posed by passive resistance as Nero's fiddling to the burning of Rome. They replied to the charge of Government responsibility for civil disobedience by the counter-charge that this criticism implied a justification of passive resistance, and consequently support for, and incitement to, the breaking of law. They alleged further that it was the 'liberalistic' doctrines of the United Party itself which had sown new ideas and created dissatisfaction among an otherwise contented non-white population. Not to be outmanœuvred, United Party spokesmen declared the Nationalist Party allegations of United Party support an incitement to the non-whites. Clearly this pot-and-kettle game can go on endlessly.

Both parties played similar gambits in regard to the constitutional issues raised by the Government's devious techniques for the removal of Coloured voters from the common roll. The United Party suggested that the Government's unconstitutional actions served as a model for the non-whites. Nationalist Party propaganda denied unconstitutional action by the Government: this false allegation was itself an encouragement to defiance. The argument need not have been different if the Nationalist Party had admitted unconstitutional action; the public mention of it would turn non-whites to a similar course.

Indeed, numerous issues provided the stimulus for these standard moves. The opposition of the United Party to apartheid legislation, the suggestion that the Government negotiate with non-white leaders, criticism of the Government's handling of the riots, attacks on the proposed Criminal Law Amendment Bill and the Public Safety Bill, were all evidence of sympathy with, and encouragement for, civil disobedience. So, too, the adverse comments of overseas critics were an incitement. *Die Volksblad* ascribed to overseas demands for a change in South African policy 'the accursed effect' that the Natives were starting to murder indiscriminately 'in their blind uncivilization' their friends and benefactors. (As reported in *Press Digest*, No. 44, October 27th, 1952, p. 443.)

Irrational as this propaganda campaign may seem, its effects were to force on the United Party repeated declarations of opposition to the passive resistance movement, and hence of solidarity with the Government in this respect, and to herd the United Party toward the Government's kraals.

Fear, Aggression and Scapegoats

The Government made effective use of the curious dynamic of the South African situation that the greater the insecurity caused by its own policies, the more assured its position with the white electorate. The strong fears of the white electorate seek out a strong government which will meet any threat to privilege by forceful counteraction. United Party Leaders, corroded as many of them are by a more universal religious ethic and contact with liberal ideas, cannot match the ruthlessness of the Nationalist Party. Hence the heightening of fear would enhance the Government's prospects of capturing white support.

It is impossible to assess the extent to which propaganda was systematically planned or a spontaneous reaction to concrete situations. But, whatever the motives of the propagandists, we can readily distinguish a number of themes which served to heighten fear and stimulate aggression.

Propaganda played on the threat to white survival. From the very start of the resistance movement, Nationalist Party spokesmen repeated this theme vigorously and endlessly. They sought to establish that passive resistance was not directed against specific laws, and hence could not be countered by the repeal of those laws, nor by a change of Government. White domination itself was at stake, and not merely white domination but the survival of the whites and their civilization. The sparks would fall on all whites, not only on the Nationalist Party. The climax of the campaign was reached in the interpretation of the riots as a manifestation of Mau Mau, and hence as a threat of unspeakable heathen atrocity.

Closely related to the challenge of violence was the libidinous challenge, and the propagandists worked tirelessly on the theme of miscegenation. Inevitably, they argued, the movement for equality would result in miscegenation. Press photographs of 'the piebald front' – that is to say, of white and black at meetings or social gatherings – played an important part in this campaign, which attained maximum expression, after the

Appellate Court's decision on railway apartheid, in lurid forecasts of the common use of amenities.

Another theme accentuated fear by the continuous assertion that passive resistance was not a specifically South African phenomenon, but a local expression of the world-wide machinations of sinister international forces. This involved also the demonstration that these sinister forces had incited world hostility against an innocent South Africa. The very injustice of world condemnation proved their power and made them seem even more sinister. Liberalism is one such hostile force, but its spokesmen are misguided rather than vicious. The real enemies of South Africa are India and Communism. The disturbances in South Africa, Rhodesia, Kenya, North Africa, Indo-China, Malaya are all facets of widespread anti-white sentiment and of world-wide international plots.

A few excerpts from the Press will show the way in which these strands are woven together:

'The brown hand of the Indian reaches out to the treasures of Southern Africa and especially to the Union. Spurred on by the Communist elements in India who find reason, in conditions of overpopulation, for the establishent of an Indian empire, the octopus tentacles of Indian imperialism are daily forcing deeper and deeper into the economic life of South Africa. . . .

'This information comes from the most trustworthy source, and is only a little of the true facts. The organization is well-planned. The Indian Congress Party has already called for the establishment of a fund of some two million pounds to promote Indian interests in Africa. Indian life and affairs are ruled from a harbour on the East Coast of Africa, where the nerve centre of the Indian organization in Africa is located.' (Translated from *Die Transvaler*, December 5th, 1952.)

'What is happening in South Africa is related to the Mau Mau movement and to signs of unrest in Northern

Rhodesia. (It is all part of an anti-European feeling which has not arisen as a result of any particular Government's policy.) I have no hesitation in saying that a main contributory cause has been encouragement received from the United Nations, from so-called liberals in Europe and the United States, and from British socialists, to say nothing of the aid and comfort received from certain misguided clerics both there and in South Africa. They all must share the responsibility for the bloodshed that has taken place recently.' Further causes were local Communists and propaganda from Addis Ababa and Pretoria. And over it all hangs the shadow of India. (The Minister of Economic Affairs, as reported in the *Sunday Tribune*, November 23rd, 1952, and *Press Digest*, No. 48, p. 488.)

'The pattern of unrest in different parts of Africa was so similar that it was difficult to escape the conclusion that the racial tensions were interconnected and part of a plan. "One would not be far wrong if one said that the master plan was Communist-inspired and Indian-directed . . ." In the past 30 years, liberalists had been used as instruments of the Communist technique of sowing unrest and suspicion. Local agitators had been used to further this design, and press publicity and the platform of the United Nations had helped to intensify the campaign of fostering unrest.' (The Minister of the Interior, as reported in the *Natal Daily News*, December 4th, 1952.)

'The whole inquiry [by the United Nations Commission into the implications of apartheid] is an inquisition of India, supported by the rest of the Asiatic-Arabic Group.' (*Die Transvaler*, *Christmas Eve*, 1952.)

Fear, if it is not to be an incoherent and random reaction, requires a focus against which resentment and aggression can be mobilized. The African population as a whole might have provided the necessary focus, since fear of the African majority is the generalized basis for the manipulation of race attitudes.

Two factors, however, militated against this solution. First, the white population tends to have a very deep-seated contempt for the African. Ideas of freedom, of passive resistance, of human rights, could hardly come from the Africans themselves: they must have been planted by agitators. The Minister of the Interior expressed this contemptuous attitude when he likened the leaders of the resistance movement to 'bell-wethers', that is to say, castrated rams leading the flocks of sheep. Second, since white domination is a moral and just order for most white South Africans, African discontentment with this order, as distinct from minor, perhaps justifiable, grievances, can only arise from the actions, again, of agitators. Hence the channelling of fear reactions, of anger and aggression against scapegoats, served the usual function of diverting attention from the Government's own responsibility for the passive resistance campaign, and also the added function of establishing the necessity and the moral justification for white domination over easily misguided Africans.

The mechanisms of this complex of attitude and action are clearly illustrated in an article by the Moderator of the Dutch Reformed Church in the Transvaal.

'It is one thing to plan constructively for the future and to use all our faculties in an attempt to work for the common good according to a well-formulated and national plan. It is quite another to indulge in a flood of emotional thinking and suggestive talk against a background of irresponsible human elements who cannot all be expected, at this stage of their development, to distinguish between right and wrong.

'In a certain boarding school some years ago a member of the staff was pleading the case of a few boys who had infringed a minor rule of the establishment. They overheard him remarking to the head master: "In my time we would have gone out on strike over a matter like this." The next day the boys refused their meals. When the chairman of the board of governors was consulted, he advised: "Leave the boys alone, but pull the assistant who made the suggestion over your desk and thrash him, thrash him soundly!" . . .

'The words of Bishop W. J. Carey recently published in the *Star* do not apply to Kenya alone. He is reported as having said: "Indeed I have found that the African is almost always happy until politicians tell him that he is not. . . . Yes, when I look round I feel no less than burning indignation towards politicians who egg on agitators whose work results in sheer murder . . . sometimes in my bitter moments, I feel that these interferers are only excused from being knaves by the fact that they are fools." Some of us share Bishop Carey's feeling of indignation and disgust. We have the same experience in South Africa, except that here the task of inciting people to irrational acts and creating a feeling of discontent and unrest is not confined to politicians only. There are others who apparently feel called upon to grasp this sorry scheme of things entire and mould it nearer to their hearts' desire.' ('Four Reasons for Optimism', *The Forum*, December, 1952.)

The Africans are thus likened to children, not yet able to distinguish clearly between right and wrong, living contentedly in a just society, until disturbed by agitators. Violent counteraction against the inciters is the appropriate response.

The identity of the inciters to passive resistance was indicated in Government propaganda: this portrayed the white South African in single-handed combat against world hostility, provoked by the powerful international forces of liberalism, Indian imperialism and world communism. The obvious scapegoats were thus liberals, Indians, and communists. Moreover, the South African counterparts of these dangerous international forces were ideally cast for the role of scapegoats. Liberalism in South Africa is weak. The Communists are only a handful; the list compiled by the Liquidator under the

Suppression of Communism Act, based largely on the records of the Communist Party itself, numbers 574. The Indians are a small minority, about 3% of the total population of South Africa. Hence the stirred-up fears and aggressions were readily directed against the 'inciters', that is to say, liberals and educated non-whites, communists and Indians.

The preferred scapegoat was the Indian. South African social structure provides not only a favourable setting for propaganda among the whites against Indian business rivals, but also the opportunity of playing on African hostility to the Indians. Propaganda round the theme of Indians exploiting Africans was calculated to sow suspicion, and to drive a wedge between them. The Prime Minister, for example, stated that there was fortunately 'a growing realization among our Bantu of the role for which they are being cast, and a reluctance to be used as a pawn to further Indian national aspirations in Africa, to the permanent detriment of the indigenous population'. (As reported in the *Natal Mercury*, October 15th, 1952.) The Minister of Native Affairs declared that the Indian wished to preserve his trade with the Bantu and therefore opposed the extension of opportunities to Bantu traders in their own areas; he was dragging the Bantu masses away from their own national development. (*Die Transvaler*, November 29th, 1952.) Other statements charged the trouble-makers with wishing to sell the Bantu to India, or claimed that the Indian realized that apartheid meant the end of his exploitation of the Bantu, or that the anti-British and anti-Afrikaans sentiments of the East Coast Indian derived from the fact that the South African whites had prevented him coming to exploit the Bantu.

The theme of Indian exploitation found expression in a magistrate's court trial during the resistance campaign, no doubt inadvertently, since it is rooted in the attitudes of whites. South African Survey reported that the public prosecutor advanced in mitigation of the offence of the accused Natives the argument that they were urged on by an Indian leader. The prosecutor hoped that the Court would take into account

the fact that the Indian had used the accused to pull his
political chestnuts out of the fire, while he carefully kept out of
danger himself. The Natives were not to blame: they were like
a flock of misguided sheep. In reply, the magistrate declared
that he felt as though he were attending a funeral, because by
behaving in this way the Natives were burying their rights.

'I can see you are good Natives and believe that you do
your work well. I can never believe that you did this of
your own accord. The man who has brought you here has
gone. He is now laughing at you, because he has made fools
of you. If you are unhappy, if you want anything, don't
use other Coloured elements – go to the Government yourselves and state your grievances, and the results will be far
more satisfactory. Don't allow yourselves to be tricked into
being the dupes of others.' (October 30th, 1952.)

The Magistrate thereupon cautioned and discharged the
accused.

The United Party also felt the need for a local scapegoat,
and paid court to public opinion by using the Indians as a
whipping-horse. This was so marked that an editorial in *Indian
Opinion* commented that there was hardly any difference
between the policy of the Nationalist Party and the United
Party in regard to the Indians. 'However unpleasant the
Nationalist Party may appear to be, if there is to be a choice
between the two Parties, we would rather prefer the Nationalist
Party. For it is better to deal with an enemy you know, than
with a friend you do not know: it is better to be beheaded right
out than to die inch by inch through slow poisoning.' (*Press
Digest*, No. 49, November 28th, 1952, p. 500.) The racialism of
all groups converged on the Indian, who became all things to
all men – the communist, the capitalist exploiter, the imperialist adventurer, the Oriental, the Jew-surrogate.

The success of the Government in shifting responsibility for
passive resistance to liberals (and hence ironically enough to
the United Party), to communists, and above all to Indians,

assured its success on the remaining issues. Against a world background of international plots, the question of a judicial inquiry into the riots or of consultation with non-white leaders might well seem trivial.

The Government gave scant consideration to the demands for a commission of inquiry. The Minister of Justice declared there was only one thing these law-breakers understood and that was to hit hard when you did hit; he would not want to be Minister of Justice if he could not suppress violence with violence; he had given the police instructions to take no risks, as it was high time that the police stopped being a target for these people; a judicial commission in a time of murder and arson would achieve nothing, but provide a platform for the agitators to make propaganda for themselves and for unfriendly people in the United Nations. (The *Star*, November 28th, 1952.) The Prime Minister stated that the question of holding an inquiry could only be decided after certain cases had come before the Courts (*Press Digest*, No. 48, November 19th, 1952, p. 485), and the Minister of the Interior demonstrated the respectability of this point of view by reference to the British Colonial Secretary's refusal of an inquiry into the disturbances in Kenya until the ringleaders had been tried and punished. (*Natal Daily News*, November 22nd, 1952.) *Die Volksblad* put forward the argument that the Government could not do anything which might show lack of confidence in the ability of the police to trace the causes of, and the culprits in, this gross crime. (*Press Digest*, No. 44, p. 438.)

Pressure for consultation with non-white leaders was so consistently maintained that the Government could not ignore it. Answering propaganda developed the theme that negotiation would indicate weakness and encourage disturbances. It would undermine the foundations of law and order to consult with people who wilfully broke laws. The alternatives were either to negotiate with communist-incited organizations and refuse their requests or not to negotiate at all. Indeed, official sources declared that the Government was in contact with moderate leaders through the Native Affairs Department. The dilemma of the Government lies precisely in the circumstance that the leaders whom it refuses to consult are, in fact, leaders of their people, while the so-called moderate leaders, that is disciples of apartheid, are not leaders at all.[1]

In the result, the Government did not meet the non-white leaders, nor appoint a commission to inquire into the riots. It persisted in a policy of unilateral action, which culminated in the Criminal Law Amendment Bill and the Public Safety Bill. The United Party, through its press and supporters, started by blowing up a veritable tidal wave of propaganda against these Bills as the usurping by the executive of judicial and legislative functions, as laws to end laws, as despotism and dictatorship. But it ended by accepting the Bills in principle, and voting for them, though proposing safeguards which were arbitrarily rejected. The Government had won the battle for public opinion.

The victory of the Government in this campaign may have been partly the reward for its greater skill in propaganda. It also reflected a more fundamental influence, the trend to white solidarity, a force strong enough to counteract the initial disadvantages of the Government in the contest for public support.

White Solidarity

The basis for white solidarity is the common interest of the overwhelming majority of the whites in race domination. They are determined to maintain their domination, which they are also convinced is for the benefit of the non-whites. Few of them could view with equanimity the challenge of the passive resistance movement. Hence it was inevitable that both United Party and Nationalist Party supporters should draw together in defence of their privileges. The intensity of the resentment and anger against so insolent a threat to their material interests

[1] Chief Albert Luthuli quoted a statement by the Minister of Justice during the debate on the Public Safety Bill and the Criminal Law Amendment Bill: 'There was no one to consult since moderate Natives had no following.' (Speech at the Sixth Annual Conference of the Natal Indian Congress, February 21st, 1953.)

evoked precisely that desire for severe punitive action which the Government crystallized in its legislation.

An additional basis for a common front is the shared resentment against the criticism of the outside world and of the English churches, two of the higher tribunals of the conscience. English-speaking white South Africans join with the Afrikaner in bitter counter-attacks on the outside world and the United Nations. They cannot so readily attack their own local English pastors, but the outside criticism of overseas ministers, such as Canon Collins, Chancellor of St Paul's Cathedral, provides a channel through which the banked-up resentment can flow. Passive resistance focused overseas attention on South Africa and intensified criticism. Hence, again, it was inevitable that English and Afrikaner should man their positions, shoulder to shoulder, this time against the world and the faint stirrings of conscience.

With so wide a basis for a common front, the Nationalist Party could readily drive home the need for white solidarity. At a time when South Africa stood alone against the world, it was the duty of every white person to support the Government. Indeed, Government spokesmen linked the plea for solidarity with arguments which demonstrate the trend towards a dictatorship by the whites. Criticism of apartheid becomes an incitement to rebellion; the policy of slighting and belittling the Government and its actions can only result in a belittling of its authority. Divisions between the whites, exaggerated and misinterpreted by non-whites, have the effect of arousing wild expectations; political parties and political divisions are a luxury the whites can no longer afford.

Against this background, the United Party had no constructive alternative to offer. It condemned the passive resistance movement, and viewed its continuation with alarm, realizing that the effect would be to strengthen the Government. The United Party was therefore at one with the Government in its desire to halt the campaign, and it was forced repeatedly by Government propaganda to proclaim this unity of purpose, and the necessity and desirability of white domination. There was thus no clear point of difference which might have served as a focus for counter-propaganda. The United Party merely proposed different means to attain the same end, the termination of the resistance campaign. United Party leaders in their call for a national convention and an agreed policy which would remove non-white affairs from politics were, in fact, suggesting machinery by which a common front could be maintained. Inevitably, therefore, in the course of the resistance campaign and under pressure of Nationalist Party propaganda and of white public opinion, the United Party moved toward the assimilation of its non-European policy with that of the Government, and United Party supporters moved into the ranks of the Nationalist Party.

Only small groups of whites resisted this trend to solidarity. The participation of white resisters in the civil disobedience campaign, the founding of the Liberal Party and of the left-wing Congress of Democrats, were a reaction to the ranging of white against non-white. Their significance lies precisely in the demonstration that political affiliation cuts across colour lines. But these whites and their 'fellow travellers' are a small vessel in the main bloodstream of white solidarity and white dictatorship.

VIII

COUNTERACTION

THE Government's counteraction against passive resistance must be seen as a minor exercise in the broad strategy of race domination. By the propaganda campaigns described in the last chapter, and by the use of a wide range of routine and extraordinary sanctions, the Government consolidated white supremacy.

Routine Measures

In all probability, the ordinary routine procedures gave adequate powers for the control of the resistance movement. Resisters were arrested, charged before the Courts, and sentenced as a rule to terms of imprisonment with the option of a fine; juveniles were punished by whipping. Some public prosecutors, in addressing the Court on the question of sentence, mentioned instructions to press for severe penalties. There may have been some such general instruction from the Attorney-General, though the sentences could not, in fact, be severe, since the offences themselves were trivial. Sentences varied considerably throughout the country; magistrates exercised judicial discretion, and their own personal reactions to passive resistance must have been an important factor in the sentences they passed.

The police and prison warders could enhance the deterrent effect of the punishments. The resisters alleged that they were sometimes assaulted, or humiliated by abusive treatment and indecent exposure, or subjected to additional penalties, such as the loss of meals, on the slightest grounds. These allegations were denied. I have discussed the question with reliable informants in Durban, who confirm that warders often went out of their way to make prison life intolerable for the resisters. No doubt, treatment varied in the many police centres and gaols of the Union, but, in general, it is clear that policemen and warders, drawn, as they are, from an underprivileged section of the white group, must have felt and expressed a special antagonism against the resisters. Nor would the many statements by Government spokesmen of the need for drastic punitive measures encourage the pulling of punches or the barring of holds.

The support of whites not involved in the administration of Courts, police stations and prisons, automatically helped to make sanctions more effective. Other state departments played their part by threatening the loss of certain privileges to ministers of religion who participated in the resistance movement, or the withdrawal of subsidies from schools where teachers engaged in political propaganda. Municipal officials had it in their power to use the facilities under their control in a punishing way against active resisters, as, for example, by cancellation of the right to live in a location. The principal of a school might refuse readmission to students who defied the laws. Most drastic of all, some employers (Government, municipal and private) withheld employment where workers absented themselves so as to take part in demonstrations. Others replaced workers of one race by members of another. The power of employers to play off one racial group of employees against another acts as a further deterrent, and fosters antagonism among the employees themselves.

Cat-and-mouse manœuvres accompanied the routine measures against the resistance movement. Prison officials experimented with the confiscation of monies found on resisters and the application of these monies in reduction of fines, even though the resisters had refused the option of a fine. Much against their will, resisters were hustled out of gaol. This was declared to be the Government's answer to the flood-the-gaols campaign; the gaols would be emptied as fast as they were filled. (*Rand Daily Mail*, July 25th, 1952.) Inevitably the experiment was doomed to failure; the resisters needed only to ensure that they carried no money on their persons when arrested. So, too, failure attended the police experiment with non-arrest; refusal to arrest resisters for breach of the curfew laws would have given rise to the absurd anomaly of immunity, where there was the deliberate intention to defy the law, and of arrest, where the breach of law was accidental. Police measures to prevent acts of civil disobedience also miscarried. South Africa cannot afford to police the infinitely varied manifestations of apartheid; the economy of the country demands a large measure of consent from the subordinate non-whites. To cordon off public places in which defiance acts might be committed would have added considerably to the already vast unproductive expenditure on race domination.

On their side, the resisters played with the slack in their legal bonds. To defend oneself against charges rising out of deliberate acts of passive resistance is in conflict with the spirit of voluntary submission to punishment. Nevertheless, some resisters, helped by the ingenuity of their legal advisers, raised purely technical objections to the charges, while others raised substantive issues of varying importance. For example, since the validity of post-office apartheid had already been successfully challenged, public prosecutors could not charge the resisters with being in a section of the post office reserved for whites. They therefore charged them with obstructing the business of the post office, and consequently invited the defence that for a non-white to request service at a counter reserved for whites did not in itself constitute obstruction. Or, again, in the case of railway-apartheid as we have seen, the resisters established that the railway administration did not have the legislative authority to discriminate against non-whites. The immediate effect of this play was to secure the discharge of a number of resisters, to impede punitive action a little, and, at the same time, to provide the Government with ammunition for propaganda. The long-term effect was to constrict the legal bonds round the non-whites by systematic elimination of loopholes.

In all this routine administrative counteraction, the Government acted with a caution which belied the public fulminations of its spokesmen. Perhaps it was sensitive to a hostile world opinion focused on its policies as a result of the resistance drama, or it may have felt that the resistance movement would attract little support from the non-whites, and in dismal failure discredit the sponsoring Congresses. In any event, Government applied only routine measures against the rank and file of the resistance movement, while reserving for use against the leaders and the two Congresses the more extraordinary powers under the Riotous Assemblies and Criminal Law Amendment Act, No. 27 of 1914, and the Suppression of Communism Act, No. 44 of 1950.

Banned, Named and 'Liquidated'

The Riotous Assemblies Act gives wide powers for the control of public gatherings. A magistrate, acting under special authority of the Minister of Justice, may prohibit a *particular* public gathering in any public place in his district, whenever he has reason to fear a serious threat to public peace. Wider powers vest in the Minister of Justice. He may prohibit within an area and for a stated period *any* public gathering in *any* place to which the public has access, if he is of opinion that there is reason to believe that feelings of hostility would be aroused between white and non-white. His powers relate only to public gatherings in places open to the public, and their exercise does not affect the right of private assembly.

In addition, the Riotous Assemblies Act gives the Minister control over the actions of individuals. Under circumstances of apprehended hostility between whites and non-whites, he may prohibit any person from *attending* any public gathering in

184

Volunteers lead the procession to Berea Road station

They gather outside the European entrance, while the procession forms around them

Above: Detectives seize documents from the offices of the African National Congress

Left: Detectives waiting outside the Transvaal Indian Congress offices, because the key could not be found

an area for a stated period. Indeed, if the Minister is satisfied that any person is promoting feelings of hostility between white and non-white, he may prohibit him from *being* in a specified area for a stated period. This means that the Minister may limit movement to a narrowly defined area, remote from the place where the person follows his normal calling, in which case the Minister may provide for costs of removal and subsistence. In effect, then, the Minister has the power of exile![1] An order confining a person to particular areas reads as follows:

PROHIBITION

WITH REGARD TO SECTION I (12) OF THE RIOTOUS ASSEMBLIES AND CRIMINAL LAW AMENDMENT ACT OF 1914 (Act No. 27 of 1914) AS AMENDED.

Whereas, I, Charles Robberts Swart, Minister of Justice of the Union of South Africa, find that you arouse animosity between the European section of the Union and another section, i.e. Non-European.

Now therefore by virtue of powers given to me in subsection 12 of Section 1 of the Riotous Assemblies and Criminal Law Amendment Act, 1914, (Act No. 27 of 1914) as amended, I forbid you, for a period of twelve months, to be present at any place in the Province of Natal or Transvaal,[2] with the exception of that portion of the Magisterial District, Dundee, which is not a Native town or location as defined by the Native Urban Areas Consolidation Act, 1945 (Act No. 25 of 1945) or any part of the Declared Areas Nos. 41, 42, and 43 as defined in

[1] More direct powers of exile, but only in respect of Africans, are given to the Governor-General under the Native Administration Act, No. 38 of 1927, 'whenever he deems it expedient in the general public interest'.

[2] This order was issued to an Indian. Since Indians require permits to move from province to province, the effect of the order is to restrict movement to the district of Dundee, at the Minister's discretion.

Part II of the first annexure to the Native Trust and Land Act, 1936 (Act No. 18 of 1936).

The period of twelve months comes into operation seven days after the notice is handed or served upon you.

Given under my hand at Cape Town on the 10th day of February, 1953.

(*sgd.*) C. R. SWART,
Minister of Justice.

Prohibitions against attendance at any public gatherings are issued in the same way. In contrast, however, to the 'exile' or 'confinement' order, the prohibition may be Union-wide, since a person can readily survive without attending public gatherings.

The two types of order are commonly issued to the same person. A national leader who received both might still attend committee and private meetings, held in the areas to which he was confined. He could retain his position as a member of his organization and as a national leader, but shorn of the activities which would make his leadership effective. Even this limited participation might be closed under the Suppression of Communism Act.

The 'Red' Act also confers on the Minister of Justice powers of control over gatherings and individual activities. The Minister may prohibit the assembly of a particular gathering, or the *attendance* of a particular person at any gathering within an area and during a period specified, if he has reason to believe that the achievement of any of the objects of communism would be furthered. He may forbid the mere *presence* of a person in any area for a stated period of time, if he is satisfied that such person is 'advocating, advising, defending or encouraging the achievement of any of the objects of communism', or is *likely* to do so. The definition of communism, it should be remembered, includes not merely Marxist communism, but also unlawful acts or omissions, actual or threatened, aimed at bringing about any political, industrial, social or economic change.

These powers amplify the powers of the Minister of Justice under the Riotous Assemblies Act. By extending his control over gatherings to include *private* gatherings, and by extending the fields of activity over which he presides to include 'statutory communism', the area of individual freedom is more rigidly restricted. In addition, the 'Red' Act introduces new and extensive powers of control over both organizations and individuals. Organizations are dealt with by 'proscription' and individuals by 'naming'.

The Act proscribes the Communist Party as an unlawful organization and establishes machinery for its liquidation. It empowers the Governor-General to declare unlawful any other organization, or body controlled by an organization, which propagates 'communism', or is engaged in activities which are calculated to further the achievement of the objects of 'communism'. If the Minister of Justice has reason to suspect that any organization should be declared unlawful, he may appoint an officer to enter premises and to demand and seize documents which afford evidence of activities and personnel – office-bearers, officers, members or active supporters. The exercise of this power, reinforced by the power to prohibit gatherings and attendance at gatherings, gives the Minister control over organizations. He need not go so far as to request proscription of these organizations by the Governor-General, since he can effectively apply a brake to their activities by police raids and the implied threat of proscription, by the prohibition of meetings, and by the removal of records. Few, if any, organizations are able to manage without bureaucratic files.

The entirely novel procedure under the 'Red' Act is that of 'naming'. When an organization is declared unlawful, the Liquidator may be required by the Minister to compile a list of persons who are or have been office-bearers, officers, members, or active supporters. Some protection is afforded against the arbitrary listing of names, since a person must be given a reasonable opportunity of showing that his name should not be included in the list.

Superficially, the mere naming of a person would appear to be innocuous enough; if applied to a leader, it might place him in cold storage, but hardly in deep freeze. In fact, however, the psychological consequences are extensive. The fear of being 'named' acts, in itself, as a powerful deterrent. Many potential white liberals, only mildly racialist in outlook, are so paralysed by the faintly remote possibility that they might conceivably become eligible for 'naming' that they withdraw from all participation in mixed white and non-white organizations; they cease their subscriptions to left-wing periodicals, carefully refrain from attacks on the Government's racial policies or 'sickly o'er' their public statements with the 'pale cast' of sweet reasonableness. Even a man of courage, if he has a family and depends on others for a livelihood, is likely to be deterred by the fear of being 'named'. For most whites, a 'named' person bears a permanent social stigma; he is not acceptable as an employee, or in ordinary intercourse. Like the charge of witchcraft, the label 'communist' is so peculiarly horrifying as to suffice for damnation.

An individual once 'named' retains the full right of participation in his previous organizations. Should he persist, however, in the exercise of this right, then he exposes himself to the danger of 'liquidation'[3] by the Minister. The latter, that is to say, has the power to require a 'named' person to resign from, or not to join, any organization or specified kinds of organization; he may also order him not to become a member of Parliament or Provincial Council or other public body; or, subject to certain safeguards, he may compel him, if already a member, to resign.

The following is the form of order issued under the Suppression of Communism Act:

[3] The Act refers to the liquidation of organizations and the listing of individuals by the Liquidator. It does not apply the term 'liquidation' to individuals, as I have done.

COUNTERACTION

THE SUPPRESSION OF COMMUNISM ACT NO. 44 OF 1950 AS AMENDED
Whereas your name appears on the list in the custody of the officer referred to in Section 8, please take notice that:

1. *Under the powers vested in me by Section 5 of the Suppression of Communism Act, (Act No. 44 of 1950 as amended), you are hereby requested:*

   (*a*) to resign within a period of 30 days from date hereof as an office-bearer, officer or member of the following organizations and not again to become an office-bearer, officer or member thereof and not to take part in their activities:

   FRANCHISE ACTION COUNCIL
   CAPE TOWN PEACE COUNCIL

   (*b*) not to become an office-bearer, officer or member and not to take part in the activities of the organization called

   AFRICAN NATIONAL CONGRESS

(2) Under the powers vested in me by section 9 of the Suppression of Communism Act (Act No. 44 of 1950 as amended), you are hereby prohibited from attending any gathering whatever within the Union of South Africa and the Territory of South-West Africa for a period of two years from date hereof other than gatherings of a *bona-fide* religious, recreational or social nature.

(3) Under the powers vested in me by section 10 of the Act and after thirty days from date hereof you are hereby prohibited for a period of two years from being within any province in the Union of South Africa, or the Territory of South-West Africa, other than the province of the Cape of Good Hope.

Given under my hand at CAPE TOWN this 28th Day of April, 1952.

(*sgd.*) C. R. SWART,
Minister of Justice.

This would effectively terminate participation in the organizations mentioned and in public political life. A person 'named' and 'liquidated' under the Suppression of Communism Act might as well resign himself to bird-watching and other simple pleasures of nature . . . or go underground.

Leader-culling

Clearly, the two organizations which sponsored the passive resistance movement might have been proscribed under the 'Red' Act, since they were advocating social change by unlawful means. Yet the Government refrained from taking this step. Presumably it did not wish to drive the movement underground, and thus render control more difficult; or it may have been unwilling to expose the true nature of the 'Red' Act, as an instrument of white domination rather than a measure against communism.

Instead of direct proscription, Government sought to achieve the same result by indirect means. These included the harassing of the Congresses by police raids, spies and demonstrations of strength; the castration of Congress leadership by convictions, bannings, and 'liquidations'; and the assumption of additional repressive powers.

The first police raids were carried out towards the end of July 1952. Throughout the country, detectives of the Special (Political) Branch of the Criminal Investigation Department searched the offices of the Congresses and non-white trade unions, and the homes of officials of these organizations. According to police accounts, the raids were exploratory, an attempt to gather evidence of incitement or conspiracy under the provisions of the Riotous Assemblies Act and the Suppression of Communism Act. The secretary of the African National Congress (Natal) commented that the police gained no information from these raids that they could not have obtained at a public meeting. Nevertheless, organization must have been impeded by the removal of records, and fear as to the shape of things to come.

Spying is an insidious weapon, even in the case of a passive resistance movement which publicly proclaims both ends and means, and indeed seeks to make generally known the motives and conduct of the campaign. To find that a trusted worker, 'named' in a notice purporting to be signed by the Liquidator, is in fact a police agent,[4] means a good deal more than writing off a supporter. It sows doubt and suspicion, undermining the mutual confidence so necessary to co-workers in a movement over which hangs the threat of drastic reprisals. Moreover, the role of the police agent may go beyond spying to that of *provocateur*, forcing on the resistance leaders the need to scrutinize all proposals with suspicion. and to seek, behind apparent sincerity, the possibility of a police trap. Officials of the South Indian Congress know most of their members; they are better able to detect, and hence to counter, the spy than the African National Congress, whose rapid growth of membership makes it especially vulnerable to the police agent.

Police demonstrations of strength accompanied every phase of the resistance movement. The presence of armed police and of police agents, the recording of speeches, the occasional arrest of a leader at meetings, discouraged appearances in public; the situation was such as to demand a resolute determination to face whatever consequences might ensue. Even the courageous leader felt that his speeches were expanding his police record and the dockets of the public prosecutor. Further demonstrations of strength were the use of the Riotous Assemblies Act to prohibit meetings; the rough dispersal of processions and gatherings; the drafting of additional police reinforcements to Port Elizabeth and East London some two months before the riots; and the severe police measures in the riots. These were certainly intended to put the Africans firmly in their place, to drive home once and for all the lesson that the white man is master, to enforce a 'Rest in Peace' on the resistance movement.

Police spies, raids, the displays and use of force not only

[4] Preparatory Examination, W. M. Sisulu and Others, pp. 277-85.

harassed, but also discredited, the Congresses. Most people are so well-trained to law and order that they believe there must be something disreputable about an organization of which the police disapprove. Police action reinforced Government propaganda.

A second line of attack against the Congresses was directed at their leaders. Government indicted Congress leaders before the Courts, and used the Riotous Assemblies Act and the 'Red' Act to suppress their political activities.

Most of the national leaders (African and Indian, including all the members of the Joint Planning Council) and many provincial leaders in the Cape and Transvaal were charged with encouraging the achievement of an object of communism. They were found guilty and received sentences of imprisonment suspended for a number of years,[5] on condition that, during the period of their suspended sentence, they did not again commit an offence under the Act. This had the effect of removing these leaders from active roles in the resistance movement. It also made them subject to the Minister's powers in much the same way as if they were 'named' communists on the Liquidator's list.

In an attempt to place responsibility for the riots on the resistance movement, the Government charged a number of African leaders with incitement to public violence. These charges failed. The Government was not able to produce evidence linking the Congresses with the riots. The Crown case in Regina v. S. P. Sesedi and Others, which followed on the Kimberley riots, makes wondrous strange reading.

The powers of the Minister under the Riotous Assemblies

[5] In August, 1954, one of the resistance leaders was sentenced to eighteen months imprisonment in the Worcester Magistrate's Court in respect of speeches made during the resistance campaign. The conviction, that is to say, was for offences committed two years previously, offences of the same type for which the major leaders had received suspended sentences of nine months. The Appellate Division decided that it could not interfere with the sentence, although it considered that a suspended sentence might have been more appropriate. (R. v. Alwyn, 1955 A.D., p. 207.)

Act arise when there is the danger of hostility between whites and non-whites. Any challenge to white domination will certainly provoke hostile reactions from the whites. The Minister of Justice is therefore in a position to suppress action by the non-whites for political rights, unless the action takes the acceptable form of petition or supplication. The Riotous Assemblies Act is a key instrument of white domination and was clearly applicable to the passive resistance movement. The 'Red' Act was equally applicable to the 'statutory communism' of passive resistance. Hence the Minister acted within his power in banning a number of leaders under both Acts. To the best of my knowledge, the Minister distinguished at this stage between 'named' communists and non-communists, subjecting only the former to the more drastic restrictions of the 'Red' Act.

As a result of banning orders and convictions, the Congresses suffered a serious check. Many of the leaders were arrested in August 1952, at the height of the resistance campaign. From that date, until the first large-scale convictions at the beginning of December 1952, they worked under the threat of heavy penalties. Their effectiveness as leaders must have been seriously impaired. By the time of their conviction, the resistance campaign was past its peak, and the Government had already assumed additional repressive powers.

On November 28th, 1952, the Governor-General issued a proclamation dealing with the incitement of Natives. Any person who at any time uses language, or behaves in a manner, calculated to cause Natives to resist and contravene any law, or obstruct its administration, is guilty of an offence, and liable, on conviction, to a fine not exceeding £300 or, failing payment, to imprisonment for a maximum of three years. The white resisters who entered Germiston Location on December 8th were charged and convicted under these regulations.[6] The

[6] The effect is to create, by *regulations* under the authority of a Native Administration Act, a new and serious crime for whites as well as non-whites. Counsel for the defence argued that, if the regulations were valid, the 'rule of law' would have ceased for whites. An appeal was noted, but abandoned.

proclamation also makes provision for the control of meetings of more than ten Natives in any Native area, the Governor-General being empowered to extend the area of control at any time by notice in the Government *Gazette*. The prior permission of the chief or headman and the approval in writing of the Native Commissioner or Magistrate are now required. Any person who holds, presides at, addresses, or permits any such meeting without permission commits an offence, and becomes liable to the same penalties as for incitement.[7]

This proclamation effectively countered the plans of the African National Congress to spread the resistance movement among rural Africans. The only alternative to public meetings was propaganda from home to home. Newcomers to the area would be clearly conspicuous and vulnerable to deportation. The Government had not only met the challenge of the resistance movement in the rural areas, but checked the national organizations in their policy of developing political consciousness among the reserve Africans.

Piling power on power, the Government added the Public Safety Act and the Criminal Law Amendment Act to its stock. The Criminal Law Amendment Act introduces the penalty of lashes for what are essentially political crimes. It also establishes a number of new procedures and crimes to counter some of the successful manœuvres by the resistance leaders. The Government failed in its attempt to secure payment of fines from monies found on the resisters; there is now special provision for the attachment and sale of the convicted person's property to cover the amount of the fine. The ingenious device of playing the wire-recorded speeches of banned leaders becomes an offence both for the leader and for those who receive the recording. To solicit, accept, receive, offer or give money for a civil disobedience campaign is also an offence, and

---

[7] Exceptions are made in the case of meetings in Native areas for the purposes of a *bona-fide* religious service or funeral, the regulation of domestic affairs or of statutory affairs, a *bona-fide* sports gathering, concert, entertainment or wedding, and meetings addressed by a Senator, Member of Parliament, or Member of a Provincial Council.

officials of the Department of Post and Telegraphs may detain and forward suspected postal articles to the Postmaster-General for examination. The Government is in a position to know the contents of all postal communications.

The Criminal Law Amendment Act is specifically focused on civil disobedience and incitement to civil disobedience, but overlaps to an appreciable extent with the Riotous Assemblies Act and the 'Red' Act. Thus civil disobedience, in the form practised during the resistance campaign, is an offence under the 'Red' Act, and also under the Criminal Law Amendment Act. Incitement to civil disobedience can readily be handled in terms of the provisions of both these Acts as well as the Riotous Assemblies Act, and, if the incitement is addressed to Natives, the Governor-General's proclamation. The powers of exile over convicted persons which the Criminal Law Amendment Act confers on the Minister of Justice triplicate, to some extent, the powers he already enjoys. Indeed, such is the overlap of powers that nine officials of the African National Congress were told, on arrest by the police, that they would be charged under the Riotous Assemblies Act: at the charge office, this was altered to the Criminal Law Amendment Act; and they were finally indicted for contraventions of the Suppression of Communism Act. (According to a report in the *Bantu World*, May 23rd, 1953.)

The Government has not, as yet, found grounds for declaring a state of emergency under the Public Safety Act, and few charges have been laid under the Criminal Law Amendment Act. In one case, an African was convicted in the Magistrate's Court on a charge of soliciting funds for the defiance campaign and sentenced to twelve months imprisonment with hard labour and eight lashes: such, however, was the indecent haste of the prosecution that the sentence was set aside by the Appeal Court on the ground that the Act had not yet become law when the accused committed the alleged offence. (According to reports in the *Bantu World*, April 4th, and September 5th, 1953.) In another case, two Indians were acquitted of a charge of malicious injury to property; the indictment alleged that they had printed the slogan 'Defend our homes' on one wall, and the letters 'DE' on another. (*Natal Mercury*, October 13th, 1953.) The Act is still too recent and unused for the police and prosecutors to have acquired proficiency.

The Public Safety Act and the Criminal Law Amendment Act are an investment for the future, when the struggle against white domination becomes more intense. There was no need to use the new far-reaching powers. The mere assumption of these powers, combined with the vigorous exercise of the routine and extraordinary powers already vested in the Government, sufficed to suppress the resistance movement. It could not long survive in the existing state of organization among the non-whites. Moreover, the existence of the non-white national organizations is now rendered even more precarious by the liquidation of their leadership, and by the experience the Government has gained in the efficient use of its vast armoury of sanctions. If at any time indirect means of control should prove inadequate, the Government can always play its trump card by declaring the Congresses unlawful organizations, and placing them in liquidation.

Aftermath

The struggle still goes on. After the passive resistance movement, the African National Congress in the Cape Eastern area experimented with an economic boycott, designed to secure better treatment for Africans in shops and to open up employment opportunities. Still a minor experiment, the economic boycott is potentially a powerful weapon and, as yet, a legal form of action. It is not, however, accepted policy by the Congresses. Some leaders fear that the boycott might readily take the form of promoting African interests at the expense of other groups, and in this way become an instrument of African nationalism. Others feel that the boycott is premature, requiring a more highly developed organization than the Congresses can command.

The campaign against the Western Areas Removal Scheme was of more immediate importance. The Government was determined to remove non-whites from the Western areas of Johannesburg in pursuance of its policy of apartheid, and especially of its policy of ensuring that Africans should not hold any stake in the urban areas. In apartheid theory, Africans are purely migrants in the cities, there to serve the white man in the lower occupational spheres for, and only, as long as they are needed. The threatened loss of freehold rights to land in the Western Areas and the proposed transplanting of settled communities provide an emotional focus for resistance. The first stages of the removal have now been completed without resistance; many of the tenants, living in slum conditions, clearly wished to move, and the police were present in great force.

More national in scope was the campaign known as the Congress of the People, sponsored by the African and Indian Congresses, the South African Congress of Democrats, and the South African Coloured People's Organization. Provincial and local committees were established throughout the country, and held meetings to discuss the aspirations and frustrations of the people, and to arrange for the election of representatives. These representatives then attended a national congress and drafted a 'Freedom Charter'. The campaign, launched under the slogan, 'Let us Speak Together of Freedom', was clearly designed to awaken political consciousness, and to crystallize its expression in a declaration of rights. The *volkswil*, or people's will, was to be heard from the millions of unrepresented people, the overwhelming majority of the country. The sponsors are now organizing the collection of 1,000,000 signatures to the Freedom Charter.

The campaign against the Bantu Education Act is also national in scope, affecting, however, only Africans. Sponsored by the African National Congress, it seeks to boycott the School Boards now being established for the administration of the Act. In some areas, children were withdrawn from school, and private teaching arranged. There is not sufficient solidarity to make the boycott of the School Boards really effective and, in any event, African opinion is divided on the question of the desirability of the boycott. The temporary withdrawal by the Government of school privileges from children who absented themselves from school beyond a certain date, and the prosecution of teachers in the unauthorized new schools, are powerful counter-measures.

These campaigns are facets of the broader struggle by the non-whites to develop their organizational strength. The passive resistance movement itself may be viewed as an aspect of the struggle for organizational strength and unity. Enthusiasm was stirred by the tensions and sacrifices of the campaign, many new members were enrolled, and the Congresses now face the difficult problem of maintaining interest through effective action. They cannot hope for a change in white domination, save through strong national organizations, united in purpose.

The Government is determined to prevent the growth of the national organizations of the non-whites and to deny them the opportunity for action. It was firmly resolved to stamp out the Congress of the People and the resistance to the Western Areas Removal Scheme before they took root, and to prevent political collaboration between whites and non-whites. It continues to harass the Congresses, and to liquidate their leaders and officials, and the white and non-white officials of non-European trade unions. The Congress of Democrats, in particular, is under very heavy attack. This organization of whites was sponsored by the African and Indian Congresses, and identifies itself with the Congresses in their struggle.

During the election campaign in the early part of 1953, the Minister of Justice relaxed his attacks on the leaders, only to issue wave after wave of banning and resignation orders when the Nationalist Party was returned to power. Many of the leaders earned a respite as the result of an Appellate Court decision in November 1953.[8] It was short-lived, the Government responding in its customary way to adverse judgments by new legislation.

The Minister has changed his procedure for the issue of orders against attendance at meetings. He is now applying the provisions of the 'Red' Act to persons whose names do not appear on the liquidator's list and who were never members of the Communist Party.[9] Whereas in the past this type of order was issued to non-communists under the Riotous Assemblies Act and therefore did not affect private meetings, the new orders apply to both public and private meetings. It becomes more clear that the purpose of the 'Red' Act is to maintain white domination.

The Minister has also altered the form of the notice, which originally excluded gatherings of a social, recreational and religious nature. This allowed the banned person some scope for disguised political activity. The Minister now issues orders under the 'Red' Act, forbidding attendance for two years or five years at all gatherings without exception. Initially, the effect on those banned was not unlike that of outcasting – the removal of a person from group life – since a gathering is

[8] In Johnson Ngwevela v. Regina, the Court held that before the Minister exercises his powers under the 'Red' Act to prohibit attendance at meetings, he must give the affected person the opportunity of a hearing. Where the Minister had failed to provide for a hearing, the banning orders issued by him were invalid. The Government thereupon amended the Act. The banning orders were reinstated, and the relevant sections now provide that in the case of 'named' persons or persons convicted under the Suppression of Communism Act, the Minister need not provide the opportunity for representations by the affected persons, nor need he furnish reasons. In the case of persons not listed, nor convicted, the Minister, on request, must give his reasons for the issue of an order, and so much of the information on which his decision was based, as can be disclosed without detriment to public policy. It remains to be seen whether this amendment affords any protection against the arbitrary exercise of dictatorial powers. (See *A Survey of Race Relations in South Africa* 1953-4, compiled by Muriel Horrell, Johannesburg, South African Institute of Race Relations, 1954, pp. 35-6.)

[9] The Acting Minister of Justice stated that ninety named communists and sixty-eight other persons were prohibited from attending gatherings in terms of the Suppression of Communism Act. Eighty-eight named persons were ordered to resign from trade unions and other bodies, while forty-seven persons were convicted under the Act. (*Hansard, House of Assembly Debates*, January 28th, 1955, p. 182.)

defined as any gathering, concourse or procession in, through, or along any place of any number of persons having a common purpose, whether such purpose be lawful or unlawful.[10] Recently, however, the Appellate Division interpreted the term 'gathering' as an assembly of persons to achieve some common object by concerted action, with the result that banned persons are now free to take part in ordinary social activities.[11] Amending legislation is to be anticipated.

The list of organizations from which the Minister orders people to resign steadily grows. Most of these organizations are radical, but the list has also included bodies which are liberal in outlook and conciliatory in their approach to the white public. At least one person, for example, has been ordered to resign from the South African Institute of Race Relations. (*Advance*, September 30th, 1954.)

The Government is tightening its control over public information. In March, 1954, the Torch Printing and Publishing Company (Pty) Ltd was charged with promoting hostility between Natives and Europeans. The charge rested on the contents of an editorial in *The Torch* attacking the Government's education policy. The Magistrate commented that if the prosecutor's contention was correct, it would be difficult for anyone to criticize laws affecting non-whites differently from

[10] The banned ex-Secretary of the African National Congress was charged with having attended a gathering at Bloemfontein on July 24th, 1954. The Crown alleged that five other persons were present at one time or another. The purpose of the gathering was 'to partake of or be present whilst others partake of refreshment (in the nature of tea and/or some such other liquid refreshment, and/or edibles and/or a meal)', and/or to discuss matters relating to the African National Congress, and/or to make arrangements regarding a meeting, and/or to discuss and/or to be present during the discussion of matters to the prosecutor unknown, and/or to listen to what one or more of the persons present had to say about any matter (the matter to the prosecutor unknown), and/or to inform one or more of the persons present about any matter (also unknown) and/or to have social intercourse. (As reported in *Advance*, September 30th, and the *Leader*, December 3rd, 1954.)

[11] R. *v.* Kahn, 1955 A.D., p. 177. On the interpretation of the term 'gathering', Counsel for the Crown argued 'that if the appellant had a meal in his own house with his own family he would not be attending a "gathering" but if his brother, who did not live in the same house as the appellant, shared a meal with him and his family he would then be attending a "gathering" ' (p. 183).

whites. (*The Torch*, March 2nd, 1954.) The accused was discharged, but the prosecution itself serves as a warning to editors. In October, 1954, the Government banned, under the provisions of the Suppression of Communism Act, the weekly periodical *Advance*, one of the few sources of information about non-white political movements.[12] The national newspapers give meagre news of non-white political activities, the English papers imposing self-censorship to avoid conflict with the Government. On the other hand, the Government is now using State information services to propagate apartheid, as, for example, by *Bantu*, 'an informal publication of the Department of Native Affairs'.

At the same time, the police have developed further their techniques for the control of public meetings. The presence of representatives of the Special Branch of the Criminal Investigation Department is becoming routine at public meetings called to oppose the Government's apartheid policy. In June, 1954, the police gave a new turn to this technique. More than a hundred policemen armed with Sten guns, rifles, and batons invaded a conference called to oppose the Western Areas removal scheme and convened by the organizations sponsoring the Congress of the People. The police took up positions inside and outside the building, prevented anyone from entering or leaving, and recorded the names and addresses of those present. In explanation, the police stated that they were investigating a case of treason. The display of force, and the recording of names by the police, repeated also at a later meeting, are sufficient to deter most people from supporting causes of which the Government disapproves, and indeed to prevent them even hearing the case for support of such causes.

Recently the police received a setback when they forcibly entered a private meeting of delegates called by the Congress of the People, and were ordered by the Court to leave. The Government responded first by the issue of more banning orders, on the ground that the Court's decision made it difficult

[12] It has now been succeeded by *New Age*.

for the police to investigate and control the activities of suspect persons, and later by extending the powers of the police.[13]

Lists of persons 'named' have been made available to all the 18,000 members of the police force, ostensibly because 'they were in a position where unknown to themselves they might have discussed some matter with a named person about which it would have been very incorrect to talk'. (Commissioner of Police, according to a report in the *Natal Daily News*, October 22nd, 1954.) It is clear that the steps from circulating these lists to supplementing them with lists of other opponents of apartheid, to continuous police surveillance and, indeed, to persecution, are easily taken.

In this way, democratic values are steadily corroded. Through continued exercise, the extraordinary powers of the Government become routine. The field of police control over political activity extends daily. For the average white person, South Africa is a supremely free society; he is quite unaware of the extent of police activity, or, if aware, approves. It is primarily the Africans, and the active opponents of apartheid, both white and non-white, who suffer under growing police intimidation. They feel the trend toward the police State, not fully realized under present conditions, when the non-whites are too disorganized for a serious challenge to white domination, but almost inevitable as the struggle becomes more acute.

We usually think of a police State as a highly secular State, and the approach of the South African Government to legislation and to the use of the police in the purely rational terms of efficient means to apartheid ends is indeed essentially secular. But the belief in the sanctity of apartheid, in the God-given mission of the Afrikaner people, adds a sacred element. It is this combination of the sacred and secular which suggests that South Africa may evolve that curious political form – the Sacred Police State.

[13] The Police Amendment Act, No. 15 of 1955.

CONCLUSION

IX

TRIBAL ETHIC AND UNIVERSAL ETHIC

THE consequences of the passive resistance campaign are difficult to assess. Certainly, the institutions supporting white domination have increased in number and in the range of their application; and white domination is apparently more firmly established.

During the course of the campaign and in the year following, the Government extended its control over political activity. It assumed powers which effectively limit freedom of association among the African peasants. It amended the criminal law so as to provide more severe sanctions against any illegal challenge to white domination, and it developed its police techniques for the intimidation and suppression of non-white political organization and leadership, under the cloak of action against treason and communism. Behind these sanctions and techniques lie the wide powers taken by the Government for the suspension of normal legal and administrative process in times of emergency.

During the same period, the Government extended the administrative centralization of non-European affairs by the transfer of African education from the provinces to the Native Affairs Department and by the adoption of an educational system compatible with apartheid. The political potential of the African trade-union movement was diverted, in theory at any rate, to the relatively safe level of administrative routine by the Native Labour (Settlement of Disputes) Act.

So, too, the principle of unequal-status contact between white and non-white was reinforced by the Reservation of Separate Amenities Act, which confers on administrators and private persons the right to discriminate in access to amenities. And, at the present time, the Government is carrying out the separation of races under the Group Areas Act, and proposing to reserve occupations for whites and non-whites, in somewhat the same way that caste restricts choice of occupation.

Thus, in each of the major techniques of white domination, there has been a development since the commencement of the resistance campaign. Indeed, the institutional framework of apartheid is now so near completion that new issues must be sought as a focus for political organization and propaganda – issues within the white group itself, such as the Republican issue, rather than the issue of apartheid between the races.

Yet we cannot conclude that the resistance campaign materially influenced the pattern of institutional change. The law for the reservation of separate amenities is a clear example of a link between passive resistance and legislation. The occasion for its enactment was the successful establishment by passive resisters of their legal right to equal facilities, in the absence of express legislative authority to the contrary. But this law did not introduce discrimination by administrators; it merely gave legal sanction to accepted practice. Its significance lies at the ideological level, the frank avowal of the legitimacy of racial discrimination.

For the rest, the main institutional changes directly linked with passive resistance relate to the more effective application of force and repressive action. This is, however, only a seeming paradox. In all probability it was the resistance to domination, rather than the non-violent character of the resistance, which provoked a passionate and forceful response. Force is implicit in white domination: the resistance campaign made it explicit.

In any event, the disturbances at Kimberley, Denver, Port Elizabeth, and East London intervened between the commencement of the resistance campaign and the passage of the Criminal

Law Amendment Act and the Public Safety Act. The amendments to the criminal law deal specifically with civil disobedience and are, presumably, a consequence of the resistance campaign, while the wide powers assumed against any threat to public safety flow presumably from the disturbances. Whether these laws would have been enacted and, if so, in the same terms, without a supporting public opinion inflamed by the loss of life and destruction of property in the disturbances, cannot be known with certainty.

Assessment of the effect of the passive resistance campaign on the attitudes of the white population is even more complex. There can be little doubt that the attitudes supporting apartheid are expressed in a wider range of situations and by a greater number of public bodies and private associations than in the past. Social organization and social problems are defined more and more in purely racial terms. Differentiation on the basis of race carries with it official moral approval, while the opposition to this principle is identified with communism or categorized as a device of Indian imperialism.

Among many English groups, apartheid has gained an everyday currency, and numbers of local authorities and administrators in English centres eagerly translate the theory into practice. Increasingly, the supporters of the opposition United Party accept the more consistent policy of apartheid. Concepts which carried a ludicrous connotation – such as a 'buffer zone', a 'no-man's land' between racial groups, or 'racial zones' for line fishermen on the beaches – are applied earnestly and without embarrassment. Even men relatively free from racial modes of thought may be obliged to work with race categories, and liberal judges solemnly declare people to be white or non-white for purposes of a particular law. Minor officials, classifying coloured persons in one centre, apply physical tests based on a crude mythology of race characteristics, and the magical transformations of race in South African society have a Grimm's-fairy-tale quality.

From lay sources, not connected with administration or the

struggle for political power, come many suggestions for the extension of apartheid – such as separate containers in laundries for the clothes of whites and non-whites; and apartheid in separators for the milk of European-owned cows and African-owned cows. Apartheid is a simple doctrine to understand and apply; under the kindly light of Government favour, the most untutored mind can, and does, make an original contribution to its practice.

At the same time, a contrary process has taken place – the crystallization or public expression of anti-racialist attitudes. This is demonstrated among many English churchmen by the sympathy they extended to the passive resistance campaign; their testing of Government legislation, more particularly the Criminal Law Amendment Act and the Bantu Education Act, against the ethic of Christianity; and their open denunciation of apartheid. The main platform of the Liberal Party and of the Congress of Democrats is the rejection of race as a valid criterion of social organization. This is certainly the conviction of others who are not willing to commit themselves openly. It is clear that there has been a polarization of attitudes; the great majority of whites are strongly committed to racial exclusiveness and discrimination, while a small minority assert the right of individuals to participate on equal terms in a common society.

The passive resistance campaign assisted in the crystallization of these conflicting attitudes. It provided an occasion for the identification of the non-white political movements with Indian imperialism and world communism, thus intensifying the antagonisms of the whites. This identification was made in the past; it was already explicit in the definition of communism as change by illegal means; and any resistance to domination, whatever its form, would have been labelled communist. The resistance campaign, however, by reason of its long duration and the participation of people of different races, provided extended opportunities for public condemnation of the movement as communist or Indian-inspired, and, by continuous reiteration, established this reaction as a conventional mode of response by the white populace.

Similarly, the founding of the Liberal Party and of the Congress of Democrats seems to have been a reaction to passive resistance and the growing gulf between white and non-white. The time of their establishment is related to the repressive powers assumed by the Government for the suppression of the campaign. The denunciations of apartheid by English churchmen were influenced by the readiness of so many resisters to undergo voluntary suffering. English churchmen were gravely troubled by passive resistance. On the other hand, the intensification of apartheid sentiment would have sharpened the democratic reaction, even if there had been no resistance campaign, though the voluntary submission to suffering for an ideal certainly contributed to this result.

It seems clear, therefore, that the role of passive resistance in the institutional changes and in the changes of attitudes among the whites was not fundamental. Apartheid is a consistent totalitarian ideology, and the necessary laws for its implementation were systematically planned. Passive resistance modified the details of the institutional changes, the tempo and the voting in Parliament. It assisted the Government to give effect to apartheid, but did not shape the ideology of apartheid in any way. Nor did it shape the attitudes supporting apartheid, which received a reinforcement from the institutional changes themselves. The passage of the new laws established the principles of apartheid in the law-abiding sentiments of the whites, and involved more and more people in the administration of apartheid, converting its basic concepts into the routine of office. Institutional changes acted upon attitudes to heighten apartheid sentiment, and this heightened apartheid sentiment, stimulated by material advantages, supported the institutional changes.

This is the position to-day when there seems to be no point of entry for democratic action in a field dominated by the mutual reinforcement of apartheid institutions and attitudes.

CONCLUSION

Apartheid and democracy are radically opposed doctrines. Apartheid provides a political philosophy for the ordering of a multi-racial society by preserving the separate identity of the races and ranking them on a well-defined scale of superiority and inferiority. Democracy, on the contrary, reduces the significance of race differences by an emphasis on the common human rights of all individuals.

Again, apartheid is an exclusive or tribal ethic with the familiar emphasis on one's own group as *the* people; the Afrikaners are *die volk*, the chosen of God, with a heavenly mission in Africa. There is also the familiar double standard of morality. Apartheid idealizes the white man and debases the non-white; it offers the former unbounded opportunities and the monopoly of the developed industrial wealth of the country, while it carefully restricts the life-chances of the non-white, and compensates for this restriction by the illusory promise of opportunities in areas still to be developed. Within the white group apartheid emphasizes solidarity, respect for person and property; outside the white group, it compels separation and denies personal and property rights which do not fit within the master plan.

In all these respects, apartheid runs counter to the inclusive ethics of Christianity and democracy, with their single standard of morality, applicable to all men irrespective of race. Hence the ascendancy of apartheid has necessitated the increasing rejection of democratic concepts and an adherence to a highly individual interpretation of Christianity. This rejection is given further impetus, as we have seen, by the very appeal of democracy for the non-whites, to whom it offers emancipation. In a broad way, the conflict between the races in South Africa is a conflict between the exclusive ethic of apartheid and the universal ethic of democracy. The non-whites are moving away from caste and tribalism, while the whites are moving toward these systems; the non-whites increasingly give their allegiance to a universal ethic, the whites proclaim an exclusive ethic.

Thus, among the Indians, caste differences have ceased to constitute important lines of division. Endogamy is the main surviving characteristic, and even endogamy is interpreted far less rigidly than in traditional Hindu society. Caste status has relevance for prestige, but less so than occupation, choice of which is not restricted by caste. Prohibitions against social intercourse are largely disregarded, and Indians of different castes, religions and language-groups mix freely, join the same organizations and attend the same schools, speak English and assimilate Western culture. The Indian political organizations promote contact not only within the Indian community but also with other races, and have, as their objective, equal rights in an integrated society. The position of the Indians as a small minority, dependent for survival on racial tolerance, ensures their active co-operation with other races.

So, too, among the Africans, tribal divisions are diminishing in importance, partly as a result of urbanization which promotes contact between people of different tribes in factory and location, and partly as a result of the deliberate policy of African leaders. For many years now, the African National Congress has fostered African nationalism as a means of combating tribalism. It is because African nationalism represents a major step away from tribalism toward a wider unity that Congress leaders often resent the suggestion that it may develop into racial exclusiveness on the pattern of apartheid. In any event, both the African National Congress and the All-African Convention attack race discrimination, and seek co-operation and equal rights in a common society. The main ambiguity among the non-white groups is in the position of the Coloureds, the majority of whom fear greater opportunity for the African, lest it diminish their own status.

In the governing white group, the movement of ideas is in the opposite direction, a reversal of the trend toward racial integration resulting from industrial growth. Tribalism is to prevail among the Africans, subdivision among the Coloureds, while the Indians are treated as a 'pariah' people. The division of locations into linguistic areas, the greater emphasis on school teaching in the home language, the establishment of Bantu authorities, are all means to tribal ends and to tribal exclusiveness. Even the process of fusion between the Afrikaans- and English-speaking whites has been disturbed, and the founding of the Federal party in 1953 marks the reappearance of organized English sentiment in opposition to Afrikaner nationalism.

This general picture of the conflicting ideological allegiances of white and non-white is complicated by the fact that many forces contribute to invest democratic values with significance for the white group. Conversely, among the non-whites, race, language and tribal divisions provide a basis for group exclusiveness. The ideological conflict is waged not only between white and non-white, but within each of the racial groups.

Liberal democratic ideology, notwithstanding the small number of its adherents among the white voters of South Africa, is raised to the level of a rival political philosophy by outside opinion, hostile to apartheid. In consequence, the Government is forced to attack liberalism, thus enhancing its local importance, and to defend apartheid by emphasizing its 'positive' aspects. Apartheid can be interpreted quite simply as the ideology of a class seeking to convert political power to wealth, by direct appropriation of resources from the non-whites under legislative mandate, and by mobilization of nationalist sentiment for competition against other whites. The industrial expansion of South Africa is, however, such as to impose upon the Government some 'positive' aspects of apartheid, in the sense of a measure of responsible work for non-whites in public service and industry. There are not enough whites to go around, nor can they all be used in skilled occupations, even with free technical education and lowered standards.

Reinforcing the 'positive' aspects of apartheid is the survival of democratic sentiment among the Afrikaner Nationalists themselves. Apartheid is represented as just, designed in the interests of the non-whites to protect them from exploitation by the whites. The indoctrination of consenting attitudes in the

African population by means of the Bantu Education Act is linked with educational reform. So, too, the removal of non-whites from areas desired by the whites in the Western Areas of Johannesburg was coupled with slum clearance. It is only rarely, as in the reservation of separate amenities, that the Government deliberately demolishes the façade of justice.

Thus sensitivity to the democratic criticism of apartheid, heightened by the survival of democratic sentiments, has the effect of elevating propaganda about the 'positive' aspects of apartheid to the level of a principle, while the industrial expansion of South Africa provides opportunities for demonstrating the practicable applications of this principle, meagre though they are. To the extent that criticism forces the Government to emphasize the 'positive' aspects, the principle becomes more firmly established, and mitigates the exclusiveness of apartheid. Non-whites are people, though far removed from *the* people, and they have some human rights, though largely to what is left over.

The need for white solidarity further mitigates the exclusiveness of apartheid. Anti-Semitism, as a means to power along Nazis lines, is now latent, perhaps abandoned. Instead, the Nationalist Party extends the benefits of apartheid to the English and Jewish populations, which respond increasingly by assimilating the theories with the benefits. Issues which might divide the whites, such as the Republican issue, are played with caution, and the main political leaders, Government and opposition, call for white solidarity.

The counterpart of white solidarity is the growing co-operation among non-whites, a consequence which is the very opposite of what the Government intends, but flows inevitably from a policy which draws a rigid line between white and non-white. On the other hand, there is the familiar phenomenon of the strength of the dominant group exposing the weaknesses of the subordinates. The frustrations of the struggle against apartheid turn inward along the natural lines of cleavage, while the success of apartheid attracts imitation.

This is less marked among the Indians, who have faced insecurity for many years. There is a history of political dissension in the Indian community, and the present disagreements, mainly on the issue of negotiation with the Government, are not a new phenomenon. The recent revival, however, of interest in vernacular and religious teaching, and in cultural traditions, especially among the Tamil and the Telegu, was no doubt stimulated by the independence of India and by social movements within India. It coincides, however, with the establishment of apartheid as official policy, and may indicate a measure of withdrawal from the South African society under a government for whom the non-assimilability of the Indian is dogma. In any event, there is the potentiality of increasing division within the Indian community, even though all Indian organizations are aware of this and plead for integration.

Among the Africans, the possibility of administrative and other rewards under apartheid introduces a bitter cleavage between the political leaders who favour the boycott and those who wish to work with the Government. The use of tribal and linguistic divisions as a basis for community, school and residential policies may accentuate tribal divisions, more particularly since the support of many chiefs is assured by the illusion of an enhanced authority. The success of Afrikaner Nationalism provides a stimulus for exclusive African Nationalism modelled on apartheid, and expressed in anti-Indian sentiment. There is nothing to choose between the demands of an African trading class for the removal of Indian traders from their areas, and the proposals of European town councils for race zones, which banish Indian traders from the town. Both are techniques for the acquisition of Indian businesses without payment of good-will.

Against this background of actual and potential division within and between the non-white groups, which is the necessary foundation for continued white domination, the passive resistance movement assumes added significance. It spread an ethic of racial tolerance among the non-whites, and an understanding of the political technique of group tension. It strengthened the Congresses and established a method of interracial co-operation. Close bonds were forged between resisters of different races by the shared experience of voluntary suffering and exposure to Government retaliation, while the technique of non-violence provided a discipline based on broad humanitarian principles.

The emphasis on non-violence and interracial co-operation in the present struggle reflects the continuing influence of the passive resistance movement. It provides a link between white and non-white, a narrow bridge, battered on one side by Afrikaner Nationalism and on the other by African Nationalism.

APPENDICES

APPENDIX A

The Prime Minister's Letter to Rev. John Piersma and the Letter sent to the Prime Minister by the S.A. Institute of Race Relations in reply to his Letter to Rev. John Piersma

In a letter dated December 15th, 1953, the Rev. John H. Piersma, of Grand Rapids, U.S.A., asked Dr D. F. Malan, then Prime Minister of the Union of South Africa, for 'a frank description of apartheid' which could be used 'to convince the American public'. Dr Malan replied on February 12th, 1954, and on April 21st, 1954, the South African Institute of Race Relations sent a reply to him. These two letters are printed below.

OFFICE OF THE PRIME MINISTER,
CAPE TOWN.
12 February, 1954.

Reverend John Piersma,
Oakdale Park Christian Reformed Church,
1313 E. Butler Avenue, S.E.,
Grand Rapids 7,
Michigan, U.S.A.

DEAR SIR, – It was indeed heartening to receive a letter such as yours of the 15th December, asking me for a statement on the much disputed and misunderstood Apartheid policy of the South African Government. Such a request is almost unique in an imperfect world which claims the right to judge others by standards of perfection without prior knowledge of the circumstances which have in the course of centuries contributed to the creation of particular problems.

It must be appreciated from the outset that Apartheid, separation, segregation or differentiation – whatever the name given the traditional racial policy of South Africa – is part and parcel of the South African tradition as practised since the first Dutch settlement at the Cape in 1652, and still supported by the large majority of white South Africans of the main political parties.

The deep-rooted colour consciousness of the White South Africans – a phenomenon quite beyond the comprehension of the uninformed – arises from the fundamental difference between the two groups, White and Black. The difference in colour is merely the physical manifestation of the contrast between two irreconcilable ways of life, between barbarism and civilization, between heathenism and Christianity, and finally between overwhelming numerical odds on the one hand and insignificant numbers on the other. Such it was in the early beginnings and such it largely remains. The racial differences are as pronounced to-day as they were 300 years ago. Small wonder that the instinct of self-preservation is so inherent in the White South African. He has retained his identity all these years. He is not willing to surrender it now.

From the outset the European colonists were far out-numbered; there is no doubt that if they had succumbed to the temptation of assimilation, they would have been submerged in the Black heathendom of Africa as effectively as if they had been completely annihilated. Of necessity they had to arm and protect themselves against this evergrowing menace, and how could it better be done than by throwing an impenetrable armour around themselves – the armour of racial purity and self-preservation?

As Lord Balfour stated on a famous occasion: 'In South Africa a White nation has established itself in a Black continent, which is something that has never before presented itself in the history of mankind.' He might have added that there is no parallel for the South African racial record of non-extermination, non-miscegenation, non-assimilation, but of preaching and practising Christianity with the retention of racial identity and of mutual respect.

This then is the basis of Apartheid. But let me point out that there is another and more positive aspect of this creed.

Essentially a positive and non-repressive policy as applied in our enlightened day, Apartheid is based on what the Afrikaner believes to be his divine calling and his privilege – to convert the heathen to Christianity without obliterating his national identity. And as you have addressed me in the first place as a Christian and a churchman, let me at the outset summarize for your consideration the point of view of the Dutch Reformed Church with which the other Afrikaans churches are fundamentally in agreement.

A considered statement on behalf of the leaders of the Dutch Reformed Church, much the largest church in South Africa, with whose doctrine your own Christian Reformed Church is in main agreement, was issued a few months ago on the occasion of an interdenominational conference called by the Missionary Council of the Dutch Reformed Church. The principles therein enunciated fairly reflect the basis upon which the Afrikaans Churches have, ever since their establishment, approached South Africa's complex, multi-racial problem. With due regard to their historical background, I may summarize these principles as follows:

1. Missionary work has been practised in this country from the early beginnings as being the Christian duty of the settlers to the heathen. Only afterwards were the principles formulated which govern the racial policy of the State and of the established Churches here.

2. The Church believes that God in His Wisdom so disposed it that the first White men and women who settled at the foot of the Black continent were profoundly religious people, imbued with a very real zeal to bring the light of the Gospel to the

heathen nations of Africa. These first South Africans lit a torch which was carried to the farthest corners of the sub-continent in the course of the last three centuries and whose light now shines upon the greater part of all non-White peoples south of the Equator.

3. Whilst the Church regards the conversion of the heathen as a primary step in his march to civilization it is prepared to face and, in fact, to implement the implications of christianizing the heathen. Not only has it been busily employed all these many years in establishing mission congregations throughout the length and breadth of the country and far beyond its confines, it has also established separate Churches for the various non-White groups, all of which are fast approaching the stage of complete autonomy.

4. In the early beginnings the Church used the blessings of civilization as a means to attract the heathen, but to-day the traditional concept of European guardianship has taken the form of fostering and financing to the full the social, educational and economic development of the non-White. And whilst believing that God helps him who helps himself and, therefore, encouraging and assisting the non-European also to exert himself in this general movement of uplift and enlightenment, the Church has at all times vouchsafed the various Black races the right and duty to retain their national identities. Christianity must not rob the non-White of his language and culture. Its function is to permeate and penetrate to the depths of his nationalism, whilst encouraging him to retain and refine those national customs and traditions which do not clash with the Christian tenets.

5. The traditional fear of the Afrikaner of racial equality (equalitarianism) between White and Black derives from his aversion to miscegenation. The Afrikaner has always believed very firmly that if he is to be true to his primary calling of bringing Christianity to the heathen, he must preserve his racial identity intact. The Church is, therefore, entirely opposed to intermarriage between Black and White and is committed to

withstand everything that is calculated to facilitate it. At the same time it does not begrudge the non-White the attainments of a social status commensurate with his highest aspirations. Whereas the Church, therefore, opposes the social equalitarianism which ignores racial and colour differences between White and Black in everyday life, it is prepared to do all in its power to implement a social and cultural segregation which will rebound to the benefit of both sections.

6. But the duty of the Church has its bounds. It is wrong to expect the Church to enunciate a racial policy for the peoples of South Africa. It is not for the Church to define what the mutual relationships of races and racial groups should be politically. True, the Church is the guardian of the truth, the protector of the down-trodden, the keeper of the nation's conscience and the denunciator of evil practices, but there its duty ends. To Caesar must be rendered the things that are Caesar's.

7. The Bible is accepted as being the Word of God and the Dutch Reformed Church accepts the authority of Holy Writ as normative for all the political, social, cultural and religious activities in which man indulges. The Church acknowledges the basic rights of the State as a particular divine institution to regulate the lives and actions of its citizens.

Passing then from the historical and spiritual basis of apartheid to its everyday political application as practised by the present South African Government, let me remind you that government is the art of the possible. It makes no sense, therefore, to criticize the policy of apartheid in the abstract and without due regard to facts and conditions as they exist and as they have been allowed to develop through the centuries. And may I emphasize that to consider only the rights of the Blacks would be precisely as immoral as to have regard only for the rights of the Whites.

I must ask you to give White South Africans credit for not being a nation of scheming reactionaries imbued with base and inhuman motives, nor a nation of fools, blind to the gravity of their vital problem. They are normal human beings. They are a small nation, grappling with one of the most difficult problems in the world. To them millions of semi-barbarous Blacks look for guidance, justice and the Christian way of life.

Here a tremendous experiment is being tried; not that fraught with the bloodshed of annihilation, nor that coloured by assimilation, but that inspired by a belief in the logical differentiation, with the acceptance of the basic human rights and responsibilities. Human rights and responsibilities can, however, only be exercised by human beings who are capable of appreciating their significance and it is here that my Government, dealing as it does with a still primitive non-White population, is faced with a major educational problem. In order that you should realize how serious is our appreciation of this problem, let me give you some idea of the progress made since the National Party Government came into power just over five years ago.

Since 1947-8 the Government has increased its expenditure on non-White education from £3,665,600 to an estimated £8,190,000 for the financial year 1953-4. To-day nearly 800,000 Bantu children are given their schooling free of charge, whereas many more attend technical and industrial schools and an ever-increasing number are being fitted at universities, hospitals and training establishments for the profession of doctors, nurses, policemen, clerks, demonstrators, artisans and builders.

In all nearly £14,000,000 is spent annually on the education of non-Whites in South Africa, of which the lion's share is provided by White South African taxpayers. It is computed that every European taxpayer in our country 'carries' more than four non-Whites in order to provide the latter with the essential services involving education, hospitalization, housing, etc.

For, apart from education, much is done for the physical rehabilitation of the Bantu in his own reserves – in many cases the best agricultural land available in our comparatively poor country. So an amount of £3,500,000 was set aside during the past financial year for betterment works in these areas, where more than 200,000 acres of land have already been reclaimed from the ravishing soil erosion to which it had been exposed as a result of the ignorance of the Black peoples. More than 1,000 storage dams have been built here, 2,000 bore-holes sunk, 7,700 miles of fencing erected and 10,000 miles of roads built. In all these areas irrigation schemes are being undertaken and every effort made, including the improvement of stocks by the introduction of quality bulls (already 2,000 in number), to teach a primitive people the rudiments of sound agricultural practice.

In the field of human rehabilitation an even more ambitious project is being tackled. Disability grants and old-age pensions are available to the Bantu in the same way as to the Whites. Almost £2,000,000 was made available to the Bantu for old-age pensions this past year, whereas many public bodies have exercised themselves to meet the many needs of the non-Whites in regard to the disabilities to which they are heir.

The housing of the non-White population is one of the most urgent and complex problems the various authorities have had to face in our country, suddenly confronted with considerable industrial expansion. My Government has employed its limited resources to the full in order to meet the emergency created in this field by the quadrupling of our industrial production since the war. In this way £18½ millions have been granted by way of loans for Bantu housing since 1945 and 40,000 sub-economic houses have been erected for Bantu workers since 1935.

The more than a million Coloured people (people of mixed race) in our country are another tremendous responsibility to the Government and a constant drain on the country's exchequer, filled almost entirely by the White taxpayer. A Coloured man may follow any trade or profession he desires. We have Coloured lawyers, doctors, teachers, merchants, journalists, artisans, etc.

Nor does most of our industrial legislation make any distinction on the grounds of colour. Workers of all races enjoy the same protection under our factory and labour legislation; and

Wage Boards, in determining wages, are forbidden by law to discriminate on the grounds of race.

Furthermore the non-Whites of South Africa have full access to all health services. These services have done much to improve their general health. In all major centres well-equipped clinics, with properly trained nurses and doctors in attendance, cater for their needs. In addition they normally receive free hospital treatment.

Allegations that the country's non-Whites are not accorded political rights are untrue. In the urban areas, Advisory Boards whose members are elected by the residents of Black urban residential areas, provide an adequate mouthpiece, whilst tribal authorities are now being established in terms of the Bantu Authorities Act in the rural areas. Through this means the Bantu are given the opportunity to play an active part in the administration of their own affairs and, as they develop, more responsibilities and duties, as well as privileges, are granted them until they are proved to be competent to govern themselves.

Local, District and General Councils are firmly established in the Transkei and Ciskei. These Councils play a major part in the administration of the Reserves, at the same time offering the Bantu ample opportunity for self-government, self-expression and increasing development. In addition the Bantu are represented in both Houses of Parliament by White representatives, elected by themselves and given very specific charges.

Contrary to popular belief abroad, the Whites and Blacks are practically contemporary settlers in South Africa, the former migrating from Europe, the latter fleeing from the terror of Central African internecine wars of extermination.

It is only fifty years since South Africa, until then a poor country, has, through the discovery of its vast mineral resources, emerged from its pastoral era. Half a century of intense development has brought about the upliftment also of the Bantu far beyond that reached by him in any other country on the sub-continent. The result has been a large-scale, illegal migration of Black peoples from the northern territories beyond our borders to South Africa with an ever-increasing aggravation of our non-White problems.

Small wonder that despite the efforts of authorities, central and local, to uplift the Black population, an immense task still awaits them. The recent, unparalleled industrial development of our cities has laid too great a burden on our municipal government, with resultant deplorable slum conditions. And marching with housing, educational demands for the non-Whites, of whom a larger percentage are provided with free education than anywhere else in Africa, or for that matter in most Asiatic countries, including India and Pakistan, have become a real burden on the White taxpayer.

But, however heavy the burden, White South Africa is committed to a policy of Bantu development, in keeping with the positive tenets of apartheid, which I would summarize as follows:

1. Energetically to develop the Bantu reserves, both agriculturally and industrially. In industries within the reserves Bantu are to be trained eventually to fill all positions. At the moment a Commission is investigating methods to foster this industrial development.

2. Gradually to extend the powers and functions of local government within the reserves, either through the local councils where these exist, or by adapting and modernizing the traditional Bantu form of government by chief and counsellors.

3. Gradually to replace the White officials, professional men, traders, etc. within the reserves by Bantu.

Theoretically the object of the policy of Apartheid could be fully achieved by dividing the country into two states, with all the Whites in one, all the Blacks in the other. For the foreseeable future, however, this is simply not practical politics. Whether in time to come we shall reach a stage where some such division, say on a federal basis, will be possible, is a matter we must leave to the future.

In any case, the full implementation of the policy of separate racial development will take very many years. Call it an experiment, if you like, and one could say it is an experiment which is as yet only in its initial stages. Many aspects of the problem are certainly still far from clear, and it would be unwise, even if it were possible, to draw up a blue-print for 50 years ahead. In more than one respect progress will have to be by trial and error. And if in this process we should err, I ask you and your countrymen not to judge our efforts only by our incidental failures nor to reproach us for what you may at this great distance judge as being lack of the spirit of Christ.

Yours sincerely,

(*Sgd.*) D. F. MALAN.

The Letter sent to the Prime Minister by the S.A. Institute of Race Relations in reply to his Letter to Rev. John Piersma

21st April, 1954.

The Honourable the Prime Minister,
House of Assembly,
Cape Town.

DEAR DR MALAN, – Like you we were heartened to learn that an American clergyman had asked you to interpret the apartheid policy of the present South African Government. We felt that your decision to do so would help to clarify the complicated issues of our racial situation, and we greatly appreciated that as Prime Minister of South Africa you had undertaken this important task.

We have read your published letter to the Reverend John Piersma with the greatest care, and appreciate the sincerity with which it was written. But we feel obliged, as an Institute whose work for many years has been to study the facts of race relations, to state certain points of disagreement.

You state at the outset that a 'fundamental difference' exists between Black and White and that 'the difference in colour is merely the physical manifestation of the contrast between two irreconcilable ways of life, between barbarism and civilization and between heathenism and Christianity'. Yet you refer, rightly, to the great work of the Afrikaner (in which he was not alone) in following 'his divine calling and his privilege – to convert the heathen to Christianity'. We must submit that the missionary who seeks to convert the heathen denies, in so doing, that differences are 'fundamental' and 'irreconcilable', for his action rests on the belief that man can be and often is fundamentally changed. We hold, with the missionary, that the barbarian and heathen does by conversion and faith aided by education, environment and example become, in fact, a 'new man'. If this were not true those South Africans who, as you say, 'lit a torch which was carried to the farthest corners of the sub-continent' lit the torch in vain: for, according to your view, the fully qualified African doctor remains fundamentally a barbarian and the African Minister of a Christian Church is still a heathen.

Your initial statement, therefore, contradicts your affirmation of the historic mission of the Afrikaner to 'preach and practise Christianity' among the Natives. You continue to equate 'Black' with 'barbarism', and to deny the possibility of changing the Native in any 'fundamental' sense, even through the agency of Christianity. The whole history of the Western world, which is one of progress from tribal barbarism to civilization and from heathenism to Christianity, is evidence against this contention.

The identification of skin colour with permanent cultural difference is not valid scientifically. Race and culture cannot be equated; and Christianity – provided that it is not allied with a political philosophy of 'cultural segregation' – is one of the most powerful solvents of primitive or backward cultures. We must for all these reasons reject your view that the differences between different ethnic groups are unchangeable. For this is the implication of your statement.

This basic premise of yours seems to us to underlie your whole concept of 'separate development', and of the consequent duty of the Church to help preserve 'intact' what you call the 'national identity' of the black group. Such national identity, in so far as it is defined, would seem, according to your theory, to rest on tribal – and therefore primitive – foundations, with social and economic rights pegged permanently at a lower level than those of the Europeans. To that extent the theory is already an anachronism: vast numbers of Africans, permanently settled in the towns, are no longer tribal in their habits and outlook; among them a growing proportion have already assimilated – wholly or partially – Western culture. But such persons do not desire to be RACIALLY assimilated. Their sense of separate race identity is as strong as the Europeans', and there is no reason to assume, therefore, that cultural and economic advancement will lead to miscegenation and inter-marriage. We remark in passing that your statement that miscegenation did not take place in South Africa is refuted by your later reference to 'a million coloured people (people of mixed race) in our country'. Miscegenation did take place; but it was checked early in our history, and the strong public opinion that exists to-day, in both groups, against race-inter-mixture, is an effective safeguard for the preservation of race purity.

You say that apartheid furthers 'basic human rights', and 'does not begrudge the non-White the attainment of a social status commensurate with his highest aspirations'. Nowhere in the present political and economic structure of South Africa are possibilities of such attainment to be discovered. We would instance as direct contradictions of basic rights the restrictions on freedom of movement and of the right to seek work; the Separate Amenities Act which legalizes separate but UNEQUAL facilities; the refusal of the right to freehold title in urban areas. These restrictions, be it noted, apply to all Natives, however developed. Nowhere, moreover, in your Government's policies is any relaxation of such restrictions envisaged in the areas where the ferments of civilization are most rapidly at work. The trend is towards further curtailment: the only concessions promised are in the reserves, and that these must be very limited is substantiated by your own denial of the feasibility of territorial apartheid 'within the foreseeable future'. Sixty per cent. of the Native population live outside the reserves and you give this majority group no hope of basic human rights. We are, therefore, driven to the conclusion that the only interpretation possible of the phrase 'basic human rights' compatible with the policy of apartheid is one which would assign inferior human rights to the black group because it is black.

In your analysis of 'the everyday political application' of apartheid, we find a number of statements which may seriously mislead persons not fully acquainted with the South African situation. You state, for instance, that 'the Bantu are represented in both Houses of Parliament by White representatives'. You omit to state, however, that $8\frac{1}{2}$ million people are represented by 4 out of 44 Senators and 3 out of 159 Members of the House of Assembly. The latter three are returned only for the Cape; and members of your Party have repeatedly threatened to abolish this representation. Nor could we agree that Advisory Boards in the locations constitute an 'adequate mouthpiece' or that Natives in the reserves enjoy 'ample opportunity for self-government'.

You deny that 'most of our industrial legislation makes any distinction on the grounds of colour'. We cite the statutory colour bar on the gold mines imposed in terms of the Mines and Works Amendment Act; the Industrial Conciliation Act which excludes pass-bearing Natives from its definition of 'employee'; and your own Government's Native Labour (Settlement of Disputes) Act, which sets up separate conciliation machinery for Natives, prevents direct collective bargaining between Native employees and European employers, denies official recognition to Native trade unions and prohibits strikes by Natives.

In regard to education, we welcome the progress made and the increase in expenditure and enrolment. But the 800,000 Native children you cite are still only 41 per cent. of Native children of school-going age. The expenditure per head was £7·58 for Natives and £43·88 for Europeans in 1951-2 (later figures are not available). The total expenditure on European education was £21,858,316 in that year. This year, of the £8½ million voted for Native education £2 million will come directly from Native taxation and £6½ million from general revenue. The Minister of Finance announced in the budget speech last month that the State's financial contribution to Native education would be pegged at this amount and that future expansion would be directly chargeable to the Natives themselves. It is clear that the past rate of progress for which you take credit in your statement will not be maintained without additional expenditure far beyond what the African can bear at his present rates of pay.

You claim, nevertheless, that the Europeans finance 'to the full the social, educational and economic development of the non-White'. You argue that 'every European taxpayer in our country "carries" more than four non-Whites' and that not only the Natives, but the million Coloured people are a 'constant drain on the country's exchequer'. There is, however, another side to this. As 82% of the country's labour force is non-White, it could be said that, as far as work is concerned, every White is dependent on four non-Whites. You ignore the immense contribution of the non-White to the exchequer, through direct and indirect taxation. It has, for example, been estimated that over 20,000 Natives are income-tax payers. You appear to deny, in respect of non-Whites, the validity of the universally accepted principles of public finance that the most prosperous sections of the community should make the larger contribution to the public purse and 'carry' the poorer sections.

This, in fact, is the basis of the grants and pensions introduced by the previous Government, the existence of which is an evident cause of satisfaction to you. For you refer to the 'ambitious project' being tackled in the field of human re-habilitation. We feel compelled, however, to point out that although 'disability grants and old-age pensions are available to the Bantu in the same way as to the Whites', there is a vast difference in rates. The average amounts paid out last year on old-age pensions were £99 for Europeans, £37 for Coloured, £36 for Asiatics and £10 for Africans: average blind pensions were £100 for Europeans and £11 for Africans; disability grants, £84 and £10. These are only some examples of the wide disparity in social services. Furthermore, your Government abolished family allowances for Asiatics, and excluded Natives whose earnings are less than £182 per annum from the Unemployment Insurance Act. It reduced the Native school-feeding grant from £870,000 in 1948-49 to £628,000 in 1954-55, in spite of the fact that an inter-departmental committee appointed by your former Minister of Health and Social Welfare in 1948 to investigate the scheme reported that the minimum required for its efficient working was £1,200,000.

Another questionable statement is that 'a Coloured man may follow any trade or profession he desires'. We wish to point out that the Cape Coloured people meet increasing difficulty in obtaining skilled work in the printing industry and in the rapidly expanding engineering industry, and that in many other industries it is extremely difficult, if not impossible, for a Cape Coloured youth to become apprenticed.

While we appreciate the efforts that are being made to improve health services, we consider that it is misleading to state that 'the non-Whites of South Africa have full access to all health services'. We would only remind you of the tragically inadequate facilities for dealing with the estimated number of 70,000 non-White tuberculotics, of whom roughly 15,000 die each year. Admittedly, voluntary organizations, assisted by Government subsidies, are making strenuous efforts to provide settlements to which active T.B. cases may be sent, but mean-while active tuberculotics, due to lack of accommodation, have to be discharged from hospitals to their homes, there to spread the infection. There is no provision at all for the institutional care of non-European mentally defective children or any non-European epileptics. We would also point out that it has been estimated that of the total number of medical practitioners in South Africa, fifty per cent. are engaged in looking after the ten per cent. of the population in the upper income group, forty-five per cent. in looking after twenty per cent. of the middle income group, and only five per cent. in looking after seventy per cent. of the population in the lower income group, which consists overwhelmingly of non-Whites.

We assure you that we are deeply conscious of the difficulties that confront this country. We agree with you that 'government is the art of the possible'. We are not visionary 'perfectionists' who believe that satisfactory living conditions can be provided for the mere asking. On the contrary, we have consistently emphasized the interdependence of productivity and standard of living and have repeatedly urged the need to utilize our resources in manpower and its potential skills more effectively. What we regret in your statement is that it breathes an air of complacency, that its factual statements are unrelated to the total situation, that it, above all, gives no grounds for hope to the millions of non-Whites who are not in a Native reserve. Your statement gives the impression that the non-Whites of South Africa should be happy and contented; it fails to recognize the large number that have emerged from barbarism and heathenism and have earned a place in our society as civilized persons. Most unhappily it shows no understanding of the hopelessness and bitterness in the hearts of many of our people or of the mounting racial tensions that threaten the peace of our country.

Yours sincerely,
(*sgd.*) QUINTIN WHYTE, *Director.*
(*sgd.*) ELLEN HELLMANN, *President.*

[Reprinted by permission of the South African Institute of Race Relations.]

APPENDIX B

African National Congress,
2-3 New Court Chambers,
44 Commissioner Street,
JOHANNESBURG.

The Prime Minister of the Union of South Africa,
Parliament,
Capetown.

SIR, – In terms of the resolution adopted by the 39th session of the African National Congress held at Bloemfontein we have been instructed to address you as follows: The African National Congress was established in 1912 to protect and advance the interests of the African people in all matters affecting them, and to attain their freedom from all discriminatory laws whatsoever. To this end, the African National Congress has, since its establishment, endeavoured by every constitutional method to bring to the notice of the Government the legitimate demands of the African people and has repeatedly pressed, in particular, their inherent right to be directly represented in Parliament, Provincial and the Municipal Councils and in all Councils of State. This attitude was a demonstration not only of the willingness and readiness of the African people to co-operate with the Government but also evidence of their sincere desire for peace, harmony and friendship amongst all sections of our population. As is well known, the Government through its repressive policy of trusteeship, segregation and apartheid, and through legislation that continues to insult and degrade the African people by depriving them of fundamental human rights enjoyed in all democratic communities, have categorically rejected our offer of co-operation. The consequence has been the gradual worsening of the social, economic and political position of the African people and a rising tide of racial bitterness and tension. The position has been aggravated in recent times by the Pass Laws, Stock Limitation, the Suppression of Communism Act of 1950, the Group Areas Act of 1950, the Bantu Authorities Act of 1951 and the Voters Act of 1951. The cumulative effect of this legislation is to crush the National Organizations of the oppressed people; to destroy the economic position of the people and to create a reservoir of cheap labour for the farms and the gold mines; to prevent the unity and development of the African people towards full nationhood and to humiliate them in a host of other manners. The African National Congress as the National Organization of the African people cannot remain quiet on an issue that is a matter of life and death to the people; to do so would be a betrayal of the trust and confidence placed upon it by the African people. At the recent annual conference of the African National Congress held in Bloemfontein from 15th to 17th December, 1951, the whole policy of the Government was reviewed, and, after serious and careful consideration of the matter, conference unanimously resolved to call upon your Government, as we hereby do, to repeal the aforementioned Acts by NOT LATER THAN THE 29TH DAY OF FEBRUARY, 1952, failing which the African National Congress will hold protest demonstrations and meetings on the 6th day of April, 1952, as a prelude to the implementation of the plan for the defiance of unjust laws. In the light of the Conference resolution we also considered the statement made by the Prime Minister at Ohrigstad on the 5th instant, in which he appealed to all sections of our population, irrespective of colour and creed, to participate fully in the forthcoming Jan Van Riebeeck cele-brations. It is considered opinion that the African people cannot participate in any shape or form in such celebrations, unless the aforementioned Acts which constitute an insult and humiliation to them are removed from the Statute Book. We firmly believe that the freedom of the African people, the elimination of the exploitation of man by man and the restitution of democracy, liberty and harmony in South Africa are such vital and fundamental matters that the Government and the Public must know that we are fully resolved to achieve them in our lifetime. The struggle which our people are about to begin is not directed against any race or national group but against the unjust laws which keep in perpetual subjection and misery vast sections of the population. In this connection, it is a source of supreme satisfaction to us to know that we have the full support and sympathy of enlightened and honest men and women, black and white, in our country and across the seas and that the present tension and crises have been brought about not by the African leaders but by the Government themselves. We are instructed to point out that we have taken this decision in full appreciation of the consequences it entails and we must emphasize that whatever reaction is provoked from certain circles in this country, posterity will judge that this action we are about to begin was in the interest of all in our country and will inspire our people for long ages to come. We decide to place on record that, for our part, we have endeavoured over the last 40 years to bring about conditions for genuine progress and true democracy.

Yours faithfully,
Dr J. S. MOROKA (*President-General*).
W. M. SISULU (*Secretary-General*).

(*From the Office of the Prime Minister.*)

CAPETOWN.
29th January, 1952.

DEAR SIR, – I am directed to acknowledge the receipt of your undated letter addressed to the Prime Minister and to reply as follows: It is noted that your submission is framed in terms of a resolution adopted at its recent session in Bloemfontein of the

African National Congress. Resolutions adopted by the African National Congress at its annual meetings were, in the past, sent to and dealt with by the Minister of Native Affairs and his Department. On this occasion, however, there has been a definite departure from the traditional procedure in as much as you have addressed yourself directly to the Prime Minister in order to present him with an ultimatum. This new approach is probably accounted for by the recent rift or purge in Congress circles, after which it is doubtful whether you can claim to speak authoritatively on behalf of the body known to the Government as the African National Congress. The Prime Minister is, however, prepared to waive this point and to reply to various points raised by you and also to your ultimatum as he feels that the Government's attitude in the matter should be clearly stated. The first point which stands out clearly in your letter is that your organization maintains that since 1912, although no government in the past has even been able to consider this, the objective has been the abolition of all differentiating laws. It now demands such abolition as well as consequential direct representation in Parliament, provincial and municipal councils in all provinces, and in all councils of State as an inherent right. You will realize, I think, that it is self-contradictory to claim as an inherent right of the Bantu, who differ in many ways from the Europeans, that they should be regarded as not different, especially when it is borne in mind that these differences are permanent and not man-made. If this is a matter of indifference to you and if you do not value your racial characteristics, you cannot in any case dispute the Europeans' right, which in this case is definitely an inherent right, to take the opposite view and to adopt the necessary measures to preserve their identity as a separate community. It should be understood clearly that the Government will under no circumstances entertain the idea of giving administrative or executive or legislative powers over Europeans, or within an European community, to Bantu men and women, or to other smaller non-European groups. The Government, therefore, has no intention of repealing the long existing laws differentiating between European and Bantu. You demand that the Union should no longer remain a State controlled by the Europeans who developed it to the advantage of all groups of the population. You demand that it should be placed under the jurisdiction of the Bantu, Indian and other non-European groups together with the Europeans without any distinction whatsoever, and with no restriction on the possible gradual development of a completely mixed community. Nevertheless, you apparently wish to create the impression that such demands should be regarded as a generous gesture of goodwill towards the European community of this country. It is quite clear that the very opposite is true. This is not a genuine offer of co-operation, but an attempt to embark on the first steps towards supplanting European rule in the course of time. Racial harmony cannot be attained in this manner. Compliance with such demands must inevitably lead to disaster for all population groups. Not only temporary racial tension, due to misunderstanding, but worse would follow and the Bantu would suffer first and most. For instance, if the latter were to be exposed to full competition, without their present protection, they would soon lose the land now safeguarded and being increased for them. The masses would suffer misery indeed, if they lost the many privileges which the Union of South Africa – in contrast to other countries – provides for them. They would pay the price in order to satisfy the political ambitions of the few who are prepared to tear loose from the background of their own nation. The road to peace and goodwill lies in the acceptance of the fact that separate population groups exist, and in giving each group the opportunity of developing its ambitions and capacities, in its own areas, or within its own community, on its own lines, in the service of its own people. Your third point is that the differentiating laws are of an oppressive and degrading nature. This again is a totally incorrect statement. The laws are largely of a protective nature. Even those laws which are regarded as particularly irksome by the Bantu people have not been made in order to persecute them, but for the purpose of training them in the performance of those duties which must be fully observed by all who wish to claim rights. The fact that you refer to a betterment law (stock limitation) as being one of the oppressive laws is a clear indication of your failure to understand that the function of such laws is to protect the interests and the land of the Bantu community, both present and in future. It is even more significant that you should condemn the Bantu Authorities Act, which was designed to give the Bantu people the opportunity for enlightened administration of their own affairs in accordance with their own heritage and institutions, adapted to modern conditions. It should be clearly understood that while the Government is not prepared to grant the Bantu political equality within the European community, it is only too willing to encourage the Bantu initiative, Bantu services, and Bantu administration within the Bantu community, and there to allow the Bantu people full scope for all his potentialities. I must, now, refer to your ultimatum. Notwithstanding your statement that your Congress has taken the decision to present its ultimatum to the Government in full appreciation of the consequences it entails, the Prime Minister wishes to call your attention to the extreme gravity of pursuing the course indicated by you. In the interests of the Bantu he advises you to re-consider your decision. Should you adhere to your expressed intention of embarking on a campaign of defiance and disobedience to the Government, and should you, in the implementation thereof, incite the Bantu population to defy law and order, the Government will make full use of the machinery at its disposal to quell any disturbances, and, thereafter, deal adequately with those responsible for initiating subversive activities of any nature whatsoever. The Prime Minister has instructed me to urge you to let wiser counsels prevail, and to devote your energies to constructive programmes of development for the Bantu people. This can be done by using the opportunities offered by the Government for building up local Bantu government and administration within all spheres of Bantu life. This could be co-operation in the real sense of the word. Your organization could render a lasting service to the Bantu population of South Africa by helping the Government to carry out this programme of goodwill. The Prime Minister trusts that you will take these words to heart, and that you will decide to work for the welfare of your people in a constructive way.

Yours faithfully,
M. W. W. AUCAMP, *Private Secretary.*

AFRICAN NATIONAL CONGRESS.
11th February, 1952.

The Honourable the Prime Minister of the
     Union of South Africa,
Parliament,
Cape Town.

SIR, – We, the undersigned, have the honour to acknowledge receipt of your letter of the 29th January, 1952. The National Executive of the African National Congress, at a special conference convened for the purpose, has given careful consideration to the contents of your letter, and has instructed us to address you as follows. It is noted that exception is taken in your letter to the fact that the resolution adopted by the A.N.C. at its 1951 Conference was directed to the Prime Minister instead of the Minister of Native Affairs and his Department. The A.N.C. has at no time accepted the position that the Native Affairs Department is the channel of communication between the African people and the State. In any event the subject of our communication to you was not a Departmental matter, but one of such general importance and gravity affecting the fundamental principles of the policy practised by the Union Government, and its effect on the relations between Black and White, that it was considered appropriate to bring these matters directly to the notice of the Prime Minister. The suggestion that we were actuated by a so-called 'recent rift or purge in Congress circles' is without foundation and entirely beside the point as far as the substance of our case is concerned. In reply to our demand for the abolition of differentiating laws, it is suggested in your letter that there are 'permanent and not man-made' differences between Africans and Europeans which justify the maintenance of these laws. The question at issue is not one of biological differences, but one of citizenship rights which are granted in full measure to one section of the population and completely denied to the other by means of man-made laws artificially imposed, not to preserve the identity of Europeans as a separate community, but to perpetuate the systematic exploitation of the African people. The African people yield to no one as far as pride of race is concerned, and it is precisely for this reason that they are striving for the attainment of fundamental human rights in the land of their birth. It is observed that your Government rejects out of hand our claim for direct representation in Parliament and other Councils of State. This is the kernel of the policy of apartheid which is condemned not only by the African, Indian and Coloured people, but also by a large section of white South Africa. It is precisely because of this policy that South Africa is losing caste in international circles. Your letter suggests that the policy of your Government is motivated by a desire to protect the interests of the African people in various spheres of life, e.g. land rights, and unspecified privileges not enjoyed by them in other countries. The Reserve land policy has always been designed to protect the European rather than African land rights, and even within the so-called Reserves, Africans hold only occupancy privileges at the discretion of the Government, and these Reserves are notoriously congested and overcrowded, and the so-called rehabilitation scheme, in spite of the protestations of just intention with which it is camouflaged, has aggravated the misery of the people and rendered thousands destitute and homeless, and has exposed them to vexatious regimentation by Native Commissioners and petty Trust officials. In this connection we note that even the Native Laws Amendment Bill, which is now before Parliament, in spite of all its harsh and draconian provisions, has been described as a 'protective' measure. There can be no doubt that, like similar measures, passed hitherto, this Bill is intended to protect and advance the interests of Europeans and not those of Africans. It is these discriminatory laws that are preventing the African people from developing their ambitions and capacities, and along lines satisfactory to themselves. As far as the Bantu Authorities Act is concerned, it is clear that this Act is part of the policy to which we are opposed, namely that 'the Government is not prepared to grant the Africans political equality', and is not, as you suggest, 'designed to give the Africans the opportunity of enlightened administration of their own affairs'. Nothing contained in the Bantu Authorities Act can be a substitute for direct representation in the Councils of State. With reference to the campaign of mass action which the A.N.C. intends to launch, we would point out that, as a defenceless and voteless people, we have explored other channels without success. The African people are left with no alternative but to embark upon the campaign referred to above. We desire to state emphatically that it is our intention to conduct this campaign in a peaceful manner, and that any disturbances, if they should occur, will not be of our making. In reiterating our claim for direct representation, we desire to place on record our firm determination to redouble our efforts for the attainment of full citizenship rights. In conclusion we regret that the Prime Minister has seen fit to reject our genuine offer of co-operation on the basis of full equality, and express the hope that in the interests of all concerned the Government may yet reconsider its attitude.

Signed: DR J. S. MOROKA (*President General*), *and* W. M. SISULU (*Secretary-General*).

SOUTH AFRICAN INDIAN CONGRESS,
P.O. BOX 2948,
JOHANNESBURG.
20th February, 1952.

The Honourable the Prime Minister of the
   Union of South Africa,
House of Assembly,
Cape Town.

SIR, – We, the undersigned, in terms of the resolution adopted at the 20th Conference of the S.A. Indian Congress held at Johannesburg on the 25th, 26th and 27th January, 1952, are enjoined to address you as follows: The S.A. Indian Congress, as the representative organization and mouthpiece of the S.A. Indian Community, has at all times striven to protect and safeguard the interests of the Indian people against discriminatory legislation and to ensure their honourable and legitimate share in the development and progress of the land of their birth and adoption, in common with all sections of the population, both white and non-white. In spite of all its attempts, however, the position of the Indians, together with the rest of the non-European people, has been rendered intolerable by the discriminatory laws of the country. Indeed, their position had become so precarious by the passing of the Asiatic Land Tenure Act of 1946 that the South African Indian Congress had no alternative but to embark on a Passive Resistance struggle as a protest, and to request the Government of India to raise this question at the United Nations Assembly. It is to be noted that when a change of government took place as a result of the General Elections of 1948 and your Government assumed office, the Passive Resistance struggle was suspended and an approach was made to you in your capacity as the Prime Minister for a statement of government policy. This offer, as you may well recollect, was rejected and the Congress was informed through the Honourable the Minister of the Interior, Dr. Donges, that the Government was not prepared to grant the requested interview. This attitude was no doubt the outcome of the policy of your party as formulated in its Election Manifesto which laid the main stress on Apartheid which meant the compulsory segregation of all Non-European national groups into separate compartments or ghettoes, and which specifically stated: 'The Party holds the view that Indians are a foreign and outlandish element which is un-assimilable. They can never become part of the country and must therefore be treated as an immigrant community. The Party accepts as a basis of its policy the repatriation of as many Indians as possible and proposes a proper investigation into the practicability of such a policy on a large scale in co-operation with India and other countries.' The Group Areas Act, which the Prime Minister has claimed to be the 'kernel' of Apartheid, is a law which runs contrary to all the fundamental principles of democracy and of Human Rights. The enforcement of this Act will cause mass uprooting of the non-European people from areas and homes which they have acquired and built through the toil and sweat of many generations. The setting aside of Group Areas will mean to the non-European an end to all progress in every sphere of life. It will bring about economic retrogression and impoverishment with all its concomitant evils of crime and degradation. In so far as the Indian people are concerned, the Act is intended as a means of expelling them from this country, (vide the Joint Departmental Committee's report on which the Group Areas Act is based). It is to be noted that even at this early stage of its enforcement untold damage has been done to the interests of the people. Their material and economic progress is coming to a halt and immovable properties and homes running into hundreds of thousands of pounds are in the process of being confiscated by the State in terms of the Act. The Minister of the Interior is using dictatorial powers by serving notices on many companies to sell their properties within a specified time, failing which the listed properties would be liable to forced sale by the State. Not only are privately owned properties affected but religious and public institutions communally acquired for the welfare of the community have also been served with such notices. The Bantu Authorities Act is aimed at denying the African people their rightful role in the affairs of the country and rendering them ineffective as a political force. The purpose of the Act in granting controlled powers to the chiefs is to split up the African people into tribal groups which could be effectively brought under rigid State control. The purpose of the Suppression of Communism Act is to suppress the fundamental rights of the South African people to organize, to criticize, and to express by written or spoken word their opposition to any aspect of Government policy which they consider repugnant to them and anti-democratic. The way in which the arbitrary powers vested in the Minister of Justice have been used to attack the freedom of speech and of the press is already evident by the attempt to unseat a Member of Parliament and a Member of the Cape Provincial Council who were constitutionally elected to their offices, and by the Minister's threat to suppress the *Guardian* newspaper. It is apparent that this Act is intended to crush the activities of all democratic organizations and trade unions which are opposed to the Apartheid and anti-democratic policies of your Government. The Separate Representation of Voters Act is yet another Apartheid measure which is depriving the Coloured voters of whatever limited franchise rights and effectiveness they possessed. This brief summary of some of the main Apartheid measures placed on the Statute Book by your Government will suffice to show that Apartheid is primarily intended for the complete suppression of the non-European people so as to procure an unlimited supply of cheap labour. With this purpose in mind the Government is endeavouring to divide forcibly the population of our country into separate racial groups and tribes. The policy of Apartheid is anti-democratic, reactionary and contrary to the laws of natural development of history and can only be imposed by means of Fascist tyranny and unrestrained dictatorship. Indeed, not only have the non-European people become the victims of this policy but it has also encroached upon the rights and liberties of the European people as evidenced by State interference with the freedom of individuals to travel abroad, with the freedom of the right of parents regarding their children's education, with the freedom of the press and with the freedom of trade unions to conduct their own affairs. It is a fact of history that since your Government came into power it has attempted to impose its Apartheid policy with callous disregard for the feelings of the people and disastrous consequences to the country as a whole. Race relations have reached the most critical stage in our country's history. There has been unbridled incitement of race animosity and prejudice between the different population groups and unremitting race propaganda. There has been a steady increase in the use of violence and intimidation by the police and the occurrence of race riots hitherto unknown. There has been a constant tendency to place unlimited and arbitrary powers in the hands of the Ministers, powers which under the provisions of the various laws enacted by your Government are being used to crush the rights and liberties, particularly of the non-European people. There has been continuous impoverishment of the people, with a steep and steady rise in the cost of living, with the brutal enforcement of the Pass Laws, the forcible deprivation of the African peasants of their only wealth, their cattle, and the further enslavement of the urban African population through the Native Laws Amendment Bill. It was in this rapidly deteriorating situation that the Conference of the African National Congress resolved to adopt a plan of action to obtain the repeal of the Group Areas Act, the Bantu Authorities Act, the Suppression of Communism Act, the Separate Representation of Voters Act, the Pass Laws, and Regulations for the culling of cattle, as an immediate step to lessen the burden of oppression of the non-European people and to save our country from the catastrophe of national chaos and ever-widening conflicts. This plan of action was endorsed by the Conference of the S.A.

Indian Congress which met in Johannesburg on January 25th, 26th and 27th, 1952. In terms of this decision we have been instructed to convey to you the full support of the S.A. Indian Congress to the call made upon your Government by the African National Congress for the repeal of the above mentioned Acts, failing which the S.A. Indian Congress will participate with the African National Congress in holding protest meetings and demonstrations on the 6th day of April, 1952, as a prelude to the implementation of the Plan for the Defiance of Unjust Laws. It is with abiding faith and calm confidence in the truth and justice of our cause and firm conviction in democratic ideals and principles that we made this supporting call notwithstanding the contents of your reply to the letter of the African National Congress. We solemnly affirm that the Indian community of South Africa is South African and that it shall live and work for the progress and prosperity of the country on the principles of equality of rights and opportunities for all sections of our population, irrespective of race, sex, colour or creed, and that it shall continue its firm alliance with the national organizations of the non-European people and all democracy-loving Europeans in the struggle for a Free and Democratic South Africa. We unhesitatingly and emphatically state that our struggle is not directed against any national group, that we bear malice or ill will to none and that our struggle is solely against unjust laws. The Indian people in South Africa bear the proud inheritance of the precepts and example of Mahatma Gandhi, of devotion to the cause of righteousness and truth, of courage and determination in the prosecution of peaceful struggles against injustice and oppression. The non-European peoples cannot allow their own destruction by accepting Apartheid – it would be a crime against man. Our ideal is clear, our duty is defined, our efforts peaceful and our resolve not to succumb to the evils of Apartheid unfaltering. In this historic era of greater democracy and of independence of peoples' rights, both large and small, we in South Africa, too, are giving expression to the natural freedom urge and democratic rights of the people – for therein lies the true *Pad van Suid Afrika*. In the interest of Peace, Humanity and the future well-being of our country and of our peoples, we expect that unbiased justice will prevail and that laws which offend the dignity of Man and retard the progress of South Africa will be repealed.

> *Signed :* Y. M. Dadoo, *President.*
>
> D. U. Mistry ⎫
> Y. A. Cachalia ⎭ *Joint Honorary Secretaries.*

APPENDIX C

*Report of the Joint Planning Council of the African National Congress
and the South African Indian Congress*

To the President-General and Members of the Executive
Committee of the African National Congress and the President
and Councillors of the South African Indian Congress:
WHEREAS the African National Congress, at the meeting of its
National Executive, held on 17th June, 1951, decided to invite
all other National Executives of the National Organizations of
the non-European people of South Africa to a Conference to
place before them a programme of direct action; and WHEREAS
a Joint Conference of the National Executives of the African
National Congress and the South African Indian Congress and
the Representatives of the Franchise Action Council (Cape)
met at Johannesburg on the 29th July, 1951; and WHEREAS
it was resolved at the aforesaid Conference: (1) to declare war
on Pass Laws and Stock Limitation, the Group Areas Act, and
the Voters' Representation Act, the Suppression of Communism Act, and the Bantu Authorities Act; (2) to embark
upon an immediate mass campaign for the repeal of these
oppressive laws; and (3) to establish a Joint Planning Council
to co-ordinate the efforts of the National Organizations of the
African, Indian and Coloured people in this mass campaign:
NOW THEREFORE, the Joint Planning Council, as constituted
by the aforegoing resolution, have the honour to report to the
African National Congress and the South African Indian
Congress as follows:

1. We the undersigned, were constituted into a Joint
Planning Council in terms of the resolution adopted at the

Joint Conference of the executives of the African National Congress and the South African Indian Congress and the representatives of the Franchise Action Council of the Cape, held at Johannesburg on the 29th July, 1951. Dr J. S. Moroka, the President-General of the African National Congress, was elected as the Chairman and of the four remaining members of the Council, two each were nominated by the Executive Organs of the African National Congress and the South African Indian Congress.

2. We are, in terms of the resolution mentioned above, charged with the task of co-ordinating the efforts of the National Organizations of the African, Indian and the Coloured people in a mass campaign agreed upon at the Joint Conference for the repeal of the Pass Laws, the Group Areas Act, the Voters' Representation Act, the Suppression of Communism Act, the Bantu Authorities Act, and for the withdrawal of the policy of stock limitation and the so-called rehabilitation scheme.

3. Having given due and serious attention to the task before us, we have great pleasure in recommending the following plan of action to the African National Congress and the South African Indian Congress for consideration and decision at their forthcoming Annual Conference.

4. The African National Congress in Conference assembled at Bloemfontein on the 15th-17th December, 1951, should call upon the Government to repeal the aforementioned Acts by NOT LATER THAN 29TH FEBRUARY 1952. This call to be supported by the Conference of the South African Indian Congress and by all other democratic organizations which find themselves in full agreement with it.

5. In the event of the Government failing to take action for the repeal of these Acts which cannot be tolerated by the people any longer, the two Congresses will embark upon mass action for a redress of the just and legitimate grievances of the majority of the South African people. It is our considered opinion that such mass action should commence on the *6th*

April, 1952, the Van Riebeeck Tercentenary. We consider this day to be most appropriate for the commencement of the struggle as it marks one of the greatest turning points in South African history by the advent of European settlers in the country, followed by colonial and imperialist exploitation which has degraded, humiliated and kept in bondage the vast masses of the non-white people. Or, alternatively, on *26th June, 1952*. We consider this day equally as significant as April the 6th for the commencement of the struggle as it also ranks as one of the greatest turning points in South African history. On this day we commemorate the National Day of Protest held on 26th June, 1950, the day on which on the call of the President-General of the African National Congress, Dr J. S. Moroka, this country witnessed the greatest demonstration of fraternal solidarity and unity of purpose on the part of all sections of the non-European people in the national protest against unjust laws. The 26th June was one of the first steps towards freedom. It is an historical duty that on this day we should pay tribute to the fighting spirit, social responsibility and political understanding of our people; remember the brave sacrifices of the people and pay our homage to all those who had given their very lives in the struggle for freedom. Although we have suggested two alternative dates, the Joint Planning Council strongly favours the earlier date as it considers that three clear calendar months would give the people ample time to set the machinery of struggle into action.

6. With regard to the form of struggle best suited to our conditions we have been constrained to bear in mind the political and economic set-up of our country, the relationship of the rural to the urban population, the development of the trade union movement with particular reference to the disabilities and state of organization of the non-white workers, the economic status of the various sections of the non-white people and the level of organization of the National Liberatory movements. We are therefore of the opinion that in these given historical conditions the forms of struggle for obtaining the

repeal of unjust laws which should be considered are: (*a*) defiance of unjust laws and (*b*) industrial action.

7. In dealing with the two forms of struggle mentioned in paragraph 6, we feel it necessary to reiterate the following fundamental principle which is the kernel of our struggle for freedom. We believe that without the realization of this principle race hatred and bitterness cannot be eliminated and the overwhelming majority of the people cannot find a firm foundation for progress and happiness. It is to be noted, however, that the present campaign of defiance of unjust laws is only directed for the purposes of securing the repeal of those unjust laws mentioned in the resolution of the Joint Conference. ALL PEOPLE, IRRESPECTIVE OF THE NATIONAL GROUPS THEY MAY BELONG TO AND IRRESPECTIVE OF THE COLOUR OF THEIR SKIN, ARE ENTITLED TO LIVE A FULL AND FREE LIFE ON THE BASIS OF THE FULLEST EQUALITY. FULL DEMOCRATIC RIGHTS WITH A DIRECT SAY IN THE AFFAIRS OF THE GOVERNMENT ARE THE INALIENABLE RIGHTS OF EVERY MAN — A RIGHT WHICH IN SOUTH AFRICA MUST BE REALIZED NOW IF THE COUNTRY IS TO BE SAVED FROM SOCIAL CHAOS AND TYRANNY AND FROM THE EVILS ARISING OUT OF THE EXISTING DENIAL OF FRANCHISE TO VAST MASSSES OF THE POPULATION ON GROUNDS OF RACE AND COLOUR. THE STRUGGLE WHICH THE NATIONAL ORGANIZATIONS OF THE NON-EUROPEAN PEOPLE ARE CONDUCTING IS NOT DIRECTED AGAINST ANY RACE OR NATIONAL GROUP, BUT AGAINST THE UNJUST LAWS WHICH KEEP IN PERPETUAL SUBJECTION AND MISERY VAST SECTIONS OF THE POPULATION. IT IS FOR THE CREATION OF CONDITIONS WHICH WILL RESTORE HUMAN DIGNITY, EQUALITY AND FREEDOM TO EVERY SOUTH AFRICAN.

8. *Plan of Action.* We recommend that the struggle for securing the repeal of unjust laws be *DEFIANCE OF UNJUST LAWS based on Non-co-operation.* Defiance of unjust laws should take the form of committing breaches of certain selected laws and regulations which are undemocratic, unjust, racially discriminatory and repugnant to the natural rights of man. Defiance of Unjust laws should be planned into three stages —

although the timing would to a large extent depend on the progress, development and the outcome of the previous stage. Three stages of Defiance of Unjust Laws: (*a*) *First Stage*. Commencement of the struggle by calling upon the selected and trained persons to go into action in the big centres, e.g. Johannesburg, Cape Town, Bloemfontein, Port Elizabeth and Durban. (*b*) *Second Stage*. Number of volunteer corps to be increased as well as the number of centres of operation. (*c*) *Third Stage*. This is the stage of mass action during which, as far as possible, the struggle should broaden out on a country-wide scale and assume a general mass character. For its success preparations on a mass scale to cover the people both in the urban and rural areas would be necessary.

9. *Joint Planning Council*. In order to prosecute and put into effect the plan of Defiance of Unjust Laws and in order to co-ordinate the efforts of the various national groups as well as of the various centres both urban and rural, it will be necessary for the Planning Council from time to time to make recommendations to the Executive Committee of the National Organization which will jointly conduct, prosecute, direct and co-ordinate the campaign of defiance of unjust laws as agreed upon by the Conference of the African National Congress and supported by the Conference of the South African Indian Congress. The Council must be empowered:—(*a*) to co-opt members of the Council and fill vacancies with the approval of the Executive organs of the African National Congress and the South African Indian Congress; (*b*) to invite representatives from non-European organizations which are in full agreement with, and active participants in, the campaign, to serve as non-voting members of the Council; (*c*) to frame rules and regulations for the guidance of the campaign, for approval by the non-Europeans; (*d*) to set up provincial regional and/or local councils within the framework of the existing organizations; (*e*) to issue instructions for the organization of volunteer corps and frame the necessary code of discipline for these volunteers.

10. THE JOINT EXECUTIVES shall establish Provincial, Regional or where possible Local Councils, which will have the primary task of organizing and enrolling volunteers into volunteer corps on the following lines: (*a*) A leader to be in charge of each volunteer corps for maintenance of order and discipline in terms of the 'code of discipline' and for leading the corps into action when called upon to do so; (*b*) Corps to consist of members of both sexes; (*c*) The colours of the African National Congress – black, green and gold – shall be the emblem of the Volunteer Corps; (*d*) Each unit of the Volunteer Corps shall consist of members of the organization to which they belong i.e. A.N.C., S.A.I.C., and F.A.C. The Coloured Organizations in the provinces of Natal, O.F.S. and the Transvaal participating in the campaign with the approval of the Joint Planning and Directing Council shall also be allowed to form units of the Volunteer Corps; (*e*) In certain cases, where a law or regulation to be defied applies commonly to all groups, a mixed unit may be allowed to be formed of members of various organizations participating in the campaign.

11. *Laws to be Tackled*. In recommending laws and regulations which should be tackled we have borne in mind the Laws which were most obnoxious and which are capable of being defied.

The African National Congress. In so far as the African National Congress is concerned, the laws which stand out for attack are naturally the Pass Laws, and Regulations relating to Stock limitation.

Method of Struggle on the Pass Laws. (*a*) A Unit of Volunteer Corps should be called upon to defy a certain aspect of the pass law, e.g. enter a Location without a permit. The Unit chosen goes into action on the appointed day, enters the location and holds a meeting. If confronted by the authorities, the leader and all the members of the Unit court arrest and bear the penalty of imprisonment; (*b*) Selected leaders to declare that they will not carry any form of passes including the Exemption Pass and thus be prepared to bear the penalty of the law;

(*c*) Other forms of struggle on the Pass Laws can also be undertaken depending on the conditions in the different areas throughout the country.

Rural Action. Whilst the Volunteers go into action on the Pass Laws in the Urban Areas, the people in the rural areas should be mobilized to resist the culling of the cattle and stock limitation: (*a*) Stock Limitation: People in the rural areas to be asked not to co-operate with the authorities in any way in culling cattle or limiting livestock; (*b*) Meetings and demonstrations to be held; (*c*) Regional Conferences: Such conferences in the rural areas should be called to discuss the problems of the people and to decide on the most suitable form of Defiance of Unjust Laws in the area.

The South African Indian Congress. In so far as appropriate action by the South African Indian Congress is concerned, the conditions and effects of the laws vary in the three provinces, but we submit the following for the consideration of the South African Indian Congress: (*a*) Provincial Barriers; (*b*) Apartheid Laws such as train, post office, railway stations etc. (*c*) Group Areas Act – if and when possible.

The Franchise Action Council. (*a*) General Apartheid segregation in post offices, railway stations, trains etc. (*b*) Group Areas Act – if and when possible. Both (*a*) and (*b*) will apply to the Coloured people in the other provinces as well. In the Cape a strong possibility exists of having mixed units rather than having separate national organization units.

12. *The Population Registration Act.* During the conduct of the campaign it should not be forgotten that the Government is preparing the machinery for the enforcement of the Population Registration Act. This Act is repugnant to all sections of the people and the campaign must pay particular attention to the preparing of the volunteers and instructing the masses of the people to resist the enforcement of this Act. The campaign on this Act may well take the struggle from stage one and two into stage three of mass actions.

13. We cannot fail to recognize that industrial action is,

second to none, the best and most important weapon in the struggle of the people for the repeal of the unjust laws and that it is inevitable that this method of struggle has to be undertaken at one time or another during the course of a struggle. We also note that, in the present-day South African conditions, the one-day protests on May 1st and June 26th, 1950, and the one-day protest in the Cape on May 7th, 1951, against the Separate Representation of Voters' Bill, demonstrated the preparedness of the people to undertake this form of struggle with no mean success. We are nevertheless of the opinion that in this next phase of our campaign lawful industrial action should not be resorted to immediately, but it should be resorted to at a later stage in the struggle. In this new phase of the campaign a sustained form of mass action will be necessary which will gradually embrace larger groups of people, permeate both the urban and the rural areas and make possible for us to organize, discipline and lead the people in a planned manner. And, therefore, contrary to feelings in some quarters, we are not keen to advocate industrial action as the first step, but only as a later step in the campaign against Unjust Laws. It should be noted, however, that our recommendations do not preclude the use of lawful industrial action during the first stage, provided that conditions make its use possible on a local, regional, provincial or national scale.

14. It is apparent that the plan of action herein outlined cannot be put into effect without the necessary funds to back it. It is also apparent that no body of men can sit down and work out a budget estimate for such a vast national undertaking. Suffice it to say that a full-scale campaign will require thousands of pounds. Conscious of this essential requirement, we recommend with some confidence that if the African National Congress and the South African Indian Congress undertake to launch a *1 Million Shilling Drive* it can sustain the campaign. The Drive should be conducted under the slogan: '*1 Million Shillings by the end of March, 1952*' for Freedom.

15. *National Pledge.* The Council is strongly of the opinion

that an inspired National Pledge should be issued which could be read out at public, factory and group meetings and repeated by all those present. A special day – e.g. April 6th – should be set aside so that special meetings are called everywhere, in towns, villages and hamlets, in factories and locations, and special church services be held on this day where the National Pledge could be publicly read out. This day or any other day which the Conference of the African National Congress sets aside for the purpose should be called '*The National Day of Pledge and Prayer*'.

(*Sgd.*) J. S. MOROKA (*Chairman*).

Y. M. DADOO, Y. CACHALIA (*Representatives of the South African Indian Congress*).

J. B. MARKS, W. M. SISULU (*Representatives of the African National Congress*).

Thaba'Nchu, November 8th, 1951.